C-117 CAREER EXAMINATION SERIES

***This is your PASSBOOK for...***

# Public Safety Dispatcher II

***Test Preparation Study Guide Questions & Answers***

NLC®

NATIONAL LEARNING CORPORATION®

**National Learning Corporation**

212 Michael Drive, Syosset, NY 11791
(516) 921-8888 • www.passbooks.com
E-mail: info@passbooks.com

# PASSBOOK® SERIES

THE *PASSBOOK® SERIES* has been created to prepare applicants and candidates for the ultimate academic battlefield – the examination room.

At some time in our lives, each and every one of us may be required to take an examination – for validation, matriculation, admission, qualification, registration, certification, or licensure.

Based on the assumption that every applicant or candidate has met the basic formal educational standards, has taken the required number of courses, and read the necessary texts, the *PASSBOOK® SERIES* furnishes the one special preparation which may assure passing with confidence, instead of failing with insecurity. Examination questions – together with answers – are furnished as the basic vehicle for study so that the mysteries of the examination and its compounding difficulties may be eliminated or diminished by a sure method.

This book is meant to help you pass your examination provided that you qualify and are serious in your objective.

The entire field is reviewed through the huge store of content information which is succinctly presented through a provocative and challenging approach – the question-and-answer method.

A climate of success is established by furnishing the correct answers at the end of each test.

You soon learn to recognize types of questions, forms of questions, and patterns of questioning. You may even begin to anticipate expected outcomes.

You perceive that many questions are repeated or adapted so that you can gain acute insights, which may enable you to score many sure points.

You learn how to confront new questions, or types of questions, and to attack them confidently and work out the correct answers.

You note objectives and emphases, and recognize pitfalls and dangers, so that you may make positive educational adjustments.

Moreover, you are kept fully informed in relation to new concepts, methods, practices, and directions in the field.

You discover that you are actually taking the examination all the time: you are preparing for the examination by "taking" an examination, not by reading extraneous and/or supererogatory textbooks.

In short, this PASSBOOK®, used directedly, should be an important factor in helping you to pass your test.

# PUBLIC SAFETY DISPATCHER II

## DUTIES

The work involves supervision of an emergency communications center with responsibility for training personnel, supervising the work and planning adequate staff coverage. The employee monitors work performance and maintenance of activity records and participates in receiving calls and dispatching vehicles. Work is reviewed by an administrative supervisor through observation of results and review of reports. Performs related work as required.

## SCOPE OF THE EXAMINATION

The written test will cover knowledge, skills, and/or abilities in such areas as:

1. Radio operations and dispatching procedures;
2. Retaining and comprehending spoken information from calls for emergency services;
3. Coding/decoding information;
4. Understanding and interpreting written material; and
5. Supervision and training.

# HOW TO TAKE A TEST

## I. YOU MUST PASS AN EXAMINATION

### *A. WHAT EVERY CANDIDATE SHOULD KNOW*

Examination applicants often ask us for help in preparing for the written test. What can I study in advance? What kinds of questions will be asked? How will the test be given? How will the papers be graded?

As an applicant for a civil service examination, you may be wondering about some of these things. Our purpose here is to suggest effective methods of advance study and to describe civil service examinations.

Your chances for success on this examination can be increased if you know how to prepare. Those "pre-examination jitters" can be reduced if you know what to expect. You can even experience an adventure in good citizenship if you know why civil service exams are given.

### *B. WHY ARE CIVIL SERVICE EXAMINATIONS GIVEN?*

Civil service examinations are important to you in two ways. As a citizen, you want public jobs filled by employees who know how to do their work. As a job seeker, you want a fair chance to compete for that job on an equal footing with other candidates. The best-known means of accomplishing this two-fold goal is the competitive examination.

Exams are widely publicized throughout the nation. They may be administered for jobs in federal, state, city, municipal, town or village governments or agencies.

Any citizen may apply, with some limitations, such as the age or residence of applicants. Your experience and education may be reviewed to see whether you meet the requirements for the particular examination. When these requirements exist, they are reasonable and applied consistently to all applicants. Thus, a competitive examination may cause you some uneasiness now, but it is your privilege and safeguard.

### *C. HOW ARE CIVIL SERVICE EXAMS DEVELOPED?*

Examinations are carefully written by trained technicians who are specialists in the field known as "psychological measurement," in consultation with recognized authorities in the field of work that the test will cover. These experts recommend the subject matter areas or skills to be tested; only those knowledges or skills important to your success on the job are included. The most reliable books and source materials available are used as references. Together, the experts and technicians judge the difficulty level of the questions.

Test technicians know how to phrase questions so that the problem is clearly stated. Their ethics do not permit "trick" or "catch" questions. Questions may have been tried out on sample groups, or subjected to statistical analysis, to determine their usefulness.

Written tests are often used in combination with performance tests, ratings of training and experience, and oral interviews. All of these measures combine to form the best-known means of finding the right person for the right job.

## II. HOW TO PASS THE WRITTEN TEST

### *A. NATURE OF THE EXAMINATION*

To prepare intelligently for civil service examinations, you should know how they differ from school examinations you have taken. In school you were assigned certain definite pages to read or subjects to cover. The examination questions were quite detailed and usually emphasized memory. Civil service exams, on the other hand, try to discover your present ability to perform the duties of a position, plus your potentiality to learn these duties. In other words, a civil service exam attempts to predict how successful you will be. Questions cover such a broad area that they cannot be as minute and detailed as school exam questions.

In the public service similar kinds of work, or positions, are grouped together in one "class." This process is known as *position-classification.* All the positions in a class are paid according to the salary range for that class. One class title covers all of these positions, and they are all tested by the same examination.

### *B. FOUR BASIC STEPS*

**1) Study the announcement**

How, then, can you know what subjects to study? Our best answer is: "Learn as much as possible about the class of positions for which you've applied." The exam will test the knowledge, skills and abilities needed to do the work.

Your most valuable source of information about the position you want is the official exam announcement. This announcement lists the training and experience qualifications. Check these standards and apply only if you come reasonably close to meeting them.

The brief description of the position in the examination announcement offers some clues to the subjects which will be tested. Think about the job itself. Review the duties in your mind. Can you perform them, or are there some in which you are rusty? Fill in the blank spots in your preparation.

Many jurisdictions preview the written test in the exam announcement by including a section called "Knowledge and Abilities Required," "Scope of the Examination," or some similar heading. Here you will find out specifically what fields will be tested.

**2) Review your own background**

Once you learn in general what the position is all about, and what you need to know to do the work, ask yourself which subjects you already know fairly well and which need improvement. You may wonder whether to concentrate on improving your strong areas or on building some background in your fields of weakness. When the announcement has specified "some knowledge" or "considerable knowledge," or has used adjectives like "beginning principles of..." or "advanced ... methods," you can get a clue as to the number and difficulty of questions to be asked in any given field. More questions, and hence broader coverage, would be included for those subjects which are more important in the work. Now weigh your strengths and weaknesses against the job requirements and prepare accordingly.

**3) Determine the level of the position**

Another way to tell how intensively you should prepare is to understand the level of the job for which you are applying. Is it the entering level? In other words, is this the position in which beginners in a field of work are hired? Or is it an intermediate or advanced level? Sometimes this is indicated by such words as "Junior" or "Senior" in the class title. Other jurisdictions use Roman numerals to designate the level – Clerk I, Clerk II, for example. The word "Supervisor" sometimes appears in the title. If the level is not indicated by the title, check the description of duties. Will you be working under very close supervision, or will you have responsibility for independent decisions in this work?

**4) Choose appropriate study materials**

Now that you know the subjects to be examined and the relative amount of each subject to be covered, you can choose suitable study materials. For beginning level jobs, or even advanced ones, if you have a pronounced weakness in some aspect of your training, read a modern, standard textbook in that field. Be sure it is up to date and has general coverage. Such books are normally available at your library, and the librarian will be glad to help you locate one. For entry-level positions, questions of appropriate difficulty are chosen – neither highly advanced questions, nor those too simple. Such questions require careful thought but not advanced training.

If the position for which you are applying is technical or advanced, you will read more advanced, specialized material. If you are already familiar with the basic principles of your field, elementary textbooks would waste your time. Concentrate on advanced textbooks and technical periodicals. Think through the concepts and review difficult problems in your field.

These are all general sources. You can get more ideas on your own initiative, following these leads. For example, training manuals and publications of the government agency which employs workers in your field can be useful, particularly for technical and professional positions. A letter or visit to the government department involved may result in more specific study suggestions, and certainly will provide you with a more definite idea of the exact nature of the position you are seeking.

## III. KINDS OF TESTS

Tests are used for purposes other than measuring knowledge and ability to perform specified duties. For some positions, it is equally important to test ability to make adjustments to new situations or to profit from training. In others, basic mental abilities not dependent on information are essential. Questions which test these things may not appear as pertinent to the duties of the position as those which test for knowledge and information. Yet they are often highly important parts of a fair examination. For very general questions, it is almost impossible to help you direct your study efforts. What we can do is to point out some of the more common of these general abilities needed in public service positions and describe some typical questions.

1) General information

Broad, general information has been found useful for predicting job success in some kinds of work. This is tested in a variety of ways, from vocabulary lists to questions about current events. Basic background in some field of work, such as sociology or economics, may be sampled in a group of questions. Often these are principles which have become familiar to most persons through exposure rather than through formal training. It is difficult to advise you how to study for these questions; being alert to the world around you is our best suggestion.

2) Verbal ability

An example of an ability needed in many positions is verbal or language ability. Verbal ability is, in brief, the ability to use and understand words. Vocabulary and grammar tests are typical measures of this ability. Reading comprehension or paragraph interpretation questions are common in many kinds of civil service tests. You are given a paragraph of written material and asked to find its central meaning.

3) Numerical ability

Number skills can be tested by the familiar arithmetic problem, by checking paired lists of numbers to see which are alike and which are different, or by interpreting charts and graphs. In the latter test, a graph may be printed in the test booklet which you are asked to use as the basis for answering questions.

4) Observation

A popular test for law-enforcement positions is the observation test. A picture is shown to you for several minutes, then taken away. Questions about the picture test your ability to observe both details and larger elements.

5) Following directions

In many positions in the public service, the employee must be able to carry out written instructions dependably and accurately. You may be given a chart with several columns, each column listing a variety of information. The questions require you to carry out directions involving the information given in the chart.

6) Skills and aptitudes

Performance tests effectively measure some manual skills and aptitudes. When the skill is one in which you are trained, such as typing or shorthand, you can practice. These tests are often very much like those given in business school or high school courses. For many of the other skills and aptitudes, however, no short-time preparation can be made. Skills and abilities natural to you or that you have developed throughout your lifetime are being tested.

Many of the general questions just described provide all the data needed to answer the questions and ask you to use your reasoning ability to find the answers. Your best preparation for these tests, as well as for tests of facts and ideas, is to be at your physical and mental best. You, no doubt, have your own methods of getting into an exam-taking mood and keeping "in shape." The next section lists some ideas on this subject.

## IV. KINDS OF QUESTIONS

Only rarely is the "essay" question, which you answer in narrative form, used in civil service tests. Civil service tests are usually of the short-answer type. Full instructions for answering these questions will be given to you at the examination. But in case this is your first experience with short-answer questions and separate answer sheets, here is what you need to know:

**1) Multiple-choice Questions**

Most popular of the short-answer questions is the "multiple choice" or "best answer" question. It can be used, for example, to test for factual knowledge, ability to solve problems or judgment in meeting situations found at work.

A multiple-choice question is normally one of three types—

- It can begin with an incomplete statement followed by several possible endings. You are to find the one ending which *best* completes the statement, although some of the others may not be entirely wrong.
- It can also be a complete statement in the form of a question which is answered by choosing one of the statements listed.

- It can be in the form of a problem – again you select the best answer.

Here is an example of a multiple-choice question with a discussion which should give you some clues as to the method for choosing the right answer:

> When an employee has a complaint about his assignment, the action which will *best* help him overcome his difficulty is to
> A. discuss his difficulty with his coworkers
> B. take the problem to the head of the organization
> C. take the problem to the person who gave him the assignment
> D. say nothing to anyone about his complaint

In answering this question, you should study each of the choices to find which is best. Consider choice "A" – Certainly an employee may discuss his complaint with fellow employees, but no change or improvement can result, and the complaint remains unresolved. Choice "B" is a poor choice since the head of the organization probably does not know what assignment you have been given, and taking your problem to him is known as "going over the head" of the supervisor. The supervisor, or person who made the assignment, is the person who can clarify it or correct any injustice. Choice "C" is, therefore, correct. To say nothing, as in choice "D," is unwise. Supervisors have and interest in knowing the problems employees are facing, and the employee is seeking a solution to his problem.

**2) True/False Questions**

The "true/false" or "right/wrong" form of question is sometimes used. Here a complete statement is given. Your job is to decide whether the statement is right or wrong.

SAMPLE: A roaming cell-phone call to a nearby city costs less than a non-roaming call to a distant city.

This statement is wrong, or false, since roaming calls are more expensive.

This is not a complete list of all possible question forms, although most of the others are variations of these common types. You will always get complete directions for answering questions. Be sure you understand *how* to mark your answers – ask questions until you do.

## V. RECORDING YOUR ANSWERS

Computer terminals are used more and more today for many different kinds of exams.

For an examination with very few applicants, you may be told to record your answers in the test booklet itself. Separate answer sheets are much more common. If this separate answer sheet is to be scored by machine – and this is often the case – it is highly important that you mark your answers correctly in order to get credit.

An electronic scoring machine is often used in civil service offices because of the speed with which papers can be scored. Machine-scored answer sheets must be marked with a pencil, which will be given to you. This pencil has a high graphite content which responds to the electronic scoring machine. As a matter of fact, stray dots may register as answers, so do not let your pencil rest on the answer sheet while you are pondering the correct answer. Also, if your pencil lead breaks or is otherwise defective, ask for another.

Since the answer sheet will be dropped in a slot in the scoring machine, be careful not to bend the corners or get the paper crumpled.

The answer sheet normally has five vertical columns of numbers, with 30 numbers to a column. These numbers correspond to the question numbers in your test booklet. After each number, going across the page are four or five pairs of dotted lines. These short dotted lines have small letters or numbers above them. The first two pairs may also have a "T" or "F" above the letters. This indicates that the first two pairs only are to be used if the questions are of the true-false type. If the questions are multiple choice, disregard the "T" and "F" and pay attention only to the small letters or numbers.

Answer your questions in the manner of the sample that follows:

32. The largest city in the United States is
    - A. Washington, D.C.
    - B. New York City
    - C. Chicago
    - D. Detroit
    - E. San Francisco

1) Choose the answer you think is best. (New York City is the largest, so "B" is correct.)
2) Find the row of dotted lines numbered the same as the question you are answering. (Find row number 32)
3) Find the pair of dotted lines corresponding to the answer. (Find the pair of lines under the mark "B.")
4) Make a solid black mark between the dotted lines.

## VI. BEFORE THE TEST

Common sense will help you find procedures to follow to get ready for an examination. Too many of us, however, overlook these sensible measures. Indeed, nervousness and fatigue have been found to be the most serious reasons why applicants fail to do their best on civil service tests. Here is a list of reminders:

- Begin your preparation early – Don't wait until the last minute to go scurrying around for books and materials or to find out what the position is all about.
- Prepare continuously – An hour a night for a week is better than an all-night cram session. This has been definitely established. What is more, a night a week for a month will return better dividends than crowding your study into a shorter period of time.
- Locate the place of the exam – You have been sent a notice telling you when and where to report for the examination. If the location is in a different town or otherwise unfamiliar to you, it would be well to inquire the best route and learn something about the building.
- Relax the night before the test – Allow your mind to rest. Do not study at all that night. Plan some mild recreation or diversion; then go to bed early and get a good night's sleep.
- Get up early enough to make a leisurely trip to the place for the test – This way unforeseen events, traffic snarls, unfamiliar buildings, etc. will not upset you.
- Dress comfortably – A written test is not a fashion show. You will be known by number and not by name, so wear something comfortable.

- Leave excess paraphernalia at home – Shopping bags and odd bundles will get in your way. You need bring only the items mentioned in the official notice you received; usually everything you need is provided. Do not bring reference books to the exam. They will only confuse those last minutes and be taken away from you when in the test room.
- Arrive somewhat ahead of time – If because of transportation schedules you must get there very early, bring a newspaper or magazine to take your mind off yourself while waiting.
- Locate the examination room – When you have found the proper room, you will be directed to the seat or part of the room where you will sit. Sometimes you are given a sheet of instructions to read while you are waiting. Do not fill out any forms until you are told to do so; just read them and be prepared.
- Relax and prepare to listen to the instructions
- If you have any physical problem that may keep you from doing your best, be sure to tell the test administrator. If you are sick or in poor health, you really cannot do your best on the exam. You can come back and take the test some other time.

## VII. AT THE TEST

The day of the test is here and you have the test booklet in your hand. The temptation to get going is very strong. Caution! There is more to success than knowing the right answers. You must know how to identify your papers and understand variations in the type of short-answer question used in this particular examination. Follow these suggestions for maximum results from your efforts:

**1) Cooperate with the monitor**

The test administrator has a duty to create a situation in which you can be as much at ease as possible. He will give instructions, tell you when to begin, check to see that you are marking your answer sheet correctly, and so on. He is not there to guard you, although he will see that your competitors do not take unfair advantage. He wants to help you do your best.

**2) Listen to all instructions**

Don't jump the gun! Wait until you understand all directions. In most civil service tests you get more time than you need to answer the questions. So don't be in a hurry. Read each word of instructions until you clearly understand the meaning. Study the examples, listen to all announcements and follow directions. Ask questions if you do not understand what to do.

**3) Identify your papers**

Civil service exams are usually identified by number only. You will be assigned a number; you must not put your name on your test papers. Be sure to copy your number correctly. Since more than one exam may be given, copy your exact examination title.

**4) Plan your time**

Unless you are told that a test is a "speed" or "rate of work" test, speed itself is usually not important. Time enough to answer all the questions will be provided, but this does not mean that you have all day. An overall time limit has been set. Divide the total time (in minutes) by the number of questions to determine the approximate time you have for each question.

**5) Do not linger over difficult questions**

If you come across a difficult question, mark it with a paper clip (useful to have along) and come back to it when you have been through the booklet. One caution if you do this – be sure to skip a number on your answer sheet as well. Check often to be sure that you have not lost your place and that you are marking in the row numbered the same as the question you are answering.

**6) Read the questions**

Be sure you know what the question asks! Many capable people are unsuccessful because they failed to *read* the questions correctly.

**7) Answer all questions**

Unless you have been instructed that a penalty will be deducted for incorrect answers, it is better to guess than to omit a question.

**8) Speed tests**

It is often better NOT to guess on speed tests. It has been found that on timed tests people are tempted to spend the last few seconds before time is called in marking answers at random – without even reading them – in the hope of picking up a few extra points. To discourage this practice, the instructions may warn you that your score will be "corrected" for guessing. That is, a penalty will be applied. The incorrect answers will be deducted from the correct ones, or some other penalty formula will be used.

**9) Review your answers**

If you finish before time is called, go back to the questions you guessed or omitted to give them further thought. Review other answers if you have time.

**10) Return your test materials**

If you are ready to leave before others have finished or time is called, take ALL your materials to the monitor and leave quietly. Never take any test material with you. The monitor can discover whose papers are not complete, and taking a test booklet may be grounds for disqualification.

## VIII. EXAMINATION TECHNIQUES

1) Read the general instructions carefully. These are usually printed on the first page of the exam booklet. As a rule, these instructions refer to the timing of the examination; the fact that you should not start work until the signal and must stop work at a signal, etc. If there are any *special* instructions, such as a choice of questions to be answered, make sure that you note this instruction carefully.

2) When you are ready to start work on the examination, that is as soon as the signal has been given, read the instructions to each question booklet, underline any key words or phrases, such as *least, best, outline, describe* and the like. In this way you will tend to answer as requested rather than discover on reviewing your paper that you *listed without describing*, that you selected the *worst* choice rather than the *best* choice, etc.

3) If the examination is of the objective or multiple-choice type – that is, each question will also give a series of possible answers: A, B, C or D, and you are called upon to select the best answer and write the letter next to that answer on your answer paper – it is advisable to start answering each question in turn. There may be anywhere from 50 to 100 such questions in the three or four hours allotted and you can see how much time would be taken if you read through all the questions before beginning to answer any. Furthermore, if you come across a question or group of questions which you know would be difficult to answer, it would undoubtedly affect your handling of all the other questions.

4) If the examination is of the essay type and contains but a few questions, it is a moot point as to whether you should read all the questions before starting to answer any one. Of course, if you are given a choice – say five out of seven and the like – then it is essential to read all the questions so you can eliminate the two that are most difficult. If, however, you are asked to answer all the questions, there may be danger in trying to answer the easiest one first because you may find that you will spend too much time on it. The best technique is to answer the first question, then proceed to the second, etc.

5) Time your answers. Before the exam begins, write down the time it started, then add the time allowed for the examination and write down the time it must be completed, then divide the time available somewhat as follows:
   - If 3-1/2 hours are allowed, that would be 210 minutes. If you have 80 objective-type questions, that would be an average of 2-1/2 minutes per question. Allow yourself no more than 2 minutes per question, or a total of 160 minutes, which will permit about 50 minutes to review.
   - If for the time allotment of 210 minutes there are 7 essay questions to answer, that would average about 30 minutes a question. Give yourself only 25 minutes per question so that you have about 35 minutes to review.

6) The most important instruction is to *read each question* and make sure you know what is wanted. The second most important instruction is to *time yourself properly* so that you answer every question. The third most important instruction is to *answer every question*. Guess if you have to but include something for each question. Remember that you will receive no credit for a blank and will probably receive some credit if you write something in answer to an essay question. If you guess a letter – say "B" for a multiple-choice question – you may have guessed right. If you leave a blank as an answer to a multiple-choice question, the examiners may respect your feelings but it will not add a point to your score. Some exams may penalize you for wrong answers, so in such cases *only*, you may not want to guess unless you have some basis for your answer.

7) Suggestions
   a. Objective-type questions
      1. Examine the question booklet for proper sequence of pages and questions
      2. Read all instructions carefully
      3. Skip any question which seems too difficult; return to it after all other questions have been answered
      4. Apportion your time properly; do not spend too much time on any single question or group of questions

5. Note and underline key words – *all, most, fewest, least, best, worst, same, opposite,* etc.
6. Pay particular attention to negatives
7. Note unusual option, e.g., unduly long, short, complex, different or similar in content to the body of the question
8. Observe the use of "hedging" words – *probably, may, most likely,* etc.
9. Make sure that your answer is put next to the same number as the question
10. Do not second-guess unless you have good reason to believe the second answer is definitely more correct
11. Cross out original answer if you decide another answer is more accurate; do not erase until you are ready to hand your paper in
12. Answer all questions; guess unless instructed otherwise
13. Leave time for review

b. Essay questions
1. Read each question carefully
2. Determine exactly what is wanted. Underline key words or phrases.
3. Decide on outline or paragraph answer
4. Include many different points and elements unless asked to develop any one or two points or elements
5. Show impartiality by giving pros and cons unless directed to select one side only
6. Make and write down any assumptions you find necessary to answer the questions
7. Watch your English, grammar, punctuation and choice of words
8. Time your answers; don't crowd material

8) Answering the essay question

Most essay questions can be answered by framing the specific response around several key words or ideas. Here are a few such key words or ideas:

M's: manpower, materials, methods, money, management
P's: purpose, program, policy, plan, procedure, practice, problems, pitfalls, personnel, public relations

a. Six basic steps in handling problems:
1. Preliminary plan and background development
2. Collect information, data and facts
3. Analyze and interpret information, data and facts
4. Analyze and develop solutions as well as make recommendations
5. Prepare report and sell recommendations
6. Install recommendations and follow up effectiveness

b. Pitfalls to avoid
1. *Taking things for granted* – A statement of the situation does not necessarily imply that each of the elements is necessarily true; for example, a complaint may be invalid and biased so that all that can be taken for granted is that a complaint has been registered

2. *Considering only one side of a situation* – Wherever possible, indicate several alternatives and then point out the reasons you selected the best one
3. *Failing to indicate follow up* – Whenever your answer indicates action on your part, make certain that you will take proper follow-up action to see how successful your recommendations, procedures or actions turn out to be
4. *Taking too long in answering any single question* – Remember to time your answers properly

## IX. AFTER THE TEST

Scoring procedures differ in detail among civil service jurisdictions although the general principles are the same. Whether the papers are hand-scored or graded by machine we have described, they are nearly always graded by number. That is, the person who marks the paper knows only the number – never the name – of the applicant. Not until all the papers have been graded will they be matched with names. If other tests, such as training and experience or oral interview ratings have been given, scores will be combined. Different parts of the examination usually have different weights. For example, the written test might count 60 percent of the final grade, and a rating of training and experience 40 percent. In many jurisdictions, veterans will have a certain number of points added to their grades.

After the final grade has been determined, the names are placed in grade order and an eligible list is established. There are various methods for resolving ties between those who get the same final grade – probably the most common is to place first the name of the person whose application was received first. Job offers are made from the eligible list in the order the names appear on it. You will be notified of your grade and your rank as soon as all these computations have been made. This will be done as rapidly as possible.

People who are found to meet the requirements in the announcement are called "eligibles." Their names are put on a list of eligible candidates. An eligible's chances of getting a job depend on how high he stands on this list and how fast agencies are filling jobs from the list.

When a job is to be filled from a list of eligibles, the agency asks for the names of people on the list of eligibles for that job. When the civil service commission receives this request, it sends to the agency the names of the three people highest on this list. Or, if the job to be filled has specialized requirements, the office sends the agency the names of the top three persons who meet these requirements from the general list.

The appointing officer makes a choice from among the three people whose names were sent to him. If the selected person accepts the appointment, the names of the others are put back on the list to be considered for future openings.

That is the rule in hiring from all kinds of eligible lists, whether they are for typist, carpenter, chemist, or something else. For every vacancy, the appointing officer has his choice of any one of the top three eligibles on the list. This explains why the person whose name is on top of the list sometimes does not get an appointment when some of the persons lower on the list do. If the appointing officer chooses the second or third eligible, the No. 1 eligible does not get a job at once, but stays on the list until he is appointed or the list is terminated.

## X. HOW TO PASS THE INTERVIEW TEST

The examination for which you applied requires an oral interview test. You have already taken the written test and you are now being called for the interview test – the final part of the formal examination.

You may think that it is not possible to prepare for an interview test and that there are no procedures to follow during an interview. Our purpose is to point out some things you can do in advance that will help you and some good rules to follow and pitfalls to avoid while you are being interviewed.

*What is an interview supposed to test?*

The written examination is designed to test the technical knowledge and competence of the candidate; the oral is designed to evaluate intangible qualities, not readily measured otherwise, and to establish a list showing the relative fitness of each candidate – as measured against his competitors – for the position sought. Scoring is not on the basis of "right" and "wrong," but on a sliding scale of values ranging from "not passable" to "outstanding." As a matter of fact, it is possible to achieve a relatively low score without a single "incorrect" answer because of evident weakness in the qualities being measured.

Occasionally, an examination may consist entirely of an oral test – either an individual or a group oral. In such cases, information is sought concerning the technical knowledges and abilities of the candidate, since there has been no written examination for this purpose. More commonly, however, an oral test is used to supplement a written examination.

*Who conducts interviews?*

The composition of oral boards varies among different jurisdictions. In nearly all, a representative of the personnel department serves as chairman. One of the members of the board may be a representative of the department in which the candidate would work. In some cases, "outside experts" are used, and, frequently, a businessman or some other representative of the general public is asked to serve. Labor and management or other special groups may be represented. The aim is to secure the services of experts in the appropriate field.

However the board is composed, it is a good idea (and not at all improper or unethical) to ascertain in advance of the interview who the members are and what groups they represent. When you are introduced to them, you will have some idea of their backgrounds and interests, and at least you will not stutter and stammer over their names.

*What should be done before the interview?*

While knowledge about the board members is useful and takes some of the surprise element out of the interview, there is other preparation which is more substantive. It *is* possible to prepare for an oral interview – in several ways:

**1) Keep a copy of your application and review it carefully before the interview**

This may be the only document before the oral board, and the starting point of the interview. Know what education and experience you have listed there, and the sequence and dates of all of it. Sometimes the board will ask you to review the highlights of your experience for them; you should not have to hem and haw doing it.

**2) Study the class specification and the examination announcement**

Usually, the oral board has one or both of these to guide them. The qualities, characteristics or knowledges required by the position sought are stated in these documents. They offer valuable clues as to the nature of the oral interview. For example, if the job involves supervisory responsibilities, the announcement will usually indicate that knowledge of modern supervisory methods and the qualifications of the candidate as a supervisor will be tested. If so, you can expect such questions, frequently in the form of a hypothetical situation which you are expected to solve. NEVER go into an oral without knowledge of the duties and responsibilities of the job you seek.

**3) Think through each qualification required**

Try to visualize the kind of questions you would ask if you were a board member. How well could you answer them? Try especially to appraise your own knowledge and background in each area, *measured against the job sought*, and identify any areas in which you are weak. Be critical and realistic – do not flatter yourself.

**4) Do some general reading in areas in which you feel you may be weak**

For example, if the job involves supervision and your past experience has NOT, some general reading in supervisory methods and practices, particularly in the field of human relations, might be useful. Do NOT study agency procedures or detailed manuals. The oral board will be testing your understanding and capacity, not your memory.

**5) Get a good night's sleep and watch your general health and mental attitude**

You will want a clear head at the interview. Take care of a cold or any other minor ailment, and of course, no hangovers.

*What should be done on the day of the interview?*

Now comes the day of the interview itself. Give yourself plenty of time to get there. Plan to arrive somewhat ahead of the scheduled time, particularly if your appointment is in the fore part of the day. If a previous candidate fails to appear, the board might be ready for you a bit early. By early afternoon an oral board is almost invariably behind schedule if there are many candidates, and you may have to wait. Take along a book or magazine to read, or your application to review, but leave any extraneous material in the waiting room when you go in for your interview. In any event, relax and compose yourself.

The matter of dress is important. The board is forming impressions about you – from your experience, your manners, your attitude, and your appearance. Give your personal appearance careful attention. Dress your best, but not your flashiest. Choose conservative, appropriate clothing, and be sure it is immaculate. This is a business interview, and your appearance should indicate that you regard it as such. Besides, being well groomed and properly dressed will help boost your confidence.

Sooner or later, someone will call your name and escort you into the interview room. *This is it.* From here on you are on your own. It is too late for any more preparation. But remember, you asked for this opportunity to prove your fitness, and you are here because your request was granted.

*What happens when you go in?*

The usual sequence of events will be as follows: The clerk (who is often the board stenographer) will introduce you to the chairman of the oral board, who will introduce you to the other members of the board. Acknowledge the introductions before you sit down. Do not be surprised if you find a microphone facing you or a stenotypist sitting by. Oral interviews are usually recorded in the event of an appeal or other review.

Usually the chairman of the board will open the interview by reviewing the highlights of your education and work experience from your application – primarily for the benefit of the other members of the board, as well as to get the material into the record. Do not interrupt or comment unless there is an error or significant misinterpretation; if that is the case, do not hesitate. But do not quibble about insignificant matters. Also, he will usually ask you some question about your education, experience or your present job – partly to get you to start talking and to establish the interviewing "rapport." He may start the actual questioning, or turn it over to one of the other members. Frequently, each member undertakes the questioning on a particular area, one in which he is perhaps most competent, so you can expect each member to participate in the examination. Because time is limited, you may also expect some rather abrupt switches in the direction the questioning takes, so do not be upset by it. Normally, a board member will not pursue a single line of questioning unless he discovers a particular strength or weakness.

After each member has participated, the chairman will usually ask whether any member has any further questions, then will ask you if you have anything you wish to add. Unless you are expecting this question, it may floor you. Worse, it may start you off on an extended, extemporaneous speech. The board is not usually seeking more information. The question is principally to offer you a last opportunity to present further qualifications or to indicate that you have nothing to add. So, if you feel that a significant qualification or characteristic has been overlooked, it is proper to point it out in a sentence or so. Do not compliment the board on the thoroughness of their examination – they have been sketchy, and you know it. If you wish, merely say, "No thank you, I have nothing further to add." This is a point where you can "talk yourself out" of a good impression or fail to present an important bit of information. Remember, *you close the interview yourself.*

The chairman will then say, "That is all, Mr. ______, thank you." Do not be startled; the interview is over, and quicker than you think. Thank him, gather your belongings and take your leave. Save your sigh of relief for the other side of the door.

*How to put your best foot forward*

Throughout this entire process, you may feel that the board individually and collectively is trying to pierce your defenses, seek out your hidden weaknesses and embarrass and confuse you. Actually, this is not true. They are obliged to make an appraisal of your qualifications for the job you are seeking, and they want to see you in your best light. Remember, they must interview all candidates and a non-cooperative candidate may become a failure in spite of their best efforts to bring out his qualifications. Here are 15 suggestions that will help you:

**1) Be natural – Keep your attitude confident, not cocky**

If you are not confident that you can do the job, do not expect the board to be. Do not apologize for your weaknesses, try to bring out your strong points. The board is interested in a positive, not negative, presentation. Cockiness will antagonize any board member and make him wonder if you are covering up a weakness by a false show of strength.

**2) Get comfortable, but don't lounge or sprawl**

Sit erectly but not stiffly. A careless posture may lead the board to conclude that you are careless in other things, or at least that you are not impressed by the importance of the occasion. Either conclusion is natural, even if incorrect. Do not fuss with your clothing, a pencil or an ashtray. Your hands may occasionally be useful to emphasize a point; do not let them become a point of distraction.

**3) Do not wisecrack or make small talk**

This is a serious situation, and your attitude should show that you consider it as such. Further, the time of the board is limited – they do not want to waste it, and neither should you.

**4) Do not exaggerate your experience or abilities**

In the first place, from information in the application or other interviews and sources, the board may know more about you than you think. Secondly, you probably will not get away with it. An experienced board is rather adept at spotting such a situation, so do not take the chance.

**5) If you know a board member, do not make a point of it, yet do not hide it**

Certainly you are not fooling him, and probably not the other members of the board. Do not try to take advantage of your acquaintanceship – it will probably do you little good.

**6) Do not dominate the interview**

Let the board do that. They will give you the clues – do not assume that you have to do all the talking. Realize that the board has a number of questions to ask you, and do not try to take up all the interview time by showing off your extensive knowledge of the answer to the first one.

**7) Be attentive**

You only have 20 minutes or so, and you should keep your attention at its sharpest throughout. When a member is addressing a problem or question to you, give him your undivided attention. Address your reply principally to him, but do not exclude the other board members.

**8) Do not interrupt**

A board member may be stating a problem for you to analyze. He will ask you a question when the time comes. Let him state the problem, and wait for the question.

**9) Make sure you understand the question**

Do not try to answer until you are sure what the question is. If it is not clear, restate it in your own words or ask the board member to clarify it for you. However, do not haggle about minor elements.

**10) Reply promptly but not hastily**

A common entry on oral board rating sheets is "candidate responded readily," or "candidate hesitated in replies." Respond as promptly and quickly as you can, but do not jump to a hasty, ill-considered answer.

**11) Do not be peremptory in your answers**

A brief answer is proper – but do not fire your answer back. That is a losing game from your point of view. The board member can probably ask questions much faster than you can answer them.

**12) Do not try to create the answer you think the board member wants**

He is interested in what kind of mind you have and how it works – not in playing games. Furthermore, he can usually spot this practice and will actually grade you down on it.

**13) Do not switch sides in your reply merely to agree with a board member**

Frequently, a member will take a contrary position merely to draw you out and to see if you are willing and able to defend your point of view. Do not start a debate, yet do not surrender a good position. If a position is worth taking, it is worth defending.

**14) Do not be afraid to admit an error in judgment if you are shown to be wrong**

The board knows that you are forced to reply without any opportunity for careful consideration. Your answer may be demonstrably wrong. If so, admit it and get on with the interview.

**15) Do not dwell at length on your present job**

The opening question may relate to your present assignment. Answer the question but do not go into an extended discussion. You are being examined for a *new* job, not your present one. As a matter of fact, try to phrase ALL your answers in terms of the job for which you are being examined.

*Basis of Rating*

Probably you will forget most of these "do's" and "don'ts" when you walk into the oral interview room. Even remembering them all will not ensure you a passing grade. Perhaps you did not have the qualifications in the first place. But remembering them will help you to put your best foot forward, without treading on the toes of the board members.

Rumor and popular opinion to the contrary notwithstanding, an oral board wants you to make the best appearance possible. They know you are under pressure – but they also want to see how you respond to it as a guide to what your reaction would be under the pressures of the job you seek. They will be influenced by the degree of poise you display, the personal traits you show and the manner in which you respond.

ABOUT THIS BOOK

This book contains tests divided into Examination Sections. Go through each test, answering every question in the margin. We have also attached a sample answer sheet at the back of the book that can be removed and used. At the end of each test look at the answer key and check your answers. On the ones you got wrong, look at the right answer choice and learn. Do not fill in the answers first. Do not memorize the questions and answers, but understand the answer and principles involved. On your test, the questions will likely be different from the samples. Questions are changed and new ones added. If you understand these past questions you should have success with any changes that arise. Tests may consist of several types of questions. We have additional books on each subject should more study be advisable or necessary for you. Finally, the more you study, the better prepared you will be. This book is intended to be the last thing you study before you walk into the examination room. Prior study of relevant texts is also recommended. NLC publishes some of these in our Fundamental Series. Knowledge and good sense are important factors in passing your exam. Good luck also helps. So now study this Passbook, absorb the material contained within and take that knowledge into the examination. Then do your best to pass that exam.

# EXAMINATION SECTION

# EXAMINATION SECTION
# TEST 1

DIRECTIONS: Each question or incomplete statement is followed by several suggested answers or completions. Select the one that BEST answers the question or completes the statement. *PRINT THE LETTER OF THE CORRECT ANSWER IN THE SPACE AT THE RIGHT.*

1. When a signal report is referred to as *five nine plus 10 db,* 1.____

   A. its bandwidth is 10 decibels above linearity
   B. its relative signal strength reading is 10 decibels greater than strength 9
   C. its signal strength has increased by a factor of 90
   D. it should be repeated at a frequency 10 kHz higher

2. *Chirp* is a(n) 2.____

   A. overload in a receiver's audio circuit whenever CW is received
   B. slight change in a transmitter's frequency each time it is keyed
   C. gradual change in transmitter frequency as the circuit warms up
   D. high-pitched tone received with a CW signal

3. A vertical antenna sends out MOST of its radio energy 3.____

   A. in two opposite directions
   B. high into the air
   C. equally in all horizontal directions
   D. in one direction

4. For correct station identification when using a radiotelephone, FCC rules suggest using ______ as an aid. 4.____

   A. a phonetic alphabet
   B. unique words of the operator's choice
   C. Q signals
   D. a speech compressor

5. A COMMON result of an operator speaking too loudly into a hand-held FM transceiver is 5.____

   A. interference to other stations operating near the operator's frequency
   B. digital interference to computer equipment
   C. atmospheric interference in the air around the antenna
   D. interference to stations operating on a higher frequency band

6. When using a repeater to transmit a two-way radio signal, the operator should pause briefly between transmissions to 6.____

   A. dial up the repeater's autopatch
   B. listen for anyone wanting to break in
   C. prepare for recording possible third-party communications
   D. check the standing-wave ratio of the repeater

7. The USUAL input/output frequency separation for repeaters in the 2-meter band is 7.____

A. 1 MHz B. 5 MHz C. 1.5 MHz D. 600 kHz

8. What is the PROPER way to ask someone's location when using a repeater? 8.____

A. What is your QTH? B. What is your 20?
C. Where are you? D. Where's the break?

9. If an ammeter reads 4 amperes, the current flow, in milliamperes, is 9.____

A. .004 B. 4,000,000 C. 4000 D. .0004

10. The purpose of repeater operation is to 10.____

A. cut power costs by linking with another high-power system
B. help mobile and low-power stations extend their ranges
C. transmit signals for observing propagation and reception
D. make calls within a range of 50 miles

11. For two-way systems situated in and around an urban area, what block of frequencies are allocated for use by police, fire, and private industries? _____ MHz. 11.____

A. 30 B. 40 C. 470-512 D. 900

12. What causes the MAXIMUM usable frequency to vary? 12.____

A. The amount of ultraviolet radiation from the sun
B. Windspeed in the upper atmosphere
C. The temperature of the ionosphere
D. The weather just below the ionosphere

13. A transmission line that has no change in voltage or current along its full length has a standing-wave ratio of 13.____

A. less than 1 B. greater than 1
C. 1:1 D. 2:1

14. When a signal is referred to as *full quieting,* it 14.____

A. is not strong enough to be received
B. is being received, but no audio is being heard
C. contains no extraneous sound
D. is strong enough to overcome all receiver noise

15. During transmission, the antenna of a hand-held transceiver should be held pointing 15.____

A. toward the ground
B. away from the operator's head and away from others
C. toward the station the operator means to contact
D. away from the station the operator means to contact

16. A _____ system is MOST at risk of receiving a barrage of calls from different sources at the same time. 16.____

A. duplex B. simplex C. repeater D. remote

17. The device that measures standing wave ratio should be connected between the 17.____

A. transmitter and power supply
B. ground and transmitter
C. feed line and antenna
D. receiver and transmitter

18. Electrical energy at a frequency of 7120 Hz is in the _____ frequency range. 18.____

A. hyper
B. audio
C. super-high
D. radio

19. The type of system in which the transmitter and receiver are at a different location from the microphone and loudspeaker is the _____ system. 19.____

A. remote
B. repeater
C. simplex
D. duplex

20. In the radio transmission of speech, the amplification added to a signal to prevent degradation of consonant sounds is referred to as 20.____

A. preemphasis
B. deemphasis
C. loading
D. squelch

21. The bandwidth over which a receiver is capable of receiving signals is referred to as its 21.____

A. monitor band
B. sideband
C. skip zone
D. acceptance band

22. The output of a transceiver should NEVER be connected to a(n) 22.____

A. antenna switch
B. receiver
C. SWR meter
D. antenna

23. Which band may NOT be used by earth stations for satellite communications? 23.____

A. 10 meters
B. 6 meters
C. 2 meters
D. 70 centimeters

24. What is the term for the kind of interference created by sharp bursts of radio frequency voltage? 24.____

A. Chirp
B. Oscillation
C. Impulse noise
D. Fluctuation noise

25. In repeater operations, a courtesy tone 25.____

A. indicates a waiting message
B. activates a receiver in case of severe weather
C. identifies the repeater
D. indicates that the transmission has been completed

# KEY (CORRECT ANSWERS)

| | | | |
|---|---|---|---|
| 1. | B | 11. | A |
| 2. | B | 12. | A |
| 3. | C | 13. | C |
| 4. | A | 14. | D |
| 5. | A | 15. | B |
| 6. | B | 16. | B |
| 7. | D | 17. | C |
| 8. | C | 18. | D |
| 9. | C | 19. | A |
| 10. | B | 20. | A |

| | |
|---|---|
| 21. | D |
| 22. | B |
| 23. | B |
| 24. | C |
| 25. | D |

# TEST 2

DIRECTIONS: Each question or incomplete statement is followed by several suggested answers or completions. Select the one that BEST answers the question or completes the statement. *PRINT THE LETTER OF THE CORRECT ANSWER IN THE SPACE AT THE RIGHT.*

1. Maximum usable frequency means the _____ frequency signal that _____. 1.____

   A. highest; is most absorbed by the ionosphere
   B. lowest; is most absorbed by the ionosphere
   C. lowest; will reach its intended destination
   D. highest; will reach its intended destination

2. As its wavelength gets LONGER, a signal's frequency 2.____

   A. lengthens
   B. shortens
   C. stays the same
   D. disappears

3. The term for voice emissions that are radio-transmitted is 3.____

   A. RTTY
   B. CW
   C. data
   D. phone

4. A _____ is used to inject a frequency calibration signal into a receiver. 4.____

   A. calibrated voltmeter
   B. calibrated wavemeter
   C. crystal calibrator
   D. calibrated oscilloscope

5. The basic unit of electric current is the 5.____

   A. volt
   B. ampere
   C. watt
   D. ohm

6. An amateur radiotelephone station operated as a mobile station is identified by 6.____

   A. transmitting the word *mobile* after the call sign
   B. at the end of every ten minutes, transmitting the call sign followed by the word *mobile*
   C. after the call sign, transmitting the word *mobile,* followed by the call sign area in which the station is operating
   D. transmitting the area of operation after the call sign

7. Which type of repeater operation should be DISCOURAGED during commuter rush hours? 7.____

   A. Traffic information networks
   B. Low-power stations
   C. Mobile stations
   D. Third-party networks

8. The MOST effective way of checking the accuracy of a receiver's tuning dial would be to tune to 8.____

   A. one of the frequencies of station WWV or WWVH
   B. a popular amateur network frequency
   C. the frequency of a shortwave broadcasting station
   D. an amateur station and ask what frequency the operator is using

9. A(n) _____ produces a stable, low-level signal that can be set to a desired frequency. 9.____

A. oscilloscope
B. reflectometer
C. signal generator
D. wavemeter

10. What is the PROPER distress call to use when operating continuous-wave? 10.____

A. MAYDAY
B. HELP
C. QRZ
D. SOS

11. What device should be connected to a transmitter's output when an operator is making transmitter adjustments? 11.____

A. Dummy antenna
B. Reflectometer
C. Receiver
D. Multimeter

12. The BEST way to minimize on-air interference during a lengthy transmitter test procedure is by 12.____

A. using a resonant antenna that requires no loading-up
B. using a dummy load
C. using a non-resonant antenna
D. choosing an unoccupied frequency

13. At what point in an operator's station is the transceiver power measured? 13.____

A. At the power supply terminals
B. At the antenna terminals
C. On the antenna
D. At the final amplifier input terminals

14. A(n) _____ meter is used to measure relative signal strength in a receiver. 14.____

A. RST
B. signal deviation
C. S
D. SSB

15. When a signal is referred to as *five seven,* it is 15.____

A. perfectly readable, but weak
B. readable with considerable difficulty
C. perfectly readable and moderately strong
D. readable with a nearly pure tone

16. What is the result of overdeviation in an FM transmitter? 16.____

A. Increased transmitter power
B. Out-of-channel emissions
C. Increased transmitter range
D. Poor carrier suppression

17. For safety, the BEST thing to do with transmitting antennas is 17.____

A. use vertical polarization
B. use horizontal polarization
C. mount them close to the ground
D. mount them where nobody can come near them

18. _____ may be caused by a multi-band antenna connected to a poorly-tuned antenna. 18.____

A. Auroral distortion
B. Parasitic excitation
C. Harmonic radiation
D. Intermodulation

19. Using a final amplifier capable of providing a 100 W output to a transmission line that provides a 10-decibel loss, the antenna will receive _____ W of power. 19.____

A. 1
B. 10
C. 90
D. 100

20. For two-way systems situated in and around an urban area, what block of frequencies are allocated for use by land mobile services? _____ MHz. 20.____

A. 30
B. 40
C. 470-512
D. 900

21. What type of messages are sent into or out of a disaster area and concern the immediate safety of human life? _____ traffic. 21.____

A. Emergency
B. Tactical
C. Formal message
D. Health and welfare

22. 50 hertz means 50 22.____

A. meters per second
B. cycles per meter
C. cycles per second
D. cycles per minute

23. A common result of operating an FM transmitter with the microphone gain set too high is 23.____

A. atmospheric interference in the air around the antenna
B. digital interference to computer equipment
C. interference to other stations operating near the operator's frequency
D. interference to stations operating on a higher frequency band

24. Which is the SIMPLEST type of system for which simultaneous transmission and reception are possible? 24.____

A. Remote
B. Repeater
C. Duplex
D. Simplex

25. *Splatter interference* is caused by 25.____

A. overmodulation of a transmitter
B. keying a transmitter too quickly
C. routing of a transmitter's output signals back to its input circuit
D. a transmitting antenna of the wrong length

# KEY (CORRECT ANSWERS)

1. D
2. B
3. D
4. C
5. B
6. C
7. D
8. A
9. C
10. D
11. A
12. B
13. B
14. C
15. C
16. B
17. D
18. C
19. B
20. D
21. A
22. C
23. C
24. B
25. A

# EXAMINATION SECTION
# TEST 1

DIRECTIONS: Each question or incomplete statement is followed by several suggested answers or completions. Select the one that BEST answers the question or completes the statement. *PRINT THE LETTER OF THE CORRECT ANSWER IN THE SPACE AT THE RIGHT.*

1. The transmission of signals by electromagnetic waves is referred to as 1.____

   A. biotelemetry  B. radio
   C. noise  D. all of the above

2. The transmission of physiologic data, such as an ECG, from the patient to a distant point of reception is called 2.____

   A. biotelemetry  B. simplex
   C. landline  D. none of the above

3. The assembly of a transmitter, receiver, and antenna connection at a fixed location creates a 3.____

   A. transceiver  B. radio
   C. biotelemetry  D. base station

4. The portion of the radio frequency spectrum between 30 and 150 mhz is called 4.____

   A. very high frequency (VHF)  B. ultrahigh frequency (UHF)
   C. very low frequency (VLF)  D. all of the above

5. A _______ is a miniature transmitter that picks up a radio signal and rebroadcasts it, thus extending the range of a radiocommunication system. 5.____

   A. transceiver  B. repeater  C. simplex  D. duplex

6. The portion of the radio frequency spectrum falling between 300 and 3,000 mhz is called 6.____

   A. ultrahigh frequency (UHF)  B. very high frequency (VHF)
   C. very low frequency (VLF)  D. none of the above

7. One cycle per second equals one _______ in units of frequency. 7.____

   A. hertz  B. kilohertz  C. megahertz  D. gigahertz

8. The sources of noise in ECG telemetry include 8.____

   A. loose ECG electrodes
   B. muscle tremors
   C. sources of 60-cycle alternating current such as transformers, power lines, and electric equipment
   D. all of the above

9. The method of radio communications called _______ utilizes a single frequency that enables either transmission or reception of either voice or an ECG signal, but is incapable of simultaneous transmission and reception. 9.____

A. duplex
B. simplex
C. multiplex
D. none of the above

10. A terminal that receives transmissions of telemetry and voice from the field and transmits messages back through the base is referred to as a 10.____

A. transceiver
B. remote control
C. remote console
D. ten-code

11. The role of dispatcher includes 11.____

A. reception of requests for help
B. arrangements for getting the appropriate people and equipment to a situation which requires them
C. deciding upon and dispatching of the appropriate emergency vehicles
D. all of the above

12. A dispatcher should NOT 12.____

A. maintain records
B. scope a problem by requesting additional information from a caller
C. direct public safety personnel
D. receive notification of emergencies and call for assistance from both individual citizens and public safety units

13. The professional society of public safety communicators has developed a standard set of ten codes, the MOST common of which is 10- 13.____

A. 1
B. 4
C. 12
D. 18

14. What is the meaning of 10-33? 14.____

A. Help me quick
B. Arrived at scene
C. Reply to message
D. Disregard

15. One of the MAIN purposes of ten-codes is to 15.____

A. shorten air time
B. complicate the message
C. increase the likelihood of misunderstanding
D. none of the above

Questions 16-20.

DIRECTIONS: In Questions 16 through 20, match each translation of a commonly used ten-code with its appropriate code, listed in Column I.

COLUMN I

A. 10-1
B. 10-9
C. 10-18
D. 10-20
E. 10-23

16. What is your location? 16.____

17. Urgent. 17.____

18. Signal weak. 18.____

19. Arrived at the scene. 19.____

20. Please repeat. 20.____

## KEY (CORRECT ANSWERS)

| | | | |
|---|---|---|---|
| 1. | B | 11. | D |
| 2. | A | 12. | C |
| 3. | D | 13. | B |
| 4. | A | 14. | A |
| 5. | B | 15. | A |
| 6. | D | 16. | D |
| 7. | A | 17. | C |
| 8. | D | 18. | A |
| 9. | B | 19. | E |
| 10. | C | 20. | B |

# TEST 2

DIRECTIONS: Each question or incomplete statement is followed by several suggested answers or completions. Select the one that BEST answers the question or completes the statement. *PRINT THE LETTER OF THE CORRECT ANSWER IN THE SPACE AT THE RIGHT.*

1. FCC rules prohibit 1.____

   A. deceptive or unnecessary messages
   B. profanity
   C. dissemination or use of confidential information transmitted over the radio
   D. all of the above

2. Penalties for violations of FCC rules and regulations range from 2.____

   A. prison to death
   B. $20,000 to $100,000
   C. $100 to $10,000 and up to one year in prison
   D. up to 10 years in prison

3. Which of the following is NOT true about base stations? 3.____

   A. The terrain and location do not affect the function.
   B. A good high-gain antenna improves transmission and reception efficiency.
   C. Multiple frequency capability is available at the base station.
   D. Antenna should be as close as possible to the base station transmitter/receiver.

4. Radio frequencies are designated by cycles per second. 1,000,000 cycles per second equals one 4.____

   A. kilohertz B. megahertz C. gigahertz D. hertz

5. The Federal Communications Commission (FCC) is the agency of the United States government responsible for 5.____

   A. licensing and frequency allocation
   B. establishing technical standards for radio equipment
   C. establishing and enforcing rules and regulations for the operation of radio equipment
   D. all of the above

6. Information relayed to the physician should include all of the following EXCEPT 6.____

   A. patient's age, sex, and chief complaint
   B. pertinent history of present illness
   C. detailed family history
   D. pertinent physical findings

7. True statements regarding UHF band may include all of the following EXCEPT: 7.____

   A. It has better penetration in the dense metropolitan area
   B. Reception is usually quiet inside the building
   C. It has a longer range than VHF band
   D. Most medical communications occur around 450 to 470 mhz

8. Which of the following statements is NOT true regarding VHF band? 8.____

   A. Low band frequency may have ranges up to 2000 miles, but are unpredictable.
   B. VHF band may cause *skip interference,* with patchy losses in communication.
   C. High band frequency is wholly free of skip interference.
   D. High band frequencies for emergency medical purposes are in the 300 to 3000 mhz range.

9. 1000 cycles per second is equal to one 9.____

   A. hertz B. kilohertz C. megahertz D. gigahertz

10. _______ achieves simultaneous transmission of voice and ECG signals over a single radio frequency. 10.____

   A. Duplex B. Multiplex
   C. Channel D. None of the above

11. Radio equipment used for both VHF and UHF band is 11.____

   A. frequency modulated
   B. amplitude modulated
   C. double amplitude modulated
   D. all of the above

12. ECG telemetry over UHF frequencies is confined to _____ of a 12 lead ECG. 12.____

   A. 1 B. 2 C. 6 D. 12

13. All of the following further clarity and conciseness EXCEPT 13.____

   A. understandable rate of speaking
   B. knowing what you want to transmit after transmission
   C. clear presentation of numbers, names, and dates
   D. using phrases and words which are easy to copy

14. The LEAST preferred of the following words is 14.____

   A. check B. desire C. want D. advise if

15. All of the following are techniques useful during a call EXCEPT 15.____

   A. answering promptly
   B. identifying yourself and your department
   C. speaking directly into the mouthpiece
   D. none of the above

Questions 16-20.

DIRECTIONS: In Questions 16 through 20, match each definition with the term it describes, listed in Column I.

COLUMN I
A. Frequency
B. Noise
C. Patch
D. Duplex
E. Transceiver

16. A radio transmitter and receiver housed in a single unit; a two-way radio 16.____

17. The number of cycles per second of a radio signal, inversely related to the wavelength. 17.____

18. Interference in radio signals. 18.____

19. A radio system employing more than one frequency to permit simultaneous transmission and reception. 19.____

20. Connection between a telephone line and a radio communication system, enabling a caller to get *on the air* by special telephone. 20.____

# KEY (CORRECT ANSWERS)

| | | | |
|---|---|---|---|
| 1. | D | 11. | A |
| 2. | C | 12. | A |
| 3. | A | 13. | B |
| 4. | B | 14. | C |
| 5. | D | 15. | D |
| 6. | C | 16. | E |
| 7. | C | 17. | A |
| 8. | D | 18. | B |
| 9. | B | 19. | D |
| 10. | B | 20. | C |

# EXAMINATION SECTION
# ˙EST 1

DIRECTIONS: Each question or incomplete statement is followed by several suggested answers or completions. Select the one that BEST answers the question or completes the statement. *PRINT THE LETTER OF THE CORRECT ANSWER IN THE SPACE AT THE RIGHT.*

1. Police Communications Technicians Clay and Robinson are told by their supervisor that they would have to share the computer terminal on Position 77 in the overflow because the terminal at Position 78 has been removed for repair. Dispatcher Clay signs into the terminal using her tax number, 505873. A few minutes later, Dispatcher Robinson tries to sign in with her tax number, 555873, and her attempt is rejected. As her supervisor, you should instruct Dispatcher Robinson that the PROPER format to use is ____/555873/to (ENTER) 1.____

   A. BSIA  B. BSIP  C. BSIO  D. BSIB

2. On January 2, Police Communications Dispatcher Quinones receives a call on 911 from a Mrs. Turnbaum. She states that she and her husband were fighting, and her husband struck her across the face. Dispatcher Quinones asks Mrs. Turnbaum if she is injured and whether her husband is still there. Mrs. Turnbaum replies in the negative to both questions. Dispatcher Quinones asks you, the supervisor, how to handle this call. You should direct Dispatcher Quinones to 2.____

   A. enter a 10-24Q1
   B. enter a 10-52D1
   C. refer the caller to Family Court
   D. refer the caller to her local precinct

3. Police Communications Operator Lucas, assigned to 911 in Brooklyn, receives a call from a Mrs. Spano, who lives at 1205 Elm Avenue in the 70th Precinct. She states that she called twice before to report that her apartment was burglarized. She says that no police have shown up yet. Dispatcher Lucas does an Incident Query of the location. He finds that the job was previously entered in 911 and then displays it on his screen. He sees that 70SP10 is assigned to the job. Dispatcher Lucas then notifies you that he has received a third call on this incident. As the supervisor, you should instruct Dispatcher Lucas to enter the job as additional information indicating that the caller was referred to the precinct, that the supervisor was notified, and then have Dispatcher Lucas 3.____

   A. route the job R
   B. route the job Z
   C. route the job D
   D. enter the job with no routing

4. Police Communications Technician Sands receives a call from an ABC Alarm Company operator stating that they have an alarm of a hold-up or burglary in progress at Met's Jewelry Store at 1259 Broadway in Manhattan. The operator then states that a phone call she made to the Met's Jewelry Store was answered by someone who did not properly identify himself. Dispatcher Sands is unsure of what action to take and asks Supervising Police Communications Technician Rain for assistance. 4.____

Supervisor Rain should instruct Dispatcher Sands to enter the job as a

A. 10-11C4 code with all pertinent information
B. 10-10P1 for prowler on the premises
C. 10-31C code with all pertinent information
D. 10-68Q2 to meet alarm company personnel to check the premises

5. While you are working as a Supervising Dispatcher, one of your operators receives a call from a grocery store manager who states that he was held up *five minutes in the past* by two male Hispanics who took all the cash from his register and fled in a green auto that headed south on Broadway. Your operator quickly inputs a 10-30C and hotlines the job to the dispatcher concerned. 5.____
As the supervisor, you should instruct the operator to change the code to a

A. 10-20C B. 10-20Q1 C. 10-30Q1 D. 10-30Q2

6. As the Supervising Police Communications Technician, you ask Police Communications Technician Glass to prepare a list of screenable jobs that have been entered into 911 in the borough of Brooklyn in the last half hour. 6.____
The following is a list of jobs that Dispatcher Glass has before her:
A(n)
1. auto accident involving property damage
2. dead horse in the street
3. tree down on the sidewalk
4. unoccupied auto that might be stolen
5. female who has found a wallet
6. request to assist a female in serving a summons

Dispatcher Glass is not sure which of the above jobs is screenable.
Which of these incidents should you have Dispatcher Glass include in the screenable list?

A. 1, 2, 4, and 5, but not 3 and 6
B. 1, 3, 4, and 6, but not 2 and 5
C. 1, 3, 5, and 6, but not 2 and 4
D. 2, 3, 4, and 6, but not 1 and 5

7. Police Communications Dispatcher Howard, assigned to Position 38 on Brooklyn Dispatch, receives a call from a Mr. Green, Chief of Security for the Starlight Security Company. Mr. Green states that one of his uniformed guards is holding five males on a charge of shoplifting. He asks that a unit respond at once since their holding cell can accommodate only two persons. 7.____
As the Supervising Dispatcher assigned to Brooklyn, you should instruct Dispatcher Howard to input the job as follows:

A. IE/68Q1/SECURITY HOLDING 5*
B. IE/32Q1/SECURITY HOLDING 5*
C. IE/12U1/SECURITY HOLDING 5*
D. IE/68Q1/1085* NO EMERGENCY, SECURITY HOLDING 5

8. Police Communications Operator Street, assigned to Brooklyn Dispatching, receives a call on 911 from a male stating that his apartment is being flooded by a leak that is com ing from the vacant apartment above him. He insists that the police come to his home to correct the condition. Dispatcher Street asks you, the supervisor, how to handle this call. 8.____

You should instruct Dispatcher Street to

A. refer the caller to his local precinct
B. enter a 10-65S
C. enter a 10-68Q1
D. refer the caller to his superintendent

9. A male who does not wish to reveal his name calls a dispatcher to report that his landlord at 16 Hollywood River Drive, Apartment 1H, appears to be selling drugs and guns. He tells the dispatcher that this usually occurs every night after 9 P.M. The dispatcher inputs the job into Sprint as a Code 10-Y3. 9.____
Upon reviewing this job, you, as the supervisor, should

A. ensure that a patrol car is sent
B. call the Narcotics Unit and Precinct Detective Unit by landline and have them dispatch units
C. tell the operator to route the job to Citywide and the Organized Crime Control Bureau
D. tell the operator to change the code to a 10-69S defer to be referred to the Organized Crime Control Bureau

10. Police Communications Tech. Proctor receives a call on 911 from PAA Gamble of the 71st Precinct in Brooklyn. PAA Gamble is the telephone switchboard operator for the stationhouse. She states that she just received a call from an unknown male who stated that at 250 Fenimore Street, Apartment 3E, there is a male named Jack Daniels who is selling cocaine. The caller stated that when a buyer stands at the door and whistles, Daniels opens it and the deal is made. Dispatcher Proctor asks PAA Gamble to hold on. She summons you, the supervisor, for assistance on how to handle this call. 10.____
You should instruct Dispatcher Proctor to

A. enter a 10-69S defer for the Organized Crime Control Bureau
B. enter a 10-10Y3 man selling drugs
C. advise PAA Gamble to call her Precinct Detective Unit directly
D. advise PAA Gamble to call the Organized Crime Control Bureau directly

Questions 11-16.

DIRECTIONS: Questions 11 through 16 are to be answered SOLELY on the basis of the following information.

Supervising Police Communications Technician Noel is assigned to monitor Police Communications Technician Casey on dispatching. The following calls were received and handled by Dispatcher Casey during the monitoring period:

Call 1. Operator 512 from the AZU Alarm Company called to report a burglary alarm for the roof and rear door at the Zero Savings Bank at 1 Park Row in Manhattan. Dispatcher Casey asked the caller to hold on, hotlined the job as an 11B4, and then returned to Operator 512. Dispatcher Casey was advised that the alarm company was responding, and that AZU Alarm Company's phone number is 999-8888. Dispatcher Casey entered the job as follows:

IQ/7/1 PARK ROW (ENTER)
IE/11B4/ZERO SAVINGS BANK* BURGLARY ALARM FOR REAR DOOR - AZU ALARM CO. - RESPONDING - OPR. 512 - CB9998888 - HOTLINED - OPR. 52-5 (ENTER)

IF/OPR. 512/9998888 (ENTER)

Call 2. Nurse Manning from New York Hospital, located at East 68th Street and York Avenue in Manhattan, called to report an aided case in the emergency room. Mrs. Carmen, who came for emergency treatment after being beaten by her neighbor during a dispute, wanted to see the police to file a report. Dispatcher Casey asked for the phone number in the hospital emergency room. The phone number was given as 999-8989, and Dispatcher Casey told the nurse that the police would respond as soon as possible. Dispatcher Casey entered the job as follows:

IQ/7/NY HOSPITAL MD (ENTER)

IE/68Q1/AIDED CASE* SFC CARMEN IN THE EMERGENCY ROOM - REGARDING A PAST ASSAULT THAT OCCURRED AT HER RESIDENCE - OPR. 52-5=P2 (ENTER)

IF/MANNING/9998989 (ENTER)

Call 3. Security Guard Joseph called to report an explosion and fire in the lobby of the Empire State Building in Manhattan. Dispatcher Casey immediately connected the caller with the Fire Department. After giving the necessary information to Fire Department Operator 32, the caller stated that there were at least three people injured at the location. Dispatcher Casey connected the caller to Ambulance Receiving Operator 117, exchanged information, hotlined the job, and notified Supervisor Noel of the incident. Dispatcher Casey entered the job as follows:

IQ/7/EMPIRE STATE BUILDING UNK (ENTER)

IE/33/EXPLOSION AND FIRE* IN THE LOBBY - SECURITY GUARD JOSEPH STATES THAT AT LEAST THREE PEOPLE HAVE BEEN INJURED - FD 32 NTFD - RO 117 NTFD - HOTLINED - SPCT NOEL NTFD - OPR. 52-5=P9 (ENTER)

IF/JOSEPH/ (ENTER)

Call 4. Ms. Topps called 911 to report that two teenagers were drag racing in an empty parking lot. Ms. Topps told Dispatcher Casey that it was a dangerous condition and she wanted the police to respond. Dispatcher Casey told the caller that this was not a 911 emergency and referred Ms. Topps to the local precinct. Ms. Topps said she had the phone number and hung up.

Call 5. Mr. Janzen called to report that his shoe store, located at Hyland Boulevard and Robinson Avenue in Staten Island, was just robbed about six minutes in the past. Mr. Janzen said he was robbed by two males, white, both dressed in blue; they each had a gun. He did not see which way they ran and could give no further description. Dispatcher Casey asked the caller for his phone number. Mr. Janzen gave 777-9999, and Dispatcher Casey told him that the police would respond as soon as possible. Dispatcher Casey entered the job as follows:

IQ/4/HYLAND BLVD - ROBINSON AVE (ENTER)

IE/20Q1/SHOE STORE* SMC JANZEN - STATES SIX MINUTES IN PAST STORE WAS HELD UP BY TWO MALES - DRESSED IN BLUE - UNKNOWN DIRECTION OF FLIGHT - OPR. 52-5 (ENTER)

IF/JANZEN/7779999 (ENTER)

Call 6. Mr. Peters called 911 to report that, in the parking lot of Jacobi Hospital in the Bronx, an auto's horn has been blasting for the past ten minutes. The owner of the car was unable to shut off the horn. Dispatcher Casey told the caller that this was not a 911 emergency, and he could call the 43rd Precinct at 822-5611.

Call 7. Mrs. Arnold called 911 and stated that she called 15 minutes ago to request that the police respond to a dispute on the street in front of 2011 Broadway. She stated that the police had not responded yet, and now one of the males has been stabbed. Dispatcher Casey found that a 10-52D2 was entered in the system at the location, and a patrol car had been dispatched. Dispatcher Casey hotlined the new information to the dispatcher and then connected the caller to Emergency Medical Service Operator 320. The caller could give no descriptions. Dispatcher Casey notified Supervisor Noel of the incident and entered the information as follows:

II/34K2* ANOTHER CALL - CALLER STATES ONE OF THE MALES HAS BEEN STABBED - RO 320 NTFD - NO DESCRIPTIONS AVAILABLE - SPCT NOEL NTFD - HOTLINED _ OPR. 52-5=DNSP3A:SA320-HOSP-HOSQ (ENTER)

Call 8. Dispatcher Casey received a job via 911 from Telephone Switchboard Operator PAA Thomas of the 90th Precinct, advising of an anonymous call reporting gas fumes at 193 Grand Street, Brooklyn, on the 4th floor. Dispatcher Casey connected the caller to the Fire Department and entered the job as follows:

IQ/6/193 GRAND ST (ENTER)
IE/65S/GAS FUMES* FD 161 NTFD - AUTH 90 TS PAA THOMAS - RECEIVED FROM ANON CALLER - OPR. 52-5 (ENTER)
IF/PAA THOMAS/6834219 (ENTER)

The following questions are based on the monitoring of Dispatcher Casey by Supervisor Noel.

11. Supervisor Noel should identify errors in coding for which of the following calls? 11.____

A. 1, 2, 7 B. 1, 3, 8 C. 2, 3, 5 D. 2, 5, 8

12. For which of the following calls were there errors or omissions in routing? 12.____

A. 1, 3, 5 B. 1, 3, 7 C. 1, 5, 7 D. 3, 5, 7

13. Which of the following calls were handled properly according to 911 screening procedures? 13.____

A. 1, 4, 6 B. 1, 4, 8 C. 1, 6, 8 D. 4, 6, 8

14. During which of the following calls did Dispatcher Casey fail to enter pertinent data given by the caller? 14.____

A. 1, 5, 8 B. 1, 3, 7 C. 2, 3, 5 D. 2, 7, 8

15. During which of the following calls did Dispatcher Casey fail to follow established hotline procedure? 15.____

A. 3 B. 5 C. 7 D. 8

16. For which one of the following calls did Dispatcher Casey fail to walk the job into the dispatcher as required by procedure? 16.____

A. 1 B. 3 C. 5 D. 7

17. On June 6, the Sprint System suddenly ceases operation. You, as the supervisor, immediately assign Police Communications Dispatcher Black as the scanner for the borough of the Bronx. 17.____

As a scanner, the FIRST task that Dispatcher Black should do is

A. check the address file for the incident location
B. deliver slips to the radio dispatchers and other necessary locations
C. return rejected slips to operators for completion or correction
D. walk behind operators and pick up completed slips

18. Police Communications Operator Lincoln, assigned to Brooklyn Dispatching, receives a call from a Mrs. Gomez who states that she and her husband just had a violent argument. She also states that her husband was discharged from a psychiatric hospital last week and is threatening to kill himself. Mrs. Gomez further states that her husband stormed out of the house five minutes ago, and at this time she is unsure of his present location. She wants the police and an ambulance to come to her house to find her husband and take him back to the hospital. Dispatcher Lincoln is unsure of how to handle this call, and he asks you, his supervisor, for assistance. 18.____
You should direct him to

A. refer the caller to her local precinct
B. tell the caller to call 911 as soon as her husband returns
C. enter a job as a 10-54E1
D. enter a job as a 10-68Q1

19. Police Communications Dispatcher Baker, assigned to overflow Position 85, receives a call from Police Officer Marin of the 63rd Precinct. Officer Marin advises Dispatcher Baker that the precinct has just received another call regarding an alarm at 1183 Avenue He further states that he called in the alarm about an hour ago and has not yet heard the job go over the air. Dispatcher Baker enters an incident query message into Sprint and sees that a job was entered but was not dispatched because the location, 1183 Avenue H, has been designated as *chronic*. Dispatcher Baker tells Officer Marin that a car will not be sent because it is a chronic location. You, as the supervisor, overhear Dispatcher Baker's final remark to Officer Marin. 19.____
You should instruct her to

A. input a new job as a 10-11
B. input a new job as a 10-68
C. refer the job back to the precinct
D. refer Officer Marin to the FATN section

20. Police Communications Operator Milbrook calls you, her supervisor, to ask for assistance in handling a caller who is reporting a flooding condition. You advise Dispatcher Milbrook that you would not order a job input unless *possible aggravating circumstances* existed. 20.____
Which one of the following is NOT an example of a *possible aggravating circumstance?*

A. Water pressure emergency
B. Local flooding caused by a broken hydrant
C. Flooding the ground floor of a residence
D. Flooding of an intersection

21. Police Communications Technician Healy receives a call via 911 from a female who resides at a housing project located at 2340 Nostrand Avenue, Apartment 6E. The caller is angry about what she states is a dangerous condition. She reports that there is garbage strewn all over the exit steps and that someone may fall. Dispatcher Healy is not sure what to do in this situation and asks you, the supervisor, for assistance. You should instruct Dispatcher Healy to 21.____

A. input a 10-10Y3 *dangerous condition*
B. input a 10-68Q1
C. take the information and refer it to the Housing Authority Police Department
D. refer the caller to the Environmental Protection Agency

22. Police Communications Technician Zenith tells you, the overflow supervisor, that he received a call from an hysterical male who said he was traveling southbound on the Clearview Expressway in Queens. He said he was driving to the hospital with his pregnant wife, who is in labor, but his car broke down on the highway. The caller didn't know the name of the nearest exit, but he saw a mile marker listing the numbers 2076 on the bottom and 295I on the top of the marker. Dispatcher Zenith could not get the location into the system and asks you how he should enter this information. You should instruct him to use which one of the following formats? IQ/5/ 22.____

A. 295I RTE S 2076
B. RTE S 295I
C. RTE 2076I 295S
D. 2076 295I RTE S

23. On January 9, all operators are given a memo detailing a planned visit by President Bush to Manhattan during your tour of duty. At approximately 0930 hours this date, Police Communications Technician Jones, an operator assigned to the borough of Queens, receives a call from Captain Barnes of the 113th Precinct. He requests information regarding the planned time that the Presidential motorcade will pass through his precinct as indicated in the memo. Recalling the memo, Operator Jones provides him with the information requested. Operator Jones then informs you, his supervisor, that he was able to provide Captain Barnes with the requested information. As his supervisor, you should instruct Operator Jones that the CORRECT procedure is to 23.____

A. tell the caller that you cannot provide him with the information requested
B. input a 10-69S DEFER-INFO ONLY* - TIME NOTING PLANNED VISIT
C. notify the supervisor who will interview the caller providing necessary details of the memo
D. input a 10-69S DEFER - INFO ONLY* = P9N

24. Police Communications Technician Roberts receives a call from Mr. Rich requesting a Med-Evac Helicopter for an emergency transport of blood from New York Hospital in Manhattan to Smithtown Hospital in Long Island. Dispatcher Roberts is unfamiliar with the procedure for Med-Evac and requests assistance. As a supervisor, you should direct Dispatcher Roberts to 24.____

A. enter a 10Y3 and hotline to Citywide for the dispatching of a helicopter
B. connect the caller to the Emergency Medical Service and enter a 10Y3 with routing for Citywide and Notifications

C. tell the caller that Med-Evac can only be requested by a member of the service
D. tell the caller to speak to the Emergency Medical Service via their direct phone number to request Med-Evac

25. Police Communications Technician Grow, an operator, receives a call from Transit Police Officer Brown. Officer Brown states that there is an elderly female who is having difficulty breathing at the token booth at the West 50th Street Station on the IND line. Officer Brown tells Operator Grow that the transit officer on the scene wants an ambulance. However, Officer Brown cannot stay on the telephone to speak with the Emergency Medical Service because he must respond to another emergency. Operator Grow attempts to enter the location and receives an error message. 25.____
Operator Grow asked for the supervisor's assistance and was instructed according to procedures to use which one of the following formats? IQ/7/______ and process the job as a ______.

A. W 50 ST TRAN (ENTER); 10-55
B. 50 ST IND TRAN (ENTER); 10-54S1
C. IND W 50 ST TRAN (ENTER); 10-54S1
D. IND 50 ST TRAN (ENTER); 10-55

# KEY (CORRECT ANSWERS)

| | |
|---|---|
| 1. D | 11. C |
| 2. D | 12. B |
| 3. B | 13. B |
| 4. A | 14. A |
| 5. A | 15. A |
| 6. B | 16. D |
| 7. C | 17. A |
| 8. D | 18. D |
| 9. D | 19. A |
| 10. C | 20. B |

21. D
22. D
23. A
24. D
25. B

# TEST 2

DIRECTIONS: Each question or incomplete statement is followed by several suggested answers or completions. Select the one that BEST answers the question or completes the Statement. *PRINT THE LETTER OF THE CORRECT ANSWER IN THE SPACE AT THE RIGHT.*

Questions 1-5.

DIRECTIONS: Questions 1 through 5 are to be answered on the basis of the following information.

Call #1

0305 Hours

OPERATOR Police Operator 712, where is the emergency?

CALLER I'm Mrs. Piermont and I need the police.

OPERATOR Where do you need the police?

CALLER I live at 1436 Broadway, Apartment 3B, and I'm having an argument with my husband.

OPERATOR May I have your phone number?

CALLER It's 3933939. Send the police now.

OPERATOR The police will be there as soon as possible.

-- caller hangs up --

The operator entered the job as follows:

IQ/7/1436 BROADWAY (ENTER)

IE/52D1/APT 3D* SFC PIERMONT - STATES SHE IS HAVING A DISPUTE WITH HER HUSBAND - OPR. 712-2 (ENTER)

IF/PIERMONT/3933939 (ENTER)

Call #2

0315 Hours

OPERATOR Police Operator 010, where is the emergency?

CALLER Hello, my name is Mrs. Conway. I live at 1436 Broadway in Apartment 4B on the 4th floor. There's a fight going on in the apartment below. I hear a woman screaming. The voice sounds like that nice Mrs. Piermont with the two kids. Would you please send someone over to see what's going on?

OPERATOR That's 1436 Broadway, Apartment 4B as in *Boy.*

CALLER Yes.

OPERATOR What's your telephone number?

CALLER It's 3934646.

OPERATOR O.K. Madam, the police will be there as soon as possible.

CALLER Thank you.

-- caller hangs up --

The operator queries the system, finds the previous entry, and sees that no patrol car has been dispatched. She then proceeds to enter an additional information message as follows:

IQ/7/1436 BROADWAY (ENTER)

IA* ANOTHER CALL - DISPUTE IN APARTMENT BELOW 4B. FEMALE STATES SHE HEARS SCREAMING - OPR. 010-12 (ENTER)

IF/CONWAY/3934646 (ENTER)

Call #3
0327 Hours

| | |
|---|---|
| OPERATOR | Police Operator 219, where is the emergency? |
| CALLER | Help me! My mommy has been stabbed! |
| OPERATOR | How old are you? |
| CALLER | What? |
| OPERATOR | I said, how old are you? |
| CALLER | I'm nine. |
| OPERATOR | Put someone else on the phone! |
| CALLER | Just my sister and I are here. |
| OPERATOR | How old is your sister. |
| CALLER | She's six years old. |
| OPERATOR | Okay, what is the address? |
| CALLER | 1436 Broadway, on the third floor. |
| OPERATOR | We have the job already. That's between 37th and 38th Streets, right? |
| CALLER | No. I live near Eastern Parkway. |
| OPERATOR | You live in Brooklyn? |
| CALLER | Yes! |
| OPERATOR | Is your name Piermont? |
| CALLER | Yes! |
| OPERATOR | The police will be there as soon as possible. |

The operator entered the job as follows:
IC/6/1436 BROADWAY* ANOTHER CALL RECEIVED - CHILD CALLER STATES MOTHER HAS BEEN STABBED - ON THE THIRD FLOOR -NO FURTHER INFORMATION OPR. 219-85 (ENTER)

Call #4
0332 Hours

| | |
|---|---|
| OPERATOR | Police Operator 956, where is the emergency? |
| CALLER | I called before. I told you there was a violent argument downstairs. The woman has been stabbed; there's blood all over the place. |
| OPERATOR | Calm down lady! What's your address? |
| CALLER | 1436 Broadway, Apartment 4B; but the woman stabbed is in Apartment 3B. |
| OPERATOR | Is that 3*B* as in *Boy* or 3*D* as in *David?* |
| CALLER | Hurry up! I gave you all this information before. The apartment is 3B as in *Boy.* |
| OPERATOR | OK Ma'am. I see the job in the system. The police are on the way. What is your name and phone number? |
| CALLER | Please hurry! She could be dying. My name is Conway, and my phone number is 393-4646. |
| OPERATOR | Alright! Hold on for the Emergency Medical Service. |

At this point, the operator attempts to notify the Ambulance Receiving Operator. After six rings, they fail to answer. The operator subsequently tells the caller that she will process the call and that the police will be there as soon as possible. The operator then enters the message as follows:
II/34K1* APT. 3B - ANOTHER CALL - CALLER STATES FEMALE STABBED - APARTMENT CORRECTION - UNABLE TO NOTIFY ARO. CALL BACK NUMBER - 393-4646 SPCT BRUCCI NOTIFIED OPR. 956-43 = NP3DAS:HOSP-HOSQ

Supervising Police Communications Technician Brucci now has the task of reinstructing the operator or operators concerned on any or all of the four jobs entered into 911. On these calls, the various operators neglected to follow several procedures or guidelines established by the Police Department.

1. During which of the following calls did the operator fail to verify the address? 1.____

   A. 1, 2, 3 B. 1, 2, 4 C. 1, 3, 4 D. 2, 3, 4

2. During which of the following calls did the operator fail to enter the name and callback correctly? 2.____

   A. 2 B. 3 C. 1, 2 D. 2, 4

3. During which of the following calls did the operator fail to properly handle the callback? 3.____

   A. 2 B. 3 C. 2, 3 D. 3, 4

4. Which of the following calls were NOT properly routed? 4.____

   A. 2, 3 B. 1, 3 C. 2, 4 D. 3, 4

5. For which of the following calls was the operator required to walk the job into the dispatcher? 5.____

   A. 2 B. 4 C. 1, 3 D. 2, 4

6. Upon being notified of a report received by Police Communications Technician Gray regarding an AWOL (absent without leave) member of the armed forces, the supervisor should instruct the 911 operator to take which of the following actions? 6.____
   1. Refer the caller to the Military Police of the branch of the service concerned.
   2. Input a Sprint job with full details so that the first available patrol car can be sent.
   3. Refer the caller to the local precinct.
   4. Input a 69 Defer with full details and route for the Operations Unit.

   The CORRECT answer is:

   A. 1 or 4 B. 2 or 3 C. 1 or 2 D. 3 or 4

7. While on duty as an operator in the borough of Manhattan, Police Communications Technician Brown receives a call from a concerned citizen regarding a patrol car double-parked in front of an abandoned building. The caller states that two police officers are apparently transferring property from the trunk of a car into their patrol car. The caller also states that the officers' behavior is somewhat suspicious. While processing this call, Operator Brown calls for your assistance. 7.____
   As the supervisor, your FIRST task is to

   A. instruct the operator to input a 10-69 defer, detailing the incident
   B. obtain details from Operator Brown and report the complaint in writing
   C. interview the caller to obtain details of the incident
   D. instruct the operator to tell the caller to contact the Civilian Complaint Review Board

8. Police Communications Technician Jones, an operator, receives a call from a merchant describing a series of incidents in which a male, who identifies himself as a police officer, routinely collects money from merchants for what he describes as a local police fund to help support a neighborhood youth basketball team. Operator Jones does not know how to handle this call, so he asks you, the supervisor, for assistance. 8.____
As the supervisor, you should instruct Operator Jones

A. to enter a 10-68 to obtain further details
B. to tell the merchant to call his local precinct
C. that you will interview the caller and advise the patrol supervisor over landline to investigate
D. that you will interview the caller and notify the Internal Affairs Division

9. On May 12, a memo is issued and distributed to all operators concerning reoccurring incidents of youths spraypainting graffiti on subway cars. The memo essentially restates the procedure that should be followed in such cases. Police Communications Technician Benson, a newly assigned operator, receives a call regarding youths in the subway with spray cans vandalizing a station. Operator Benson asks you, the supervisor, what she should do regarding this call. 9.____
You should instruct Operator Benson that her FIRST action should be to

A. connect the caller to the Transit Authority Police Department via the add-on button
B. input a 10-39 incident code into Sprint, hotlining the incident
C. input a 10-50G2 incident code into Sprint, hotlining the incident
D. give the caller the Transit Authority Police Department's telephone number

10. Police Communications Technician Garber, a Manhattan operator, receives a call from a civil service employee who works in the emergency room at Elmhurst General Hospital. The caller states that while he was on duty a couple of hours ago, two police officers brought in a female in labor. As the nurses were preparing the female for the delivery room, the hospital clerk approached one of the officers and asked for identification of the female. The officer who was holding the female's coat and purse opened the purse to seek identification. He took out a wallet, which contained the female's drivers license. As the hospital clerk turned to leave, the caller saw the police officer take a large amount of money from the female's wallet. He gave several of the bills to the clerk and put the remainder of the money inside his holster. The caller does not wish to speak to a 911 supervisor, for fear of losing his job, but he feels it is his duty as a good citizen to report the incident. Operator Garber does not know how to handle this call and asks you, the Manhattan supervisor, for assistance. 10.____
You should instruct Operator Garber to

A. send a sergeant to Elmhurst General
B. give the caller the telephone number of the Civilian Complaint Review Board
C. insist that the caller speak to you, the supervisor
D. give the caller the special corruption number

11. Police Communications Dispatcher Reiner receives a call from a Mr. Nathan, who states that an ambulance had been sent to his friend's home but a problem arose. When the Emergency Medical Service crew arrived and learned that Mr. Nathan's friend was an AIDS patient, they refused to take him to the hospital. The ambulance crew told Mr. Nathan that they were not required to transport AIDS patients, but they would do so if they were given $25 each. Mr. Nathan refused to pay, and the ambulance crew left. Dis 11.____

patcher Reiner is unsure of the proper procedure to follow and asks you for assistance. As the supervisor, you should speak with Mr. Nathan and

A. ensure that another ambulance is sent and then refer him to the Civilian Complaint Review Board
B. connect him to the Emergency Medical Service Supervisor to handle the complaint regarding the ambulance crew
C. ensure that another ambulance is sent, and then report the details to the Internal Affairs Division
D. ensure that another ambulance is sent, and also send a patrol car to take the details of the incident

Questions 12-15.

DIRECTIONS: Questions 12 through 15 are to be answered SOLELY on the basis of the following information.

As a Supervising Dispatcher, you are required to review tapes of 10-13's and other serious jobs received by Operator 010, who was assigned to Position 58 from 1600 hours to 2000 hours on May 17.

<u>Tape for Job #1 is as follows:</u>

OPERATOR Police Operator 010, where is the emergency?

CALLER This is Police Officer Doyle from Transit. I need some help here. I was down on the southbound platform in the station on Parsons Boulevard and Hillside Avenue. There is a man on the tracks trying to catch a dog who fell from the platform. I jumped down to assist, but the dog's leg is stuck between the rails.

OPERATOR Do you know the booth number, sir?

CALLER Yes; 1 am at Booth 217, my badge number is 6006, and I am in uniform. I have already notified the Station Master to shut off the power, and the shut-off has been confirmed. I need the Police Department's Emergency Service Unit.

OPERATOR Okay, we will get help there. (HOTLINE) In the 117 Precinct, A Sector, I have a 10-13 at Parsons Boulevard and Hillside Avenue. Officer going down on the subway tracks.

DISPATCHER I got it. Put the job in, please.

<u>Entry for Job #1 is as follows:</u>
IQ/5/PARSONS BLVD - HILLSIDE AVE (ENTER)
IE/13U1/P.O. ON TRACKS* P.O. ON TRACKS WITH A DOG - REQUEST ASSISTANCE - HOTLINED - OPR. 010-58 (ENTER)
IF/DOYLE/ (ENTER)

<u>Tape for Job #2 is as follows:</u>

OPERATOR Police Operator 010, where is the emergency?

CALLER Hello, police. This is Mrs. McLina. My husband is having chest pains. He is a retired police Captain. I am at 5700 Broadway, Apartment 3F - 3rd Floor. My telephone number is 094-0606.

OPERATOR Is he unconscious, madam?

CALLER No, but he's clutching his chest.

OPERATOR Does he have a cardiac history?

| | |
|---|---|
| CALLER | Not that I know of. |
| OPERATOR | Well, loosen his clothing, begin cardiopulmonary resuscitation, and I will get a car rolling. Hold on - do not hang up. (HOTLINE) I have a 10-13, in the 27th Precinct, A Sector, 5700 Broadway. It is a retired cop having a heart attack. |
| DISPATCHER | Okay, put the job in. |
| OPERATOR | Madam, I am now connecting you to the ambulance service. CALLER I can't stay on the telephone any longer. I have to go to my husband. |
| | - caller hangs up - |

Entry for Job #2 is as follows;
IQ/7/5700 BROADWAY (ENTER)
IE/13X1/HEART ATTACK* MC MCLINA - RETIRED CAPTAIN - APT 3F - 3FL - HOTLINED - CALLER HUNG UP - UNABLE TO REACH RO - SUPERVISOR ON ANOTHER LINE - OPR. 010-58 (ENTER)
IF/MCLINA/0940606 (ENTER)

Tape for Job #3 is as follows:

| | |
|---|---|
| OPERATOR | Police Operator 010, where is the emergency? |
| CALLER | This is Police Officer Lonzo. I am off duty. I've just witnessed a break-in at 142-09 164th Street. It's a private house. I am calling from the phone booth on the corner in front of A1's Grocery Store. I am going after them. |
| OPERATOR | Wait a minute. Don't hang up. (HOTLINE) I have a 31 in progress in the 117th Precinct, B Sector, 142-09 164th Street. It was called in by an off-duty police officer who is going after them. |
| DISPATCHER | Okay, please enter the job. |
| OPERATOR | Police Officer, what are you wearing, and do you have any description on the perpetrators? |
| CALLER | I am wearing a...listen, they've spotted me.... They're firing shots at me.... I've been shot.... (phone disconnects). |

Entry for Job #3 is as follows:
IQ/5/142-09 164 ST (ENTER)
IE/31R/OFF DUTY* P.O. STATED HE WAS GOING AFTER PERPETRATORS - THEN HE SAID HE HAD BEEN SHOT - UNABLE TO REACH RO - HOTLINED - SUPV VALLEY NTFD OPR. 010-58=SWNP9 AS:HOSP-HOSQ (ENTER)
IF/P.O. LONZO/(ENTER)

Tape for Job #4 is as follows:

| | |
|---|---|
| OPERATOR | Police Operator 010, where is the emergency? |
| CALLER | This is Police Officer Thomas. I am a uniformed officer on duty. My partner and I are here at Hillside Avenue and 161st Street. We are being assaulted with bottles and rocks by a large crowd of people. Get us some help fast. |
| | - caller hangs up - |
| OPERATOR | (HOTLINE) In the 117th Precinct, G Sector, I have a 10-13 at Hillside Avenue and 161st Street. Two police officers are being assaulted by a large crowd with rocks and bottles. |
| DISPATCHER | That's Hillside and 161, in uniform? |
| OPERATOR | Yes. |

DISPATCHER Enter the job, please.

Entry for Job #4 is as follows:
IQ/5/HILLSIDE AVE - 161 ST (ENTER)
IE/13U2/P.O. ASSAULTED* TWO OFFICERS UNDER ASSAULT WITH BOTTLES AND ROCKS BY A LARGE CROWD - NFI - CALLER HUNG UP - HOTLINED - SUPV VALLEY NTFD - OPR. 010-58 (ENTER)
IF/THOMAS/(ENTER)

After listening to the tapes and reviewing the entries, you notice that the operator made several errors.

12. Which of the following jobs were coded improperly? 12.____

A. 1, 2, 3 B. 1, 2, 4 C. 1, 3, 4 D. 2, 3, 4

13. For which of the following jobs did the operator fail to notify a supervisor or fail to include appropriate routing? 13.____

A. 1, 2 B. 1, 4 C. 2, 3 D. 2, 4

14. For which of the following jobs was information excluded in the entry that should be considered extremely important in processing the call? 14.____

A. 1, 2 B. 1, 3 C. 2, 4 D. 3, 4

15. On which one of the following jobs did the operator fail to follow the proper ambulance procedure? 15.____

A. 1 B. 2 C. 3 D. 4

16. Police Communications Technician Borne receives a call from a Mrs. Hiller, who states that her landlord threw her out of the apartment that she has been renting for the past year. The landlord told her it was because she had not paid rent for the past three months. The landlord, who did not present an Eviction Notice to Mrs. Hiller, put a new lock on the door, and she then called 911. Dispatcher Borne is not familiar with the procedure covering evictions and asked Supervising Dispatcher Washington, her supervisor, for assistance. 16.____
Supervising Dispatcher Washington should direct the operator to

A. refer the caller to Landlord-Tenant Court
B. enter the job as a 39Q1
C. refer the caller to her local precinct
D. refer the caller to the Department of Building Complaints

17. Police Communications Technician James, an experienced operator, is aware of the department's Solo Unit Procedure, where one-officer units are assigned to respond to 38 different code signals. He asks you, his supervisor, which of the following code signals are considered appropriate for one officer to handle. 17.____

1. 10-24Q1
2. 10-68Q1
3. 10-11Q4
4. 10-59T

The CORRECT answer is:

A. 1, 2 B. 1, 4 C. 2, 3 D. 3, 4

18. Supervising Dispatcher Carlson is instructing one of her new operators in the procedure to follow for screening jobs received from a Housing Authority Police Service Area. All of the following jobs are appropriate for 911 entry EXCEPT a 18.____

A. request to see a complainant on found property
B. request for a patrol car to respond for a bank deposit escort
C. request for police response to a stuck occupied elevator
D. report of youths throwing firecrackers into apartment windows

19. Police Communications Dispatcher Proper does not understand the procedure set forth in the 911 Guide regarding public morals incidents. Supervising Dispatcher Gibson gives a copy of the procedure to Dispatcher Proper and instructs her in detail in the handling of particular public morals incidents. 19.____
Based on 911 procedures, in which one of the following cases did the Dispatcher handle the incident PROPERLY? A caller stated that

A. the Star Lite Bar on West 165th Street and Seventh Avenue is selling liquor to a minor seated at the bar - Dispatcher entered the job for a patrol car to be dispatched
B. in a vacant apartment on the 1st floor at 706 West 46th Street two male whites are selling drugs to people lined up in the hall - Dispatcher entered a defer job for Organized Crime Control Bureau
C. there is illegal gambling taking place in a private club at 922 West 12th Street in Manhattan - Dispatcher entered a job for a patrol car to be dispatched
D. there is a female on the corner of West 57th Street and Thirteenth Avenue soliciting for prostitution, and she is there every day from 4:00 P.M. to 8:00 P.M. - Dispatcher entered a defer job for the Organized Crime Control Bureau

20. Police Communications Technician Rossi reports to you, her supervisor, that she is sure that another dispatcher is using drugs. She believes that the drugs are kept in his locker, although she has never actually seen the drugs. 20.____
As a supervisor, what is the FIRST action you should take?

A. Request the name of the dispatcher and conduct a preliminary investigation.
B. Tell Dispatcher Rossi to observe the dispatcher; and if she sees any drugs, she should report the incident to the Internal Affairs Division.
C. Report the incident to the Internal Affairs Division.
D. Request Dispatcher Rossi to prepare a written report and submit it to you as soon as possible.

21. As a newly appointed supervisor, you are assigned to the borough of Brooklyn to supervise dispatchers. Prior to the start of your tour, you are advised by the Platoon Commander to begin a Back-up Slip Operation at approximately 0830 hours. During your tour, you assign one dispatcher runner along with one scanner. 21.____
During a Back-up Slip Operation, it is the responsibility of the scanner to

A. check the address file for the incident location
B. assist the supervisor with slip operation recovery procedures
C. deliver intact slips to radio dispatchers
D. return rejected slips to operators for completion or correction

22. The 911 operator's information area is located at the bottom left side of the screen where symbols indicate whether or not a job can be entered into the system. Police Communications Technician Wellwater is prepared to enter a 911 job. However, instead of the correct symbols being visible, only the symbol X appears on the screen. 22.____
As the supervisor, you should instruct Dispatcher Wellwater to try to correct this condition by FIRST depressing the ______ button.

A. enter B. shift C. display D. reset

23. Supervising Dispatcher Simpson is called by Police Communications Technician Eli to ask her direction regarding a caller he is holding on the line. Dispatcher Eli tells Supervising Dispatcher Simpson that the call is from a male who is a resident of Ohio and wants to report his wife missing in New York. He states that his wife has been staying at the New York Hilton for the past two weeks so she could visit her sick mother at Roosevelt Hospital. He has called the hotel, and the clerk told him that his wife had not been seen, nor has she picked up her key in the past 24 hours, but her luggage is still in the room. The caller also states that his wife is in good physical and mental health. 23.____
Supervising Dispatcher Simpson should direct Dispatcher Eli to tell the caller

A. to call the Ohio police to make the report
B. that we will send a patrol car to investigate
C. that we have no jurisdiction over his wife because she is in good physical and mental health
D. that we will not take a report because the circumstances do not indicate involuntary disappearance

24. On a Monday morning, about 0835 hours, Police Communications Technician Franklin receives a call from a young female who is very upset. She states that a Transit Authority Police Officer had taken her wallet containing her student subway pass and refused to give it back. She states that she had just put out a cigarette and was about to enter through the gate after showing the token clerk her subway pass. She was then stopped by a Transit Authority Police Officer, who informed her that he was going to write up a violation for smoking in the subway. She also states that he was very abusive, took her wallet out of her hand, and refused to return it. Dispatcher Franklin notifies you, the supervisor, about the caller on the line. 24.____
You should direct Dispatcher Franklin

A. to refer the caller to Transit Authority Police Headquarters
B. that you will take the call and refer it to the Civilian Complaint Review Board
C. that you will take the call and refer it to the Internal Affairs Division
D. to have the caller report the incident to her school authorities

25. Police Communications Technician Blakely receives a second call on a 10-13 at 5 Berkeley Place in Brooklyn. He is given a description of the perpetrator involved, enters this information into the system, and then notifies you, the supervisor, of the second call. Upon reviewing this call, you should tell Operator Blakely that he should have 25.____

A. notified you first before entering the second call into the system
B. entered the information, hotlined the information to the dispatcher, routed D, and then notified you
C. hotlined the information to the dispatcher, notified you, and then entered the information
D. hotlined the information to the dispatcher, entered it into the system, routed D, and then notified you

# KEY (CORRECT ANSWERS)

1. B
2. A
3. C
4. A
5. B
6. A
7. C
8. D
9. A
10. D
11. C
12. A
13. A
14. B
15. B
16. B
17. A
18. B
19. A
20. C
21. A
22. D
23. B
24. C
25. D

# EXAMINATION SECTION
# TEST 1

DIRECTIONS: Each question or incomplete statement is followed by several suggested answers or completions. Select the one that BEST answers the question or completes the statement. *PRINT THE LETTER OF THE CORRECT ANSWER IN THE SPACE AT THE RIGHT.*

1. A newly assigned operator tells you, his supervisor, that he thinks something is wrong with Emergency Reporting System Box Number 2515. He states that for the last minute, the box has been coming in with a series of tapping sounds, two followed by three. After you listen and hear the tapping yourself, you should direct the operator to 1.____

   A. move to the next Emergency Reporting System box and input a job so that a patrol car can be dispatched to check the condition of the first box
   B. call the Fire Department and request a test on the line
   C. input a job at the Emergency Reporting System box location as a priority run
   D. call the Fire Department and advise them that the Emergency Reporting System box is out of order

2. Police Communications Technician Cheppo, assigned to Richmond Dispatching, during the eight to four tour, receives a call from a Mr. Victor of 245 Robinson Avenue. Mr. Victor states that he is a victim of wife abuse. He tells Dispatcher Cheppo that he is a disabled veteran and his wife constantly abuses him, both physically and emotionally. Mr. Victor insists that he needs help, but he does not want the police to come to his home. His wife is not there now, but he states that she has threatened to beat him up when she returns. Dispatcher Cheppo is familiar with the Victim Services Agency referral program, but she is uncertain as to how to process the call. 2.____
You, as her immediate supervisor, should instruct her to

   A. ask Mr. Victor to hold on, and then dial transfer to 6580
   B. input a job as a 10-68
   C. input a job as a 10-52, dispute, then dial transfer to 6420
   D. ask Mr. Victor to call 911 when his wife returns home

3. Police Communications Technician Nigil receives a call from a male who states that his blind 36-year-old brother is missing. His brother was supposed to report to the New York Guild for the Blind two hours ago, but has not arrived there. The caller states that his brother also disappeared last month, and the police found him sitting in Central Park feeding the birds. Operator Nigil asks the caller to hold on while he seeks assistance from the supervisor. He asks you, the supervisor, what action he should take. 3.____
You should direct him to

   A. tell the caller that since his brother is not a minor, he must wait a while longer, but he should call back if his brother does not show up
   B. refer the caller directly to the Missing Persons Squad
   C. refer the caller to his local precinct and inform them of the situation
   D. enter a job indicating that a patrol car will be sent to the caller's location to take a report

4. Police Communications Technician Phillips, while working on 911, receives a call concerning an off-duty police officer who is having an argument with his wife. The caller states that the argument sounds violent, and the police officer has a gun. Dispatcher Phillips asks if the caller can see exactly what is going on. The caller reports that he is unable to see anything. Dispatcher Phillips, who does not know the proper code to input, brings this call to your attention. 4.____
As the Supervising Dispatcher, you should instruct Dispatcher Phillips to enter which one of the following codes?

A. 10-13Z1 B. 10-52F1 C. 10-13X1 D. 10-69S

5. Police Communications Technician Wilder approaches you, the Supervising Dispatcher, and asks you to listen to his last call. You replay the tape and hear the following situation. The caller, a Mr. Monroe, claims that he saw two police officers enter a bar at West 146th Street and 7th Avenue. He followed the officers inside to see what was going on. Once inside the bar, Mr. Monroe saw three males who were sitting at the bar drop several plastic packets to the floor. The packets appeared to contain drugs. Mr. Monroe claims that one of the police officers picked up the packets and stuffed them into his pocket. At that point, both of the officers looked around the bar as if they were searching for someone. They remained in the bar for about five minutes and then returned to their patrol car, license plate number 1269. Mr. Monroe gave his address and telephone number to Dispatcher Wilder and asked if there was anything else he wanted to know. Dispatcher Wilder stated, *No, but thank you for calling. I will relay this information to my supervisor at once.* You, as the supervisor, look at his screen and see that Dispatcher Wilder has entered an *IA* message on a previous job involving *a man with a gun* inside the same bar. A notation was made that he had *hotlined* the information. In this situation, the action taken by Dispatcher Wilder should be considered 5.____

A. *correct;* chiefly because he immediately hotlined the information and notified the supervisor of a serious incident
B. *incorrect;* chiefly because he should have given the caller the telephone number of the Internal Affairs Division
C. *correct;* chiefly because he obtained all of the pertinent information
D. *incorrect;* chiefly because he should have tried to hold the caller on the line in order to notify a supervisor

Questions 6-8.

DIRECTIONS: Questions 6 through 8 are to be answered SOLELY on the basis of the following information.

Police Communications Technician Maurice receives a call over Position 25 from Sgt. Jacobs requesting that the power be shut off on the northbound IND, A, and CC subway line at the Broadway-Nassau Station. The Sergeant states that there is a man down under a train. Dispatcher Maurice tells the Sergeant that it is not in his jurisdiction to order that power be shut off. Sgt. Jacobs then asks to speak to a supervisor, and Dispatcher Maurice calls you to the line.

6. As the supervisor, you should tell Dispatcher Maurice that the FIRST action he should take is to 6.____

A. connect the caller to the Transit Authority Police Department via the Transit Authority add-on button
B. determine if the caller is, in fact, a police sergeant
C. immediately hotline the request to the appropriate dispatcher
D. input a job and route it to Emergency Service

7. You should then tell Dispatcher Maurice that the SECOND action he should take is to 7.____

A. notify the Emergency Medical Service
B. hotline the information, input the job, and route to Emergency Service
C. maintain the connection until confirmation is received that the power has been shut off
D. connect the caller to the Transit Authority and then the Fire Department via the add-on buttons

8. What is the CORRECT entry for the job given when the proper procedure is followed? 8.____

A. IQ/7/BROADWAY NASSAU IND TRAN (ENTER)
IE/54S1/TRANSIT POWER OFF* TA011 CONFIRMED POWER SHUT OFF - MAN UNDER A TRAIN - SPCT METRO NOTIFIED - NORTHBOUND OPR. 010-15=P9S:A609 (ENTER) IF/SGT. JACOBS/(ENTER)
B. IQ/7/BROADWAY NASSAU IND TRAN (ENTER)
IE/65S/TRANSIT POWER OFF* MAN UNDER TRAIN - SPCT METRO NOTIFIED - NORTHBOUND - POWER SHUT OFF - AUTH. SGT. JACOBS -TA011 NTFD - OPR. 010-15=P9NS (ENTER) IF/JACOBS/(ENTER)
C. IQ/7/BROADWAY NASSAU IND TRAN (ENTER)
IE/66/TRANSIT POWER OFF* SGT. JACOBS N.Y.P.D. - REQUEST POWER SHUT-OFF - NORTHBOUND - MAN DOWN UNDER TRAIN -SPCT METRO NOTIFIED - OPR. 010-15=P9SWS:A609 (ENTER) IF/JACOBS/(ENTER)
D. IQ/7 BROADWAY NASSAU IND TRAN (ENTER)
IE/65S/TRANSIT POWER OFF* SGT. JACOBS N.Y.P.D. REQUEST POWER OFF, NORTHBOUND MAN DOWN UNDER A TRAIN - SPCT METRO NOTIFIED - TA 011 CONFIRMED THAT POWER HAS BEEN SHUT OFF - OPR. 010-15=P9NSAS:HOSP-HOSQ (ENTER) IF/SGT. JACOBS/(ENTER)

9. Supervisor Jan, assigned as a Manhattan Supervising Dispatcher, is monitoring Police Communications Technician Morrow when he receives a call for a test on the alarm at El Al Airlines, which is located within the boundaries of the 17th Precinct. Dispatcher Morrow enters the job as an 11C4/Test Call. 9.____
Supervisor Jan should instruct Dispatcher Morrow that he should have

A. told the caller that the Police Department does not provide this service
B. referred the caller to her supervisor
C. entered the job as a 10-69S test call for El Al Airlines
D. referred the caller to the 17th Precinct

10. Upon reporting for duty, you, the Queens supervisor, are advised by the Platoon Commander that Sprint will be inoperative for the entire tour. You assign an operator runner, a radio room runner, and a scanner, and then assign your dispatching positions. Subsequently, you remind both the radio room runner and the scanner of the procedures regarding slips involving ambulance calls. Of the following, you should emphasize to the radio room runner that it is MOST important to ensure that the 10.____

A. dispatcher gets the second copy
B. operator has identified herself by number
C. operator has noted the time the call was received
D. liaison gets the second copy

Questions 11-15.

DIRECTIONS: Questions 11 through 15 are to be answered SOLELY on the basis of the following information.

You, as a supervising dispatcher, have been assigned to review several 10-13 tapes and job inputs that have come into the borough of Brooklyn from 0730 to 1530 hours.

Job #1. At 0807 hours, Police Communications Technician Sherman receives a call from an unknown male stating that there is an accident on the corner of Coney Island Avenue and Avenue J. He also states that there is a police car involved. It is not known if there are any injuries. Dispatcher Sherman advises the caller to hold on. He hotlines a 10-13 to the Radio Dispatcher. When he goes back to the caller, he finds that the caller has been disconnected. Dispatcher Sherman enters the job as follows:

IQ/6/CONEY ISLAND AVE - J AVE (ENTER)
IE/13U2/RMP COLLISION* MALE CALLER STATES UNKNOWN INJURIES
INVOLVED - OPR. 689-36 = P9SWD (ENTER)
IF/UNKNOWN MALE/(ENTER)
IA* JOB HOTLINED - OPR 689-36 (ENTER)

Job #2. At 1135 hours, Police Communications Technician Sykes receives a call from a female who states that there is a police officer in uniform lying on the street at Campus Road and Nostrand Avenue. Dispatcher Sykes tells the female to hold on, and hotlines the call to the Radio Dispatcher as a 10-13. Dispatcher Sykes then goes back to the caller, who could provide no further information. He does, however, get the female's name and callback. He depresses the dial transfer button and phones the Emergency Medical Service. He gives them the information and enters the job. He then notifies his supervisor. Dispatcher Sykes enters the job as follows:

IQ/6/CAMPUS RD - NOSTRAND AVE (ENTER)
IE/13U2/OFFICER DOWN* FEMALE STATES AT THIS LOCATION -
ARO 617 NOTIFIED - JOB HOTLINED - OPR. 312-46=AS:A617-
HOSP-HOSQ (ENTER)
IF/FLANNERY/6897213 (ENTER)
IA*SPCT GUZMAN NOTIFIED (ENTER)

Job #3. Police Communications Technician Andrews receives a call at 1136 hours that there is a police officer in uniform who has been shot at Campus Road and Nostrand Avenue. Dispatcher Andrews queries the location. The caller states that he believes a man who ran into the Oklahoma Country Ribs Store did the shooting. Dispatcher Andrews asks the caller to hold on, and hotlines the information to the Radio Dispatcher. He then goes back to the caller. He sees that a call has already been entered into the system and dispatched. He asks the caller for his name and callback, but the male refuses. Dispatcher Andrews thanks the caller and enters the information as follows:

IA* UNKNOWN MALE CALLER STATES POLICE OFFICER SHOT AT LOCATION - POSSIBLE PERPETRATOR RAN INTO THE OKLAHOMA COUNTRY RIBS STORE - ANONYMOUS MALE CALLER - NO FURTHER INFO. OPR 809-41=SDFAS:HOSP-HOSQ (ENTER)

Job #4. At 1450 hours, Police Communications Technician Fisher receives a call from a young male stating that a man who appears to be a police officer is having trouble with another man at the corner of Ashford Street and Hegeman Avenue. Dispatcher Fisher asks the caller if the police officer is in uniform. The caller states that he is not. Dispatcher Fisher asks the caller for his name and callback, but he refuses to answer and hangs up. Dispatcher Fisher then hotlines a 10-13 to the Radio Dispatcher, enters the job, and notifies his supervisor. He enters the job as follows:

IQ/6/ASHFORD ST - HEGEMAN AVE (ENTER)
IE/13X2/P.O. FIGHTING*WITH ANOTHER MALE AT THE CORNER - NO FURTHER INFO - OPR. 248-33 (ENTER)
IF/MALE REFUSED/(ENTER)
IA* SPCT TEMPLE NOTIFIED - OPR. 248-33 (ENTER)

Job #5. At 1525 hours, Police Communications Technician Tyson receives a call from a male identifying himself as Police Officer Shore from the 90th Precinct. He states that he is off duty and just observed a male Hispanic breaking into a house at 1780 East 13th Street. He requests assistance in apprehending the perpetrator. Dispatcher Tyson asks the officer what he is wearing and his race. She then hotlines the information, indicating that she has a 10-13, and gets a full description of the perpetrator - a male Hispanic, 5 feet 6 inches to 5 feet 8 inches, wearing a blue down jacket, green pants, and white sneakers. She is also told that the perpetrator entered the house through the second floor rear window. The officer states that he will be in front of the house. Dispatcher Tyson then enters the job and notifies her supervisor. The job is entered as follows:

IQ/6/1780 E 13 ST (ENTER)
IE/13Z2/BURGLARY* SEE POLICE OFFICER IN FRONT OF LOCATION - STATES MALE HISPANIC BREAKING INTO REAR WINDOW - WEARING BLUE COAT - GREEN PANTS - SNEAKERS - MALE 5FT 6 TO 8 - OPR. 836-43 (ENTER)
IF/P.O. SHORE/(ENTER)
IA* JOB HOTLINED - SPCT TOPPER NOTIFIED - OPR 836-43 (ENTER)

As the supervisor, you must now correct the errors made on each call received and entered for the jobs described above.

11. Which of the following jobs are NOT 10-13's? 11.____

A. 1, 4  B. 1, 5  C. 2, 3  D. 4, 5

12. For which of the following jobs did the operator fail to get a necessary description of the perpetrator? 12.____

A. 2, 3  B. 2, 5  C. 3, 4  D. 4, 5

13. For which one of the following jobs did the operator fail to follow proper hotline procedure? 13.____

A. 2  B. 3  C. 4  D. 5

14. For which one of the following jobs did the operator fail to walk in to the dispatcher, as required by procedure? 14.____

A. 1 B. 2 C. 3 D. 4

15. For which of the following jobs did the operator unnecessarily route the entries? 15.____

A. 1, 3 B. 1, 4 C. 2, 4 D. 3, 5

16. Police Communications Technician Kind, a newly appointed operator, receives a call at 0910 hours from a female who reports that she repeatedly receives obscene phone calls concerning her children. Operator Kind requests the location of the caller and inputs a 10-68 code to investigate the incident. 16.____
As a Supervising Dispatcher, you should reinstruct Operator Kind that she should have

A. referred the caller to the New York Telephone Company during regular business hours
B. changed the code to 10-29Q1 *Phone Threats*
C. told the caller to contact her local precinct
D. change the code to 10-50P1 *Phone Threats*

17. As a Supervising Dispatcher, while monitoring Police Communications Technician Jones, you notice that he has made several errors involving his processing of ambulance calls. You decide to take Dispatcher Jones aside to reinstruct him in the proper ambulance procedures. 17.____
You should instruct Dispatcher Jones to do all of the following EXCEPT

A. input a 10-54 for an elderly sick called in by an aide at a nursing home
B. connect the caller to the Emergency Medical Service when hospital personnel requests a bus to transfer a patient from one hospital to another
C. release the call from the dispatching position when extended interviewing by the Ambulance Receiving Operator is necessary
D. enter a 10-55 when the Ambulance Receiving Operator advises that a nurse will call the complainant back

18. Police Communications Technician Ramos receives a call on 911 from an English-speaking male with a distinct Spanish accent. Dispatcher Ramos, who speaks Spanish, asks the caller, *Do you speak Spanish?* The male replies, *Si!* Dispatcher Ramos tells the caller, *Un momento, por favor,* and transfers the call to a Spanish translator. 18.____
As a supervisor, you should advise Dispatcher Ramos that the procedure he followed was

A. *correct,* primarily because he is not a translator
B. *incorrect,* primarily because he should have processed the call since he speaks Spanish
C. *correct,* primarily because the caller spoke with a Spanish accent
D. *incorrect,* primarily because he did not question the male

Question 19.

DIRECTIONS: Question 19 is to be answered SOLELY on the basis of the following information and the chart which appears on the following page.

As a supervisor, you have assigned Police Communications Technician Newhardt to work ERS for the day. During the tour, he received the calls listed below:

1. Spanish Assist
2. Report of a fire at 366 East 66th Street, Apt. 9
3. Request for the 14th Precinct's address and telephone number
4. Request for an ambulance for an E.D.P. in front of 1717 Broadway
5. Fire Department test call
6. Series of tapping (2-3) from ERS box 2514

Near the end of the tour (1520 hours), you inspect his ERS log, and you notice that he has failed to complete certain information.

EMERGENCY REPORTING SYSTEM LOG

DATE MARCH 21 BOROUGH MANHATTAN

TOUR 0800 X 1600 POSITION POS 10

| | A | B | C | D | E | F | G | H | I | J | K | L | M | N |
|---|---|---|---|---|---|---|---|---|---|---|---|---|---|---|
| | | | | TYPE OF CALL | | | | | | | | | | |
| | TIME | BOX# | CPR# | FRAU | INFO | TEST | NA | MISC | INPUT | JOB# | CODE SIGNAL | INCIDENT LOCATION | RMP ASSIGNED | FINAL DISPOSITION |
| 1 | 1430 | 3691 | 001 | | | | | ✓ | | | | REFERRED TO SPANISH | | |
| 2 | 1436 | 4266 | 001 | | | | | | | S2611 | | 366 E. 66 ST. | 23A | 91 |
| 3 | 1439 | | 001 | | | | | | | | | | | |
| 4 | 1445 | | 001 | | | | | | | | | 1717 BROADWAY | 34B | 90Z |
| 5 | | 4444 | 001 | | | | | | | | | | | |
| 6 | 1449 | 2514 | 001 | | | | | | ✓ | | | | 26A | 93C |
| 7 | | | | | | | | | | | | | | |
| 8 | | | | | | | | | | | | | | |
| 9 | | | | | | | | | | | | | | |
| 10 | | | | | | | | | | | | | | |
| 11 | | | | | | | | | | | | | | |
| 12 | | | | | | | | | | | | | | |
| 13 | | | | | | | | | | | | | | |
| 14 | | | | | | | | | | | | | | |
| 15 | | | | | | | | | | | | | | |
| 16 | TOTALS | | | | | | | | | | | | | |

VERIFIED BY ______________ SUPERVISOR'S SIGNATURE

PD 112-148 (11-79) (Formerly Misc. 702m)

19. Which of the following series of letters and numbers represents information omitted in the log? 19.____

    A. A5, B4, J5, MI, G16, D16, I4, F16, E3, J6, K2, G7, M4, N6, B2, L1, M2, I1, I16
    B. A5, B4, E4, K9, J6, M6, L1, M2, B5, L3, I5, C6, B3, L6, M6, L5, G6, I16
    C. A5, B4, J5, K4, E3, G5, K6, I4, I2, K2, K6, D16, B2, LI, M2, I1, G6, I16
    D. A5, B3, B4, E3, F5, J4, K2, K4, J6, K6, L6, E16, F16, H16, I16, I16, I4, I2, D16, G16

20. Police Communications Technician Gibson, assigned to dispatching position 38 in Brooklyn, receives a call from a male who states that he sees an ambulance on the scene at 1822 Clarkson Avenue. He states that the ambulance crew appears to be having a heated argument with the family of an aided victim in front of the location. Dispatcher Gibson enters the job as 10-52D1. 20.____
As the supervising dispatcher, you should reinstruct Dispatcher Gibson to correct the code to

A. 10-56S B. 10-10Y3 C. 10-58S D. 10-58D

21. The 27th Precinct calls 911 to report that Police Officer Arlen, who was assigned to Harbor High School as the security officer for the day, had picked up a youth for trespassing. The officer needs a patrol car to transport the youth to the stationhouse. 21.____
The operator turns to you, the supervisor, to ask what code he should use. You should instruct him to

A. hotline and enter a 10-13
B. have the police officer call the precinct to 10-1 a car
C. hotline and enter a 10-39
D. hotline and enter a 10-12

22. Mrs. James calls 911 demanding to speak to someone in charge. You, the supervisor, *jack-in* to your operator's position to find out what the problem is. Mrs. James tells you that she was driving along New York Boulevard when three police cars from the 117th Precinct raced past her and ran a red light. She further states that the police from the same precinct gave her a ticket last week for accidentally running a red light, and she feels something should be done to discipline the officers who drove through the red light. She asks, *What gives them the right to break the law and go unpunished? This type of corruption has to stop!* 22.____
As the supervisor, you should advise the caller that

A. she should register her complaint with the Commanding Officer of the 117th Precinct
B. she can call the Civilian Complaint Review Board to register her complaint
C. the officers were probably on their way to an emergency
D. you will send the Patrol Sergeant to take her complaint

23. Assume that the Spring system fails and all Bronx operators are told by Supervising Dispatcher Shelton that a Backup Slip Operation will be in effect. Police Communications Technician Jordan then receives a call over the Emergency Reporting System indicating a call from fire box 7215. A Mrs. Smith is on the line reporting a heavy smoke condition in her 3rd floor hallway at 6773 Daytona Drive. Operator Jordan disengages the call with Mrs. Smith and proceeds to connect to the Bronx fire operator. 23.____
Fire Operator 737 accepts the information and advises Operator Jordan that a unit will be sent, although there have been numerous unfounded alarms at this location in the past. Operator Jordan then gives the slip to Supervising Dispatcher Shelton, who is passing by her position.
The slip is shown below.

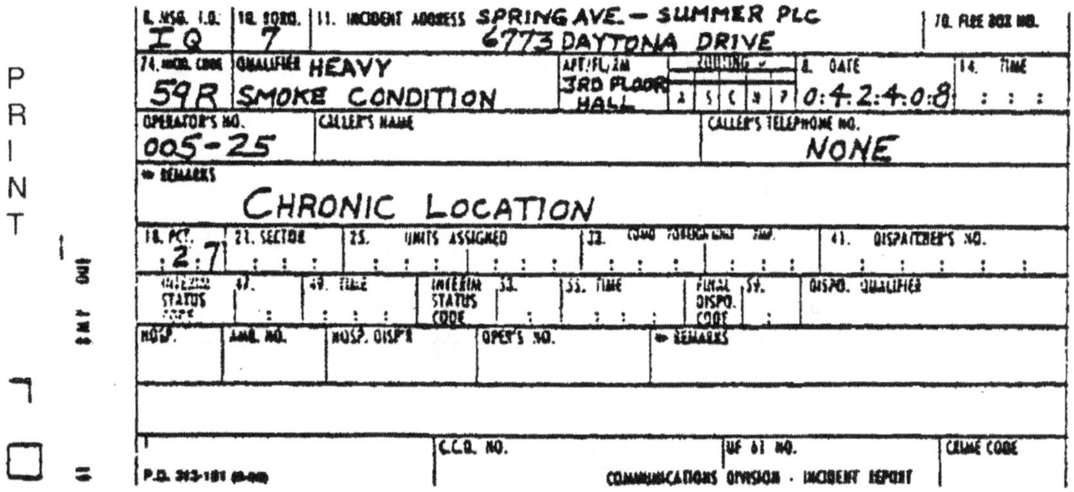


After checking the slip, Supervising Dispatcher Shelton should return it to Operator Jordan and tell her that she omitted the

A. caller's name, routing, fire box number, time, precinct
B. fire box number, caller's name, fire operator's number, time
C. fire operator's number, fire box number, sector, date
D. fire box number, precinct, intersection, time

24. As supervisor, you receive a notification from the 911 Platoon Commander that the Sprint Computer Operation will change over to a Backup Slip Operation at 0930 hours. Prior to the transition to slips, you assign two operators to serve as dispatching runners. Which one of the following is a responsibility of a dispatching runner? 24.____

A. Enter precinct and sector covering location on slip and leave it for the radio room scanner.
B. Check address file for incident location entered on slip.
C. Walk behind operators and pick up completed slips.
D. Collect slips from scanner with precinct and sector designations entered.

25. Police Communications Technician Greenwald receives a call from a male who states that he was involved in a car accident at West 204th Street and Broadway in Manhattan. He also states that he has exchanged information with the other driver, but he wants the police to respond because the bumpers of the cars are locked together and the cars cannot be moved. Dispatcher Greenwald is unsure of the procedure to follow and asks you, the supervising dispatcher, for assistance. You should direct Dispatcher Greenwald to 25.____

A. report the accident to the Motor Vehicle Department
B. tell the caller to contact the ABC Tow Company
C. enter a job indicating that the cars are locked together
D. refer the caller to the local precinct

# KEY (CORRECT ANSWERS)

1. C
2. A
3. D
4. B
5. D
6. A
7. C
8. D
9. B
10. D
11. B
12. C
13. C
14. C
15. A
16. A
17. A
18. D
19. D
20. D
21. D
22. B
23. B
24. C
25. C

# TEST 2

DIRECTIONS: Each question or incomplete statement is followed by several suggested answers or completions. Select the one that BEST answers the question or completes the statement. *PRINT THE LETTER OF THE CORRECT ANSWER IN THE SPACE AT THE RIGHT.*

1. An hysterical female calls 911 to report that she and her husband are having an argument. She tells the operator that her husband is now storming out of the house with their child, and she is afraid that her husband will do the child bodily harm. The operator has the caller's name, address, apartment number, and telephone number. The operator turns to you, the supervising dispatcher, and asks how she should handle this call. You should instruct her to 1.____

   A. input the job as a kidnapping
   B. input the job as a family or custodial dispute
   C. input the job as a possible abduction
   D. refer the caller to Family Court

2. Police Communications Technician Curtis receives a call from Fire Dispatcher 249 requesting assistance at the scene of a residence fire on West 125th Street and Amsterdam Avenue. Dispatcher 249 states that they have a disorderly group harassing firemen, requests a signal red, and hangs up. Dispatcher Curtis, uncertain of the correct code to use, requests your assistance. 2.____
   As the supervising dispatcher, you should instruct Dispatcher Curtis to enter

   A. 10-39C/CODE RED* HARASSING FIREMEN - SEND RMP -OPROO-5
   B. 10-59/CODE RED* HARASSING FIREMEN - SEND SUPERVISOR OPROO-5
   C. 10-50G2/CODE RED* HARASSING FIREMEN - OPROO-5=P9
   D. 10-59R/CODE RED* HARASSING FIREMEN - SEND RMPS AND SUPERVISOR OPROO-5=P9

3. At 0315 hours on April 1, Police Communications Technician Karter received a call on 911 of a 10-13 at the intersection of Avenue M and East 21st Street. Operator Karter entered a 10-13U2 at the above location. While reviewing the tape of the 10-13 with Operator Karter, you, the supervisor, find that the following statements made by the caller were omitted from the job: 3.____
   Statement 1. The officer said he was on the southwest corner.
   Statement 2. The officer gave his badge number.
   Statement 3. The officer gave his name, race, and rank.
   Statement 4. The officer stated that he was in trouble and requested two units as a back-up.
   Which one of the above statements should be considered the MOST serious omission?
   Statement

   A. 1 B. 2 C. 3 D. 4

4. On May 9, all operators are informed of a memo emphasizing the need to carefully screen calls not requiring an immediate response by 911. Police Communications Technician Jones, a newly assigned operator, receives a call from a female who reports that there is a large dead dog blocking a busy roadway. Operator Jones asks his supervisor what action he should take concerning this call. 4.___
As the supervisor, you should instruct Operator Jones to

A. input a job as a 67S/DEAD DOG* BLOCKING INTERSECTION=N
B. input a job as a 65S/DEAD DOG* BLOCKING INTERSECTION=N
C. input a job as a 68S/DEAD DOG* REFER TO ASPCA=N
D. refer the caller to the ASPCA

5. Police Communications Technician Ultra, assigned to Manhattan Dispatching, receives a call from a Mr. Ray, who states that there is a late model green Dodge station wagon with New Jersey license plates parked at the fire hydrant in front of his apartment building. Mr. Ray states that the vehicle has been parked there for two days. He demands that you send a patrol car at once since the automobile is illegally parked and could be stripped. Dispatcher Ultra, uncertain as to how to enter the job, requests your assistance. 5.___
As the supervising dispatcher, you should instruct her to

A. input a job as a 22V2
B. refer the caller to his local precinct
C. input a job as a 10V2 unoccupied suspicious
D. refer the caller to the Fire Department via the add-on button so they will be aware of the blocked fire hydrant

6. Police Communications Technician Whitney, a 911 operator, receives a call from a male, wishing to remain anonymous, who states that there are two police officers from the 29th Precinct drinking in an after-hours club. The caller states that the police officers have just completed their tour of duty at the precinct and are in the club in civilian clothes. The 911 operator is unsure of what procedure to follow and asks you what she should do. As the supervisor, you should tell Dispatcher Whitney 6.___

A. that you will speak to the caller and then notify the Internal Affairs Division with the details
B. to refer the caller to the Precinct Commanding Officer
C. that you will obtain the details from the caller, notify the Duty Captain, and have the Patrol Sergeant respond
D. to tell the caller that there is no violation since the officers are off-duty

7. While monitoring Police Communications Technician Reilly, you observe that he entered a job for a burglary in progress. During the conversation, the caller asked Dispatcher Reilly for his operator's number, his name, and his address. Dispatcher Reilly refused to give the information. 7.___
As a supervisor, you should instruct Dispatcher Reilly that he is required to give

A. the information as requested
B. his operator's number only
C. his operator's number, name, and 1 Police Plaza as his address
D. his operator's number and name

8. Police Officer Smith from the 5th Precinct calls 911 and states that he received a robot alarm of a hold-up or burglary in progress at 732 West 126th Street. The location is a bodega. No further information is given. The 911 operator is unsure of the correct code and asks you, the supervisor, for instruction.
You should instruct the operator that the proper code is 8.____

A. 11C4 B. 11C3 C. 11Q3 D. 11Q4

9. When Police Communications Technician Miles reports for duty at 0730 hours on Monday, Supervising Dispatcher Bell notices that she is visibly upset. Supervising Dispatcher Bell takes her aside and asks what the problem is and whether she can be of any assistance. Dispatcher Miles states that she went to a party Saturday night and saw Police Officer Denim behaving in an irrational manner. She observed the officer swallow what appeared to be a Quaalude, along with several glasses of wine. His behavior then became noticeably irrational. Dispatcher Miles states that she is concerned about Officer Denim because she had worked with him. She feels that the officer disgraced himself even though he was off-duty. Dispatcher Miles then asks Supervising Dispatcher Bell what she should do. Supervising Dispatcher Bell should tell Dispatcher Miles to 9.____

A. keep the incident to herself because Officer Denim was off-duty
B. report the incident to the Civilian Complaint Review Board
C. keep the incident to herself because there is no way to verify the story
D. report the incident to her Integrity Officer

10. Police Communications Technician Rapelye receives a call from a male who states that his uncle is having difficulty breathing. The caller also states that his uncle is experiencing chest pains and a neighbor is administering cardio-pulmonary resuscitation. Operator Rapelye, after obtaining the address, callback, and apartment number, connects the caller with Emergency Medical Service. The Ambulance Receiving Operator gets on the line and obtains the necessary information. With the call completed, Operator Rapelye must now enter a job but is unsure of what code to use.
As his supervisor, you should direct Operator Rapelye to enter the code as a 10.____

A. 10-54C1 B. 10-54S1 C. 10-54C3 D. 10-54C3PO

11. Police Communications Technician Williams, assigned to dispatching position 39 in Brooklyn, enters into the 911 terminal the following input: IQ/7/3000 BEDFORD AVE. Sprint responds with the following: 11.____

1. ID IQ
2. Boro 7 *ERROR MSG*
3. NO 3000
4. SEL ST1 Bedford Ave
   0 Bedford St

Dispatcher Williams asks you, the supervisor, to assist in getting this address into the system.
You should tell Dispatcher Williams to

A. IQ the location again
B. make a correction by entering E/L:2/6
C. clarify the location with the caller
D. make a correction by entering E/L:4/S:0

12. Police Communications Technician Parnell receives a call from Mrs. Barker, who states that she received a call from a man who identified himself as Detective Sampson of the Midtown South Precinct Detective Unit. The man told Mrs. Barker that he was working on a case of employee theft from customer accounts at the New York Savings Bank. He asked Mrs. Barker to go with him to the bank to withdraw $3,000 from her own savings account so he could observe the suspected teller's actions. Mrs. Barker agreed to meet the man in one hour in front of the bank, but now she thinks that the man is trying to swindle her out of her money. Dispatcher Parnell, unsure of what action to take, asks her supervisor for instructions. 12.____
The supervisor should

A. tell Dispatcher Parnell to advise Mrs. Barker to call the Midtown South Precinct to verify that a Detective Sampson is assigned to the precinct
B. tell Dispatcher Parnell to enter the job as a 68Q1 see complainant for a con game and male impersonating a police officer
C. take the information from the caller, enter it as 69S, and refer it to the Precinct Anti-Crime Officers by landline so they can stake out the bank
D. take the information from the caller and report the incident to the Internal Affairs Division even though it is not clear that an officer is involved

13. A call is received by Police Communications Technician Roman from Mrs. Smith, who states that two police officers responded to her house on a family dispute at 1200 Broadway. She says that one of the officers was very rude and verbally abused both her and her husband. Operator Roman refers the caller to the Internal Affairs Division and notifies her supervisor. 13.____
Her supervisor should tell Operator Roman that

A. the caller should have been referred to the Precinct Commanding Officer
B. the caller should have been interviewed by a supervisor and information forwarded to the Internal Affairs Division
C. a job should have been entered for the Patrol Supervisor to respond
D. the caller should have been referred to the Civilian Complaint Review Board directly or a report should have been taken by a supervisor

14. On March 9, a memo is distributed to all operators regarding the excessive number of jobs being input into 911 regarding flea market peddlers. The memo emphasizes the need to carefully screen all unnecessary calls to local precincts or appropriate agencies. No change in procedure is noted. At approximately 1030 hours, Police Communications Technician Greeny, an operator assigned to Brooklyn, receives a call from the owner of a jewelry store located at Fulton Street and Nostrand Avenue concerning a large crowd spilling into the street attempting to purchase items which peddlers are selling in front of his shop. 14.____
As a supervisor, you should tell Operator Greeny to

A. input a 50G2
B. input a 52D2
C. refer the caller to the local precinct
D. refer the caller to the Department of Consumer Affairs

15. While monitoring Police Communications Technician Newly, you hear a conversation involving Blockwatcher 79-1. At the end of the conversation, Dispatcher Newly requests the name, address, and phone number of the blockwatcher, but the blockwatcher refuses to give the information. 15.____
At the monitoring interview with Dispatcher Newly, you, the supervisor, should instruct her that

A. a telephone number should be requested from a block-watcher but not a name and address
B. blockwatchers are required to give only their assigned identification number but should give their address upon request
C. blockwatchers should give an address and phone number in case more information is needed regarding their calls
D. the blockwatcher should have identified herself as a member of the service since only information regarding the incident would have been requested

16. Police Dispatcher Breen asks you, a supervising dispatcher, to speak to a caller complaining about an unlicensed Las Vegas Night in the basement of a church at 600 West 20th Street. The caller states that gambling is going on now, and he is sure they do not have a license. 16.____
You should tell Dispatcher Breen to

A. send a patrol car using 10Y3, unlicensed Las Vegas Night
B. enter a 69S, to be referred to the Organized Crime Control Bureau
C. enter a 69S, to be referred to the precinct for a supervisor to investigate
D. refer the caller to the Department of Consumer Affairs for an unlicensed operation

17. Police Communications Technician Butler receives a call from Mr. Rhet, who states that a female at 300 56th Street, Apartment #3, in Brooklyn is an illegal alien. Mr. Rhet states that the female is now in front of the building, and he will meet the police to point her out. Dispatcher Butler asks the caller to hold on and asks you, the supervising dispatcher, for advice. 17.____
You should instruct the operator to

A. refer the caller to the appropriate agency
B. enter the information as a 69S, to be referred to the Organized Crime Control Bureau
C. refer the caller to Precinct Detective Unit
D. enter the information as a 68Q2 (see complainant)

18. Police Communications Technician Mark receives a recorded alarm of a medical emergency at 570 West 42nd Street in Apartment #5. No further information is given. Operator Mark is unfamiliar with the correct procedure and asks you for your assistance. 18.____
As the supervisor, you should direct the operator to enter the job as a(n)

A. 11Q4 B. 56S C. 11R4 D. 54Q1

19. During random monitoring of Police Communications Technicians, the supervising dispatcher stops to listen to a call answered by Dispatcher Belaire. An alarm company is telling Dispatcher Belaire that an alarm was called in 15 minutes ago. He is now placing another call for the same location. The supervisor hears the operator /Q the location. The roll out is as follows: 19.____

INCIDENT 19A S5 PP60 T09 2345 D3 T9049

10-11 COMMERCIAL/BURGLARY
TV TRADERS PR4
3692 WASHINGTON AVENUE
WEST 194TH STREET - WEST 195TH STREET

*2345 G + G ALARM CO. OPR 1056 - OWNER NTFD - OPR500-9
*2347 PREVIOUS INCIDENT CODE 10-11C4 - CT BROWN

Dispatcher Belaire then tells the caller, *Sir, I will place another call for you and the police will be there as soon as possible.* She enters the *IA* message and routes the job Z and At the monitoring interview with Dispatcher Belaire, the supervisor should tell her that this job was handled

A. *correctly* because you, the supervisor, should ascertain what caused the delay
B. *incorrectly* because the job should have been entered again
C. *correctly* because she routed the job Z and D
D. *incorrectly* because she should have routed the second call *R*

20. Police Communications Technician Brent receives a call from a Mr. Renna reporting that his store was just robbed. Mr. Renna states that one of his customers was shot during the robbery by a white male dressed in blue. Operator Brent asks for the location and the phone number of the store. He then connects the caller to Ambulance Receiving Operator 666 and advises the operator that the incident occurred at West 42nd Street and Broadway at the Royal Shoe Store. After the Ambulance Receiving Operator finishes his questioning of the caller, the operator asks the caller to hold on and hotlines the job to the dispatcher. When Operator Brent returns to the line, the caller had hung up. Operator Brent enters the job as a 30C with the pertinent information and the following routing - AS:A666-HOSP-HOSQ. 20.____
Supervisor Jones, who had monitored this call, should provide reinstruction because Operator Brent failed to

A. enter a direction of flight
B. follow proper hotline procedure
C. route the job properly
D. enter a description of the perpetrator

21. A new memo is issued detailing the services provided by the Victim Services Agency. Supervising Police Communications Technician Rios instructs Police Communications Technician Alonzo in the details of the memo. 21.____
Which of the following services are provided by the Victim Services Agency?

A. 1. Replacement of stolen documents
   2. Installation of window pins for senior citizens
   3. Court appearance notification
B. 1. Replacement of lost or stolen Transit Reduced Fare Cards for the elderly
   2. On-the-job injury disability insurance
   3. Property release assistance
C. 1. Crisis counseling
   2. Emergency money for crime victims
   3. Assistance with income tax relating to theft or casualty loss
D. 1. Applying for State Crime Victims Compensation
   2. Fee payments for stolen checks which were stopped
   3. Emergency services for families of homicide victims

22. While you are working as a supervising dispatcher assigned to the borough of Queens, one of your operators receives a call on 911 from a Dr. Green. He asks for a patrol car to take him from his home at 125-13 Sutphin Boulevard in Queens to 1126 President Street, a high crime area in Brooklyn, to make an emergency visit to a sick patient. Dr. Green tells the operator that he also wants the patrol car to take him back to his home when the visit is completed. The operator, unsure of how to handle the call, requests your assistance. 22.____
As the supervisor, you should instruct her to

A. tell Dr. Green that he must provide his own transportation when making house calls
B. input a job at 1126 President Street as a 68Q2/MEET DOCTOR IFO*
C. input a job at 125-13 Sutphin Boulevard as a 68Q1/ DOCTORS ESCORT*
D. tell Dr. Green that the patrol car will transport him to the location, but it cannot wait for him to complete his visit

23. Police Communications Technician Gold, newly assigned to Brooklyn Dispatching on the 12 to 8 tour, receives a call from a Mr. Jones stating that the police in the 61st Precinct are involved in a parking conditions cover-up. Mr. Jones alleges that the officers in the precinct are not issuing tickets to vehicles illegally parked in the bus stop in front of Tuckley's Tavern at Nostrand Avenue and Avenue S. He insists that a unit from an adjoining precinct respond to the location immediately to issue tickets. Dispatcher Gold enters a job into the system as a 10-67S parking condition requesting that an adjoining resource respond. 23.____
You, as the supervising dispatcher, should instruct Dispatcher Gold that she should have referred the caller to

A. the Special Corruptions number
B. her supervisor so that a written report could be forwarded to the Civilian Complaint Review Board
C. the Integrity Officer at the 61st Precinct since no particular police officer was named
D. her supervisor so that a written report could be forwarded to the Internal Affairs Division

24. Police Communications Technician Furman receives a call from a Mrs. Cannon. She states that her husband, who has a history of mental illness, is acting violently and throwing furniture out of the window. Dispatcher Furman enters the job as a 10-54E1 at the caller's location. The job is brought to the attention of Supervising Dispatcher Simmons, and she instructs Dispatcher Furman that the 10-54E1 code must have an explicit route to *S* for assignment of an Emergency Service Unit. Which one of the following could Supervising Dispatcher Simmons use as another example of a code that would require an explicit route for an Emergency Service Unit? 24.____

A. 10-10Y2
B. 10-20Q2
C. 10-54L1
D. None of the above

25. Mr. Ripple calls 911 and tells Police Communications Technician Chips that Police Officer Newton, assigned to the 70th Precinct, goes to the One Hundred and One Ice Cream Store on Ocean Avenue and Avenue M every day at 12 o'clock noon. He states that the manager always gives Officer Newton an extra scoop of ice cream because the officer has an arrangement with the manager to give special attention to his store. Dispatcher Chips refers the caller to you, the supervisor. You should tell the caller 25.____

A. that this is not a justifiable complaint
B. to contact the Commanding Officer of the 70th Precinct
C. that you will contact the Internal Affairs Division
D. to contact the Civilian Complaint Review Board

---

# KEY (CORRECT ANSWERS)

1. B
2. C
3. A
4. A
5. B
6. A
7. C
8. D
9. D
10. C
11. C
12. D
13. D
14. A
15. A
16. C
17. A
18. D
19. B
20. B
21. A
22. C
23. D
24. D
25. C

---

## READING COMPREHENSION
## UNDERSTANDING AND INTERPRETING WRITTEN MATERIAL

# EXAMINATION SECTION

# TEST 1

DIRECTIONS: Each question or incomplete statement is followed by several suggested answers or completions. Select the one that BEST answers the question or completes the statement. *PRINT THE LETTER OF THE CORRECT ANSWER IN THE SPACE AT THE RIGHT.*

Questions 1-6.

DIRECTIONS: Questions 1 through 6 are to be answered SOLELY on the basis of the following passage.

An aide assigned to the Complaint Room must be familiar with the various forms used by that office. Some of these forms and their uses are:

Complaint Report: Used to record information on or information about crimes reported to the Police Department.

Complaint Report Follow-Up: Used to record additional information after the follow-up initial complaint report has been filed.

Aided Card: Used to record information pertaining to sick and injured persons aided by the police.

Accident Report: Used to record information on or information about injuries and/or property damage involving motorized vehicles.

Property Voucher: Used to record information on or information about property which comes into possession of the Police Department. (Motorized vehicles are not included.)

Auto Voucher: Used to record information on or information about a motorized vehicle which comes into possession of the Police Department.

1. Mr. Brown walks into the police precinct and informs the Administrative Aide that, while he was at work, someone broke into his apartment and removed property belonging to him. He does not know everything that was taken, but he wants to make a report now and will make a list of what was taken and bring it in later. 1.____
According to the above passage, the CORRECT form to use in this situation should be the
   A. Property Voucher
   B. Complaint Report
   C. Complaint Report Follow-Up
   D. Aided Card

2. Mrs. Wilson telephones the precinct and informs the Administrative Aide she wishes to report additional property which was taken from her apartment. The Administrative Aide finds a Complaint Report had been previously filed for Mrs. Wilson. 2.____
According to the above passage, the CORRECT form to use in this situation should be the
   A. Property Voucher
   B. Complaint Report
   C. Complaint Report Follow-Up
   D. Aided Card

3. Police Officer Jones walks into the Complaint Room and informs he Administrative Aide that, while he was on patrol, he observed a woman fall to the sidewalk and remain there, apparently hurt. He comforted the injured woman and called for an ambulance, which came and brought the woman to the hospital. 3.____
According to the above passage, the CORRECT form on which to record this information should be the
   A. Accident Report
   B. Complaint Report
   C. Complaint Report Follow-Up
   D. Aided Card

4. Police Officer Smith informed the Administrative Aide assigned to the Complaint Room that Mr. Green, while crossing the street, was struck by a motorcycle and had to be taken to the hospital. 4.____
According to the above passage, the facts regarding this incident should be recorded on which one of the following forms?
   A. Accident Report
   B. Complaint Report
   C. Complaint Report Follow-Up
   D. Aided Card

5. Police Officer Williams reports to the Administrative Aide assigned to the Complaint Room that he and his partner, Police Officer Murphy, found an auto which was reported stolen and had the auto towed into the police garage. 5.____
Of the following forms listed in the above passage, which is the CORRECT one to use to record this information?
   A. Property Voucher
   B. Auto Voucher
   C. Complaint Report Follow-Up
   D. Complaint Report

6. Administrative Aide Lopez has been assigned to the Complaint Room. During her tour of duty, a person who does not identify herself hands Ms. Lopez a purse. The person states that she found the purse on the street. She then leaves the station house. 6.____
According to the information in the above passage, which is the CORRECT form to fill out to record the incident?
   A. Property Voucher
   B. Auto Voucher
   C. Complaint Report Follow-Up
   D. Complaint Report

Questions 7-9.

DIRECTIONS: Questions 7 through 9 are to be answered SOLELY on the basis of the following passage.

Traffic Enforcement Agent Lewis, while on patrol, received a radio call from Lieutenant Oliva instructing him to proceed to 34th Street, between Madison and Park Avenues, in order to report on the traffic condition in that area.

When Agent Lewis arrived at the assigned location, he discovered approximately 100 demonstrators on the sidewalk in front of the Bamlian Mission to the United Nations located at 135 E. 34th Street. Agent Lewis radioed Lt. Oliva and informed him that traffic was moving very slowly because the demonstration had spilled out onto the street. Lt. Oliva responded that he understood the situation and would contact the Police Department, as well as send an additional agent to the scene.

Police Sergeant Rodriguez arrived at the Bamlin Mission along with several police officers and informed Agent Lewis that he was going to seal off the street between Madison and Park Avenues to contain the demonstration and prevent any demonstrators from being injured.

Agent McMillian arrived at the scene shortly after the police. He and Agent Lewis decided that to divert traffic from 34th Street, which has east and westbound traffic, Agent McMillian would go to the intersection of 34th Street and Madison Avenue and direct eastbound traffic north onto Madison Avenue. Meanwhile, Agent Lewis would position himself at the intersection of 34th Street and Park Avenue and direct westbound traffic south onto Park Avenue.

7. Agent Lewis was sent to 34th Street to 7.____
   - A. direct traffic at the Bamlin Mission
   - B. keep demonstrators out of the street
   - C. report on the traffic condition
   - D. assist the police

8. Police Sergeant Rodriguez closed 34th Street because he wanted to 8.____
   - A. prevent injuries and wait for additional police officers
   - B. contain the demonstration and wait for instructions from Lt. Oliva
   - C. divert traffic and wait for additional police officers
   - D. prevent injuries and contain the demonstration

9. Agent McMillian directed 9.____
   - A. eastbound traffic north onto Madison Avenue
   - B. westbound traffic south onto Park Avenue
   - C. eastbound traffic south onto Madison Avenue
   - D. westbound traffic north onto Park Avenue

Questions 10-11.

DIRECTIONS: Questions 10 and 11 are to be answered SOLELY on the basis of the following passage.

Traffic Enforcement Agents who drive patrol cars are required to perform vehicle maintenance inspections twice a week. Maintenance inspections are conducted on Wednesdays and Saturdays under the direct supervision of a Traffic Enforcement Lieutenant. The main purpose of this program is to make sure that the vehicle fleet is working properly. The responsibility for vehicle maintenance lies first with the driver and then up through the supervisory chain within each command.

10. The MAIN purpose of the Vehicle Maintenance Inspections Program is to 10.____
    A. ensure that the vehicles operate properly
    B. assign responsibility for the operation of the vehicles
    C. reduce the amount of time between the initial reporting of defects and repairs
    D. set up a cost reduction policy whereby minor repairs are conducted at the command level

11. Who supervises maintenance inspections? 11.____
    A. Lieutenant
    B. Agent
    C. Maintenance Specialist
    D. Captain

Questions 12-15.

DIRECTIONS: Questions 12 through 15 are to be answered SOLELY on the basis of the following passage.

Traffic Enforcement Agent Krieg is assigned to direct traffic at the intersection of Frame and Taylor Streets, which is the only way into or out of the Reese Tunnel in the Bronx. At 2:25 P.M., a motorist, driving a blue Cadillac, exits the tunnel and informs Agent Krieg that a U.P.S. truck is on fire in an eastbound lane of the tunnel. Agent Krieg notifies Traffic Control that he has received an unconfirmed report of a fire in the Reese Tunnel. Traffic Control replies that once they receive confirmation of the fire, they will notify the Fire Department and also the District Office so that they may send additional agents and a tow truck to the scene. At 2:30 P.M., a motorist in a gray Ford exits the tunnel and informs Agent Krieg that the tunnel is filled with smoke and that driving is dangerous. Agent Krieg again informs Traffic Control of the situation. Traffic control informs Agent Krieg that they have received confirmation of the fire from the Port Authority Police and that the Fire Department is on the way, as well as six Traffic Enforcement Agents and a tow truck. When the additional agents arrive, they close the tunnel to traffic in both directions in order to clear a path for the Fire Department and other emergency vehicles. Agent Krieg notifies Traffic Control that the Fire Department arrived at 2:45 P.M. and that the tunnel is closed. At 3:15 P.M., Lt. Backman of the Fire Department informs Agent Krieg that the fire has been extinguished, but that there are three vehicles in the tunnel that have to be towed, as well as the U.P.S. truck. At 3:20 P.M., the Fire Department leaves the scene, and the westbound lane is re-opened. At 3:40 P.M., the last vehicle is towed from the tunnel, and Agent Krieg notifies Traffic Control that all lanes in the tunnel are re-opened to traffic.

12. What vehicle was reported to be on fire? 12.____
    A. Blue Cadillac
    B. U.P.S. truck
    C. Gray Ford
    D. Tow truck

13. From whom did Traffic Control receive confirmation that there was a fire? 13.____
    A. Agent Krieg
    B. A motorist
    C. Lt. Backman
    D. Port Authority Police

14. At what time was Agent Krieg informed that the fire was extinguished? 14.____
    A. 2:25
    B. 2:30
    C. 3:15
    D. 3:20

15. How many vehicles had to be towed out of the tunnel? 15.____
    A. 1
    B. 2
    C. 3
    D. 4

Questions 16-17.

DIRECTIONS: Questions 16 and 17 are to be answered SOLELY on the basis of the following passage.

Traffic Enforcement Agents Benjamin and O'Brien are assigned to direct traffic at the entrance of the eastbound side of the Smithsonian Bridge. While the agents are directing traffic, Agent Benjamin notices that eastbound traffic going onto the bridge is at a standstill. While Agent O'Brien remains at the intersection to direct traffic, Agent Benjamin goes onto the eastbound side of the bridge's lower level and observes a tractor trailer stopped in a lane. When Agent Benjamin reaches the trailer, she observes that it exceeds the height limit for vehicles to safely use the bridge. Agent Benjamin radios Traffic Control about the situation, and Traffic Control replies that they will notify the Bureau of Bridges but that, in the meantime, Agents Benjamin and O'Brien should try to handle the situation themselves. Agent Benjamin radios Agent O'Brien and tells him to stop all eastbound traffic from coming onto the bridge. Once this is done, Agent Benjamin then stops all westbound traffic at the site of the trailer. She then directs the eastbound vehicles behind the trailer to go around the trailer by using the westbound lane. Once all the traffic behind the tractor trailer has passed, Agent Benjamin has the trailer back off the bridge.

16. The tractor trailer did not proceed across the bridge because it was 16.____
    A. too high
    B. too heavy
    C. too wide
    D. out of fuel

17. Agent O'Brien was told to stop traffic heading in which direction? 17.____
    A. Northbound
    B. Southbound
    C. Eastbound
    D. Westbound

Questions 18-20.

DIRECTIONS: Questions 18 through 20 are to be answered SOLELY on the basis of the following passage.

Traffic Enforcement Agents Miner and LaBatt are assigned to direct traffic at the intersection of 181st Street and Broadway. While directing traffic, Agent LaBatt is informed by a motorist that there is a brown Ford Escort partially blocking the 181st Street exit of the Cross-Bronx Expressway. While Agent LaBatt proceeds to investigate this report, Agent Minor radios Traffic Control and informs Traffic Lieutenant Wesley that Agent LaBatt has left the intersection in order to investigate the motorist's report.

When Agent LaBatt arrives at the scene, he sees the reported vehicle partially blocking the 181st Street exit ramp. Agent LaBatt inspects the vehicle and discovers that the right front fender is missing and the left rear fender is dented. Upon further inspection, he finds that the license plates are missing, as well as the car's registration sticker. Agent LaBatt, believing that the car is abandoned, follows the procedures for an abandoned vehicle by writing his District Office number and the date and time on both rear fenders. Agent LaBatt also believes that the vehicle creates a hazard to safe traffic flow. He radios Traffic Control with this information and informs Lt. Wesley that a tow truck will be necessary. Lt. Wesley instructs Agent LaBatt to remain with the vehicle and direct exiting traffic off the expressway until the tow truck arrives.

18. The vehicle blocking the exit was missing its 18.____
    A. left rear fender, front license plate, and car registration sticker
    B. right rear fender, left rear fender, and license plates
    C. right front fender, license plates, and car registration sticker
    D. left front fender, rear license plate, and car registration sticker

19. Agent LaBatt was directed to remain with the vehicle 19.____
    A. to prevent the vehicle from being stripped
    B. so the tow truck would know where to go
    C. because traffic at 181st Street and Broadway was light
    D. to direct traffic off the expressway

20. What are the procedures to be followed regarding an abandoned vehicle? 20.____
    Write the date, time,
    A. and the District Office number on the left and right rear fenders
    B. District Office number and registration sticker number on both rear fenders
    C. and the District Office number on both front fenders
    D. the District Office number, and the license plate number on both front fenders

Questions 21-23.

DIRECTIONS: Questions 21 through 23 are to be answered SOLELY on the basis of the following passage.

Traffic Lieutenant Seaver informs Traffic Enforcement Agent Roberts that his assignment for the day is to direct traffic at the intersection of 72nd Street and Madison Avenue. At 11:30 A.M., Agent Roberts observes that the westbound lane at the corner of 120 E. 72nd Street is crumbling and water is pouring out of a huge crack in the street. Mrs. Perry, a resident at 140 E. 72nd Street is looking out her window at the time and immediately dials 911 to report the incident. Agent Roberts radios Traffic Control and informs them of the situation. He requests additional agents to respond to the scene. Traffic Control informs Agent Roberts that they will contact the appropriate utilities and city agencies. However, Agent Roberts is told that until additional agents arrive, he should handle the situation. Fortunately for Agent Roberts, Mrs. Perry's call to 911 brought Police Officers Monroe and Lanier to the scene at 11:35 A.M. Since the crack is located in the westbound lane at 72nd Street and Madison Avenue, Police Officer Monroe proceeds to 72nd Street and 5th Avenue in order to divert westbound traffic before it reaches Madison Avenue. Police Officer Lanier proceeds to 71st Street and Madison Avenue to divert northbound traffic, while Agent Roberts diverts eastbound traffic at the 72nd Street and Madison Avenue intersection.

21. Police Officers Monroe and Lanier arrived at the scene at 21.____
   A. 11:00 P.M. B. 11:15 A.M. C. 11:30 P.M. D. 11:35 A.M.

22. Who diverted traffic at 71st Street and Madison Avenue? 22.____
   A. Traffic Agent Roberts
   B. Police Officer Lanier
   C. Lieutenant Seaver
   D. Police Officer Monroe

23. The water is pouring out of the street at the corner of _____ 72nd Street. 23.____
   A. 120 W. B. 140 E. C. 120 E. D. 140 W.

Questions 24-25.

DIRECTIONS: Questions 24 and 25 are to be answered SOLELY on the basis of the following passage.

Traffic Enforcement Agent Murray was on patrol in his vehicle at the corner of Chambers and Church Streets when he noticed an accident between a white van and a green station wagon at the intersection of Church and Duane Streets. The two drivers were involved in a heated argument when Agent Murray approached them. He advised them to move their vehicles out of the intersection and over to the curb. Once at the curb, Ms. Ambrose, the driver of the station wagon, informed Agent Murray that the van had cut her off. The driver of the fan, Mr. Hope, informed Agent Murray that he was simply trying to change lanes when the station wagon hit his van. Agent Murray asked both drivers for their drivers' licenses and registrations. He informed them that since no one was injured and the damage to the vehicles was minor, they should have driven their cars from the intersection before arguing as to who was at fault. Since they failed to do so, he was going to issue both drivers a summons for obstructing traffic. At this point, Mr. Hope jumped into his van and raced up Reade Street. Agent Murray completed two summonses, one for Ms. Ambrose and the other for Mr. Hope. He issued Ms. Ambrose her summons and at the end of the day returned to his District Office and prepared a Summons Refusal Form. He then attached Mr. Hope's summons to the Summons Refusal Form so that the summons could be mailed to Mr. Hope.

24. At what intersection did the accident occur? 24.____
   A. Chambers Street and Church Street
   B. Church Street and Duane Street
   C Chambers Street and Reade Street
   D. Reade Street and Duane Street

25. When Agent Murray arrived at the scene, the drivers involved in the accident were 25.____
A. moving their vehicles to a side street
B. exchanging insurance information
C. involved in an argument
D. waiting for an ambulance

## KEY (CORRECT ANSWERS)

| | | | |
|---|---|---|---|
| 1. | B | 11. | A |
| 2. | C | 12. | B |
| 3. | D | 13. | D |
| 4. | A | 14. | C |
| 5. | B | 15. | D |
| 6. | A | 16. | A |
| 7. | C | 17. | C |
| 8. | D | 18. | C |
| 9. | A | 19. | D |
| 10. | A | 20. | A |

| | |
|---|---|
| 21. | D |
| 22. | B |
| 23. | C |
| 24. | B |
| 25. | C |

# TEST 2

DIRECTIONS: Each question or incomplete statement is followed by several suggested answers or completions. Select the one that BEST answers the question or completes the statement. *PRINT THE LETTER OF THE CORRECT ANSWER IN THE SPACE AT THE RIGHT.*

Questions 1-2.

DIRECTIONS: Questions 1 and 2 are to be answered SOLELY on the basis of the following passage.

At 2:00 P.M., Traffic Enforcement Agent Black was on foot patrol on Hack Avenue when Mrs. Herbet approached him about a faulty parking meter. She complained that for the two quarters she deposited she is supposed to get two hours of parking tie and not just the forty minutes that the meter shows. Agent Black accompanied Mrs. Herbet to her car which was parked at 243 Chief Street. He tested the meter by turning the knob and found that the meter was broken because any amount of money deposited in the meter would register forty minutes of parking time. He searched for the serial number of the meter which was P26601 and recorded it along with the location of the meter on his Daily Field Patrol Sheet. Agent Black informed Mrs. Herbet that she would have two hours of parking time, the maximum amount of time she would have received if the meter were working properly. He also informed her that he was starting this two hour limit as of 2:05 P.M. and recorded this time and her license plate number (DRE-927) on his Daily Field Patrol Sheet. The agent told Mrs. Herbet that if her car was parked at the meter past the two hour limit, he would have to issue her a summons. Mrs. Herbet thanked the agent and said she would be gone long before the limit was up.

At 4:15 P.M., Agent Black was again on Chief Street when he saw that Mrs. Herbet's car was still parked at the meter. He issued her a summons for a meter violation and continued on his patrol.

1. Which of the following is recorded on Agent Black's Daily Field Patrol Sheet? 1.____
   A. 243 Hack Avenue, P26611, 2:05 P.M., DRE-927
   B. 243 Chief Street, P26601, 2:05 P.M., DRE-927
   C. 243 Hack Street, P26661, 2:05 P.M., DRE-927
   D. 243 Chief Avenue, P26601, 2:05 P.M., DRE-927

2. Agent Black allowed Mrs. Herbet to park at the meter for two hours because 2.____
   A. it is the maximum amount of parking time allowed if the meter were working properly
   B. he felt bad that she lost her money
   C. she was complaining to him
   D. she assured him she would be gone before the two hour limit was up

Questions 2-5.

DIRECTIONS: Questions 2 through 5 are to be answered SOLELY on the basis of the following passage.

At 10:35 A.M., Police Communications Technician Ross receives a second call from Mrs. Smith who is very upset because she has been waiting for the police and an ambulance since her first call, one hour ago. Mrs. Smith was mugged, and in resisting the attack, her nose was broken. The location of the incident is the uptown side of the subway station for the IND #2 train located at Jay Street and Borough Hall. Operator Ross advises Mrs. Smith to hold on and that she will check the status of her complaint. Operator Ross calls the Emergency Medical Service (EMS) and connects Mrs. Smith to the EMS operator. The EMS operator informs Mrs. Smith that an ambulance is coming from a far distance away and will be at the location at approximately 11:03 A.M. Operator Ross then calls the Transit Authority Police Department (TAPD). The TAPD received Mrs. Smith's call at 9:37 A.M., and police arrived at location at 9:46 A.M. However, the police arrived at the downtown side of the subway station for the IND #3 train. TAPD informs Operator Ross that a police car will arrive at the correct location as soon as possible.

3. What is the CLOSEST approximate time that Mrs. Smith made her first call for help? 3.____
   A. 9:35 B. 9:46 C. 10:35 D. 11:03

4. The ambulance was delayed because 4.____
   A. the ambulance responded to the downtown side of the subway station for the IND #2 train
   B. EMS never received Mrs. Smith's request for an ambulance
   C. a broken nose is not a priority request for an ambulance
   D. the ambulance was coming from a far distance

5. There was a delay in TAPD response to the crime scene because TAPD 5.____
   A. was coming from a far distance
   B. responded on the uptown side of the subway station for the IND #2 train
   C. was waiting for the Police Department to respond first
   D. responded on the downtown side of the subway station for the IND #3 train

Questions 6-8.

DIRECTIONS: Questions 6 through 8 are to be answered SOLELY on the basis of the following passage.

Police Communications Technician Robbins receives a call at 5:15 P.M. from Mr. Adams reporting he witnessed a shooting in front of 230 Eagle Road. Mr. Adams, who lives at 234 Eagle Road, states he overheard two white males arguing with a black man. He describes one white male as having blonde hair and wearing a black jacket with blue jeans, and the other white male as having brown hair and wearing a white jacket and blue jeans.

Mr. Adams recognized the black man as John Rivers, the son of Mrs. Mary Rivers, who lives at 232 Eagle Road. At 5:10 P.M., the blonde male took a gun, shot John in the stomach, and dragged his body into the alleyway. The two males ran into the backyard of 240 Eagle Road and headed west on Randall Boulevard. Dispatcher Robbins connects Mr. Adams to the Emergency Medical Service. The Ambulance Receiving Operator processes the call at 5:25 P.M. and advises Mr. Adams that the next available ambulance will be sent.

6. Who was the witness to the shooting? 6.____
   A. Dispatcher Robbins
   B. Mr. Adams
   C. Mrs. Rivers
   D. John Rivers

7. In front of what address was John Rivers shot? 7.____
   _____ Eagle Road.
   A. 230
   B. 232
   C. 234
   D. 240

8. What is the description of the male who fired the gun? 8.____
   A _____ male wearing a _____ jacket, and blue jeans.
   A. white blonde-haired; white
   B. white brown-haired; black
   D. white blonde-haired; black
   D. black brown-haired; white

Questions 9-10.

DIRECTIONS: Questions 9 and 10 are to be answered SOLELY on the basis of the following passage.

At the beginning of their tours, Police Communications Technicians need to call the precinct to find out what patrol cars are covering which sections of the precinct and which special assignment cars are being used. Special assignment cars are used instead of regular patrol cars when certain situations arise. Special assignment cars should be assigned before a patrol car when a call comes in that is related to the car's special assignment, regardless of what section the incident is occurring in. Otherwise, a regular patrol car should be assigned.

Police Communications Technician Tanner is assigned to the 83rd Precinct. He calls the precinct and determines the following patrol cars and special assignment cars are being used:

Patrol cars are assigned as follows:
Patrol Car 83A – Covers Sections A, B, C
Patrol Car 83D – Covers Sections D, E, F
Patrol Car 83G – Covers Sections G, H, I

Special assignment cars are assigned as follows:
83SP1 – Burglary Car
83SP2 – Religious Establishment
83SP8 – Anti-Crime (plainclothes officers)

9. Dispatcher Tanner receives a call located in the 83rd Precinct in E Section Which car should be assigned? 9.____
   A. 83D
   B. 83A
   C. 83SP8
   D. 83SP2

10. Dispatcher Tanner receives a call concerning a burglary in B Section Which is the CORRECT car to be assigned? 10.____
    A. 83A B. 83G C. 83SP1 D. 83SP2

Questions 11-13.

DIRECTIONS: Questions 11 through 13 are to be answered SOLELY on the basis of the following passage.

Mrs. Arroyo returns from work one evening to find her door open and loud noise coming from her apartment. She peeks through the crack of the door and sees a white male moving rapidly through her apartment wearing blue jeans and a pink T-shirt. She runs to the nearest public telephone and dials 911. Police Communications Technician Ms. Lopez takes the call. Mrs. Arroyo informs Operator Lopez that there is a strange man in her apartment. The operator asks the caller for her address, apartment number, name, and telephone number, and then puts Mrs. Arroyo on hold. Operator Lopez enters the address in the computer and, realizing it is a high priority call, tries to notify the Radio Dispatcher directly by depressing the *hotline* button. The Radio Dispatcher does not respond, and Operator Lopez realizes the *hotline* button is not working. The operator then continues to enter the rest of the information into the computer and notifies the caller that the police will respond. Operator Lopez then walks into the dispatcher's room to make sure the dispatcher received the information entered into the computer, and then notifies the supervisor of her malfunctioning equipment.

11. The operator notified her supervisor because 11.____
    A. the suspect was still in the apartment
    B. the *hotline* button was not working
    C. she could not enter the address in the computer
    D. it was a high priority call

12. What was the FIRST action the operator took after putting the complainant on hold? 12.____
    A. Entered the caller's telephone number and name in the computer
    B. Walked into the dispatcher's room
    C. Entered the caller's address into the computer
    D. Tried to notify the Radio Dispatcher by depressing the *hotline* button

13. Operator Lopez depressed the *hotline* button 13.____
    A. to check if the *hotline* button was working properly
    B. because it was a high priority call
    C. to make sure the dispatcher received the information entered into the computer
    D. because the computer was not working properly

Questions 14-16.

DIRECTIONS: Questions 14 through 16 are to be answered SOLELY on the basis of the following passage.

Police Communications Technician John Clove receives a call from a social worker, Mrs. Norma Harris of Presbyterian Hospital, who states there is a 16-year-old teenager on the other line speaking to Dr. Samuel Johnson, a psychologist at the hospital. The teenager is threatening suicide and claims that she is an out-patient, but refuses to give her name, address, or telephone number. She further states that the teenager took 100 pills of valium and is experiencing dizziness, numbness of the lips, and heart palpitations. The teenager tells Dr. Johnson that she wants to die because her boyfriend left her because she is pregnant.

Dr. Johnson is keeping her on the line persuading her to give her name, telephone number, and address. The social worker asks the dispatcher to trace the call. The dispatcher puts the caller on hold and informs his supervisor, Mrs. Ross, of the incident. The supervisor contacts Telephone Technician Mr. Ralph Taylor. Mr. Taylor contacts the telephone company and speaks to Supervisor Wallace, asking him to trace the call between Dr. Johnson and the teenager. After approximately 10 minutes, the dispatcher gets back to the social worker and informs her that the call is being traced.

14. Why did the social worker call Dispatcher Clove? 14.____
    A. A teenager is threatening suicide
    B. Mrs. Ross took 100 pills of valium
    C. Dr. Johnson felt dizzy, numbness of the lips, and heart palpitations
    D. An unmarried teenager is pregnant

15. Who did Mr. Clove notify FIRST? 15.____
    A. Mrs. Norma Harris
    B. Dr. Samuel Johnson
    C. Mr. Wallace
    D. Mrs. Ross

16. The conversation between which two individuals is being traced? 16.____
    A. Mrs. Norma Harris and the 16-year-old teenager
    B. The Telephone Technician and Telephone Company Supervisor
    C. Dr. Johnson and the 16-year-old teenager
    D. the dispatcher and the Hospital social worker

Questions 17-19.

DIRECTIONS: Questions 17 through 19 are to be answered SOLELY on the basis of the following passage.

Police Communications Technician Flood receives a call from Mr. Michael Watkins, Program Director for *Meals On Wheels*, a program that delivers food to elderly people who cannot leave their homes. Mr. Watkins states he received a call from Rochelle Berger, whose elderly aunt, Estelle Sims, is a client of his. Rochelle Berger informed Mr. Watkins that she had just received a call from her aunt's neighbor, Sally Bowles, who told her that her aunt has not eaten in several days and is in need of medical attention.

After questioning Mr. Watkins, Dispatcher Flood is informed that Estelle Sims lives at 300 79$^{th}$ Street in Apartment 6K, and her telephone number is 686-4527; Sally Bowles lives in Apartment 6H, and her telephone number is 678-2456. Mr. Watkins further advises that if there is difficulty getting into Estelle Sims' apartment, to ring Sally Bowles bell and she will let you in.

Mr. Watkins gives his phone number as 776-0451, and Rochelle Berger's phone number is 291-7287. Dispatcher Flood advises Mr. Watkins that the appropriate medical assistance will be sent.

17. Who did Sally Bowles notify that her neighbor needed medical attention? 17.____
    A. Dispatcher Flood
    B. Michael Watkins
    C. Rochelle Berger
    D. Estelle Sims

18. If the responding medical personnel are unable to get into Apartment 6K, they should speak to 18.____
    A. Rochelle Berger
    B. Sally Bowles
    C. Dispatcher Flood
    D. Michael Watkins

19. Whose telephone number is 686-4527? 19.____
    A. Michael Watkins
    B. Estelle Sims
    C. Sally Bowles
    D. Rochelle Berger

Questions 20-22.

DIRECTIONS: Questions 20 through 22 are to be answered SOLELY on the basis of the following passage.

On May 15, 2020, at 10:15 A.M., Mr. Price was returning to his home at 220 Kings Walk when he discovered two of his neighbors' apartment doors slightly opened. One neighbor, Mrs. Kagan, who lives alone in Apartment 1C, was away on vacation. The other apartment, 1B, is occupied by Martin and Ruth Stone, an elderly couple, who usually take a walk everyday at 10:00 A.M. Fearing a robbery might be taking place, Mr. Price runs downstairs to Mr. White in Apartment B1 to call the police. Police Communications Technician Johnson received the call at 10:20 A.M. Mr. Price gave his address and stated that two apartments were possibly being burglarized. Communications Technician Johnson verified the address in the computer and then asked Mr. Price for descriptions of the suspects. He explained that he had not seen anyone, but he believed that they were still inside the building. Communications Technician Johnson immediately notified the dispatcher ho assigned two patrol cars at 10:25 A.M., while Mr. Price was still on the phone. Communications technician Johnson told Mr. Price that the police were responding to the location.

20. Who called Communications Technician Johnson? 20.____
    A. Mrs. Kagan
    B. Mr. White
    C. Mrs. Stone
    D. Mr. Price

21. What time did Communications Technician Johnson receive the call? 21.____
    _____ A.M.
    A. 10:00
    B. 10:15
    C. 10:20
    D. 10:25

22. Which tenant was away on vacation? 22.____
    The tenant in Apartment
    A. 1C
    B. 1B
    C. B1
    D. 1D

Questions 23-25.

DIRECTIONS: Questions 23 through 25 are to be answered SOLELY on the basis of the following passage.

On Tuesday, March 20, 2020, at 11:55 P.M., Dispatcher Uzel receives a call from a female stating that she immediately needs the police. The dispatcher asks the caller for her address. The excited female answers, *I cannot think of it right now.* The dispatcher tries to calm down the caller. At this point, the female caller tells the dispatcher that her address is 1934 Bedford Avenue. The caller then realizes that 1934 Bedford Avenue is her mother's address and gives her address as 3455 Bedford Avenue. Dispatcher Uzel enters the address into the computer and tells the caller that the cross streets are Myrtle and Willoughby Avenues. The caller answers, *I don't live near Willoughby Avenue.* The dispatcher repeats her address at 3455 Bedford Avenue. Then the female states that her name is Linda Harris and her correct address is 5534 Bedford Avenue. Dispatcher Uzel enters the new address into the computer and determines the cross streets to be Utica Avenue and Kings Highway. The caller agrees that these are the cross streets where she lives.

23. What is the caller's CORRECT address? 23.____
    A. Unknown
    B. 1934 Bedford Avenue
    C. 3455 Bedford Avenue
    D. 5534 Bedford Avenue

24. What are the cross streets of the correct answer? 24.____
    A. Myrtle Avenue and Willoughby Avenue
    B. Utica Avenue and Kings Highway
    C. Bedford Avenue and Myrtle Avenue
    D. Utica Avenue and Willoughby Avenue

25. Why did the female caller telephone Dispatcher Uzel? 25.____
    A. She needed the cross streets for her address
    B. Her mother needed assistance
    C. The purpose of the call was not mentioned
    D. She did not know where she lived

# KEY (CORRECT ANSWERS)

1. B
2. A
3. A
4. D
5. D

6. B
7. A
8. C
9. A
10. C

11. B
12. C
13. B
14. A
15. D

16. C
17. C
18. B
19. B
20. D

21. C
22. A
23. D
24. B
25. C

# TEST 3

DIRECTIONS: Each question or incomplete statement is followed by several suggested answers or completions. Select the one that BEST answers the question or completes the statement. *PRINT THE LETTER OF THE CORRECT ANSWER IN THE SPACE AT THE RIGHT.*

Questions 1-3.

DIRECTIONS: Questions 1 through 3 are to be answered SOLELY on the basis of the following passage.

Dispatcher Clark, who is performing a 7:30 A.M. to 3:30 P.M. tour of duty, receives a call from Mrs. Gold. Mrs. Gold states there are four people selling drugs in front of Joe's Cleaners, located at the intersection of Main Street and Broadway. After checking the location in the computer, Dispatcher Clark asks the caller to give a description of each person. She gives the following descriptions: one white male wearing a yellow shirt, green pants, and red sneakers; one Hispanic male wearing a red and white shirt, black pants, and white sneakers; one black female wearing a green and red striped dress and red sandals; and one black male wearing a green shirt, yellow pants, and green sneakers. She also states that the Hispanic male, who is standing near a blue van, has the drugs inside a small black shoulder bag. She further states that she saw the black female hide a gun inside a brown paper bag and place it under a black car parked in front of Joe's Cleaners. The drug selling goes on everyday at various times. During the week, it occurs from 7 A.M. to 1 P.M. and from 5 P.M. to 12 A.M., but on weekends it occurs from 3 P.M. until 7 A.M.

1. Which person was wearing red sneakers? 1.____
   A. Black male B. Hispanic male
   C. Black female D. White male

2. Mrs. Gold stated the drugs were located 2.____
   A. under the blue van B. inside the black shoulder bag
   C. under the black car D. inside the brown paper bag

3. At what time does Mrs. Gold state the drugs are sold on weekends? 3.____
   A. 7:30 A.M. – 3:30 P.M. B. 7:00 A.M. – 1:00 P.M.
   C. 5:00 P.M. – 12:00 A.M. D. 3:00 P.M. – 7:00 A.M.

Questions 4-6.

DIRECTIONS: Questions 4 through 6 are to be answered SOLELY on the basis of the following passage.

911 Operator Gordon receives a call from a male stating there is a bomb set to explode in the gym of Public School 85 in two hours. Realizing the urgency of the call, the Operator calls the radio dispatcher, who assigns Patrol Car 43A to the scene. Operator Gordon then notifies her supervisor, Miss Smith, who first reviews the tape of the call, then calls the Operations Unit, which is notified of all serious incidents, and she reports the facts. The Operations Unit notifies the Mayor's Information Agency and Borough Headquarters of the emergency situation.

4. Who did Operator Gordon notify FIRST? 4.____
   A. Supervisor Smith
   B. Operations Unit
   C. Patrol Car 43A
   D. Radio dispatcher

5. The Operations Unit was notified 5.____
   A. to inform school personnel of the bomb
   B. so they can arrive at the scene before the bomb is scheduled to go off
   C. to evacuate the school
   D. due to the seriousness of the incident

6. Who did Miss Smith notify? 6.____
   A. Patrol Car 43A
   B. Operations Unit
   C. Mayor's Information Agency
   D. Borough Headquarters

Questions 7-9.

DIRECTIONS: Questions 7 through 9 are to be answered SOLELY on the basis of the following passage.

Communications Operator Harris receives a call from Mrs. Stein who reports that a car accident occurred in front of her home. She states that one of the cars belongs to her neighbor, Mrs. Brown, and the other car belongs to Mrs. Stein's son, Joseph Stein. Communications Operator Harris enters Mrs. Stein's address into the computer and receives information that no such address exists. She asks Mrs. Stein to repeat her address. Mrs. Stein repeats her address and states that gasoline is leaking from the cars and that smoke is coming from their engines. She further states that people are trapped in the cars and then hangs up.

Communications Operator Harris notifies her supervisor, Jones, that she received a call but was unable to verify the address and that the caller hung up. Mrs. Jones listens to the tape of the call and finds that the caller stated 450 Park Place, not 415 Park Place. She advises Communications Operator Harris to enter the correct address, then notify Emergency Service Unit to respond to the individuals trapped in the cars, the Fire Department for the smoke condition, and Emergency Medical Service for any possible injuries.

7. Who did Communications Operator Harris notify concerning the problem with the caller's address? 7.____
   A. Mrs. Brown
   B. Joseph Stein
   C. Joseph Brown
   D. Mrs. Jones

8. Which agency was Communications Operator Harris advised to notify concerning individuals trapped in the cars? 8.____
   A. Emergency Medical Service
   B. Fire Department
   C. Emergency Service Unit
   D. NYC Police Department

9. Which agency did Supervisor Jones advise Communications Operator Harris to notify for the smoke condition? 9.____
   A. NYC Police Department
   B. Emergency Medical Service
   C. Fire Department
   D. Emergency Service Unit

Questions 10-12.

DIRECTIONS: Questions 10 through 12 are to be answered SOLELY on the basis of the following passage.

On May 12, at 3:35 P.M., Police Communications Technician Connor receives a call from a child caller requesting an ambulance for her mother, whom she cannot wake. The child did not know her address, but gave Communications Technician Connor her apartment number and telephone number. Communications Technician Connor's supervisor, Ms. Bendel, is advised of the situation and consults Cole's Director, a listing published by the Bell Telephone Company to obtain an address when only the telephone number is known. The telephone number is unlisted. Ms. Bendel asks Communications Technician Taylor to call Telco Security to obtain an address from their telephone number listing. Communications Technician Taylor speaks to Ms. Morris of Telco Security and obtains the address. Communications Technician Connor, who is still talking with the child, is given the address by Communications Technician Taylor. She enters the information into the computer system and transfers the caller to the Emergency Medical Service.

10. What information did Communications Technician Connor obtain from the child caller? 10.____
    A. Telephone number and apartment number
    B. Name and address
    C. Address and telephone number
    D. Apartment number and address

11. Communications Technician Taylor obtained the address from 11.____
    A. Communications Technician Connor
    B. Ms. Morris
    C. Supervisor Bendel
    D. the child caller

12. The caller's address was obtained by calling 12.____
    A. Cole's Directory
    B. Telco Security
    C. Emergency Medical Service
    D. the Telephone Company

Questions 13-15.

DIRECTIONS: Questions 13 through 15 are to be answered SOLELY on the basis of the following passage.

Bridge and Tunnel Officer Frankel is assigned to Post 33 inside the Main Street Tunnel. All posts in the northbound tunnel are numbered using odd numbers. All posts in the southbound tunnel are numbered with even numbers. The sergeant on duty, Sgt. Hanks, drives through the northbound tunnel at 10:30 P.M. to check on the tunnel posts before taking his meal break. When he reaches Officer Frankel, Sgt. Hanks stops the patrol car and exits from his car in order to speak with Frankel. He informs the officer that at 11:05 P.M. a truck with a wide load is expected to pass through the tunnel. Officer Frankel states he will be prepared for the vehicle and will watch for it.

Sgt. Hanks gets back into his patrol car and continues on his way to inform the other three officers in the northbound tunnel. At 10:50 P.M., Sgt. Hanks is heading to the facility building when his patrol car stalls in front of Post 44. Bridge and Tunnel Officer Torrey, stationed at the post, observes the disabled patrol car and leave his post in order to assist the sergeant. Sgt. Hanks orders Officer Torrey to call for a wrecker to remove the patrol car from the tunnel.

13. At what post did Sgt. Hanks' patrol car break down? 13.____
    A. 34, Northbound B. 44, Southbound
    C. 43, Northbound D. 33, Southbound

14. How many Bridge and Tunnel Officers were posted in the northbound tunnel? 14.____
    A. 2 B. 3 C. 4 D. 5

15. Sgt. Hanks was driving through the northbound tunnel in order to 15.____
    A. inform the posts of the *wide load* truck
    B. find where Bridge and Tunnel Officer Frankel was stationed
    C. check on the tunnel posts
    D. return to the facility building

Questions 16-18.

DIRECTIONS: Questions 16 through 18 are to be answered SOLELY on the basis of the following passage.

At 6:45 P.M., two motorists were involved in a minor accident on the toll plaza at the Cross-Bay Bridge. Tempers became short, and soon the two motorists were involved in a heated argument.

Bridge and Tunnel Officers Bender and Rourke, who were to start their tour at 6:50 P.M., arrived and broke up the altercation. The two drivers were separated and calmed. Each began to describe the accident to the officers.

Nicholas Warren informed Officer Rourke that he paid his toll in Lane 1, which is the extreme right lane. He wanted to go into the left lane on the bridge and began to move his vehicle to the left when his vehicle was struck in the rear by a vehicle leaving Toll Lane 2.

Olga Miller informed Officer Bender that she had paid her toll and was leaving Lane 2 when Mr. Warren's vehicle cut directly in front of her vehicle and caused the accident.

Ten minutes after the accident occurred, Bridge and Tunnel Officers Pena and Bickford rang their supervisor and asked when they were to be relieved since their tours were scheduled to end at 7:00 P.M. Sergeant White explained to the two officers that their relief officers were taking information on an accident. Officers Pena and Bickford told the Sergeant that they would take over for Bender and Rourke and finish taking the information. Sgt. White approved the switch. Twenty-five minutes after the accident, all information was taken, and all parties left the scene.

16. Ms. Miller FIRST spoke to Officer 16.____
    A. Bender B. Bickford C. White D. Pena

17. Officer Pena was due to end his tour at ______ P.M. 17.____
    A. 6:45 B. 6:50 C. 7:00 D. 7:10

18. In what toll lane did Mr. Warren pay the toll? 18.____
    A. 1 B. 2 C. 3 D. 4

Questions 19-20.

DIRECTIONS: Questions 19 through 20 are to be answered SOLELY on the basis of the following passage.

Bridge and Tunnel Officer Wendell is assigned to a toll plaza at the Wilson Bridge. At about 2:15 P.M., he observes John Edwards drive into the toll lane without throwing any money into the Exact Coin Machine. As Officer Wendell approaches the vehicle, Mr. Edwards starts to blow his horn. Officer Wendell instructs Mr. Edwards to place the proper toll into the machine, but Mr. Edwards refuses, stating that the bridge toll is unfair. When Officer Wendell requests Mr. Edwards' drivers license and car registration, Mr. Edwards starts to yell and use abusive language. Officer Wendell warns Mr. Edwards that he will be arrested if he continues to block the toll lane. Mr. Edwards continues to yell, refuses to leave the lane, and is arrested by Officer Wendell.

19. Officer Wendell FIRST observed Mr. Edwards when he 19.____
    A. started blowing his horn
    B. refused to leave the toll lane
    C. entered the toll lane
    D. began yelling and using abusive language

20. Officer Wendell arrested Mr. Edwards because he 20.____
    A. refused to pay the toll
    B. was yelling and using abusive language
    C. refused to give his license and registration to Officer Wendell
    D. was blocking the toll lane

# KEY (CORRECT ANSWERS)

| | | | |
|---|---|---|---|
| 1. | D | 11. | B |
| 2. | B | 12. | B |
| 3. | D | 13. | B |
| 4. | D | 14. | C |
| 5. | D | 15. | A/C |
| 6. | B | 16. | A |
| 7. | D | 17. | C |
| 8. | C | 18. | A |
| 9. | C | 19. | C |
| 10. | A | 20. | D |

# CODING

# EXAMINATION SECTION

## COMMENTARY

An ingenious question-type called coding, involving elements of alphabetizing, filing, name and number comparison, and evaluative judgment and application, has currently won wide acceptance in testing circles for measuring clerical aptitude and general ability, particularly on the senior (middle) grades (levels).

While the directions for this question usually vary in detail, the candidate is generally asked to consider groups of names, codes, and numbers, and then, according to a given plan, to arrange codes in alphabetic order; to arrange these in numerical sequence; to re-arrange columns of names and numbers in correct order; to espy errors in coding; to choose the correct coding arrangement in consonance with the given directions and examples, etc.

This question-type appear to have few parameters in respect to form, substance, or degree of difficulty.

Accordingly, acquaintance with, and practice in, the coding question is recommended for the serious candidate.

## TEST 1

DIRECTIONS: Questions 1 through 8 are to be answered on the basis of the code table and the instructions given below.

| Code Letter for Traffic Problem | B | H | Q | J | F | L | M | I |
|---|---|---|---|---|---|---|---|---|
| Code Number for Action Taken | 1 | 2 | 3 | 4 | 5 | 6 | 7 | 8 |

Assume that each of the capital letters on the above chart is a radio code for a particular traffic problem and that the number immediately below each capital letter is the radio code for the correct action to be taken to deal with the problem. For instance, "1" is the action to be taken to deal with problem "B", "2" is the action to be taken to deal with problem "H", and so forth.

In each question, a series of code letters is given in Column 1. Column 2 gives four different arrangements of code numbers. You are to pick the answer (A, B, C, or D) in Column 2 that gives the code numbers that match the code letters in the same order.

SAMPLE QUESTION

| Column 1 | Column 2 |
|---|---|
| BHLFMQ | A. 125678 |
| | B. 216573 |
| | C. 127653 |
| | D. 126573 |

According to the chart, the code numbers that correspond to these code letters are as follows: B – 1, M – 2, L – 6, F – 5, M – 7, Q – 3. Therefore, the right answer is 126573. This answer is D in Column 2.

| Column 1 | Column 2 | |
|---|---|---|
| 1. BHQLMI | A. 123456<br>B. 123567<br>C. 123678<br>D. 125678 | 1.____ |
| 2. HBJQLF | A. 214365<br>B. 213456<br>C. 213465<br>D. 214387 | 2.____ |
| 3. QHMLFJ | A. 321654<br>B. 345678<br>C. 327645<br>D. 327654 | 3.____ |
| 4. FLQJIM | A. 543287<br>B. 563487<br>C. 564378<br>D. 654378 | 4.____ |
| 5. FBIHMJ | A. 518274<br>B. 152874<br>C. 528164<br>D. 517842 | 5.____ |
| 6. MIHFQB | A. 872341<br>B. 782531<br>C. 782341<br>D. 783214 | 6.____ |
| 7. JLFHQIM | A. 465237<br>B. 456387<br>C. 4652387<br>D. 4562387 | 7.____ |
| 8. LBJQIFH | A. 614382<br>B. 6134852<br>C. 61437852<br>D. 61431852 | 8.____ |

## KEY (CORRECT ANSWERS)

| | | | |
|---|---|---|---|
| 1. | C | 5. | A |
| 2. | A | 6. | B |
| 3. | D | 7. | C |
| 4. | B | 8. | A |

# TEST 2

DIRECTIONS: Each question or incomplete statement is followed by several suggested answers or completions. Select the one that BEST answers the question or completes the statement. *PRINT THE LETTER OF THE CORRECT ANSWER IN THE SPACE AT THE RIGHT.*

Questions 1-5.

DIRECTIONS: Questions 1 through 5 are based on the following list showing the name and number of each of nine inmates.

| | | |
|---|---|---|
| 1. Johnson | 4. Thompson | 7. Gordon |
| 2. Smith | 5. Frank | 8. Porter |
| 3. Edwards | 6. Murray | 9. Lopez |

Each question consists of 3 sets of numbers and letters. Each set should consist of the numbers of three inmates and the first letter of each of their names. The letters should be in the same order as the numbers. In at least two of the three choices, there will be an error. On your answer sheet, mark only that choice in which the letters correspond with the numbers and are in the same order. If all three sets are wrong, mark choice D in your answer space.

SAMPLE QUESTION
A. 386 EPM
B. 542 FST
C. 474 LGT

Since 3 corresponds to E for Edwards, 8 corresponds to P for Porter, and 6 corresponds to M for Murray, choice A is correct and should be entered in your answer space. Choice B is wrong because letters T and S have been reversed. Choice C is wrong because the first number, which is 4, does NOT correspond with the first letter of choice C, which is L. It should have been T. If choice A were also wrong, then D would be the correct answer.

1. A. 382 EGS B. 461 TMJ C. 875 PLF 1.____

2. A. 549 FLT B. 692 MJS C. 758 GSP 2.____

3. A. 936 LEM B. 253 FSE C. 147 JTL 3.____

4. A. 569 PML B. 716 GJP C. 842 PTS 4.____

5. A. 356 FEM B. 198 JPL C. 637 MEG 5.____

Questions 6-10.

DIRECTIONS: Questions 6 through 10 are to be answered on the basis of the following information:

In order to make sure stock is properly located, incoming units are stored as follows:

| STOCK NUMBERS | BIN NUMBERS |
|---|---|
| 00100 – 39999 | D30, L44 |
| 40000 – 69999 | 14L, D38 |
| 70000 – 99999 | 41L, 80D |
| 100000 and over | 614, 83D |

Using the above table, choose the answer A, B, C, or D, which lists the correct Bin Number for the Stock Number given.

6. 17243 — 6.____
   A. 41L  B. 83D  C. 14L  D. D30

7. 9219 — 7.____
   A. D38  B. L44  C. 614  D. 41L

8. 90125 — 8.____
   A. 41L  B. 614  C. D38  D. D30

9. 10001 — 9.____
   A. L44  B. D38  C. 80D  D. 83D

10. 200100 — 10.____
   A. 41L  B. 14L  C. 83D  D. D30

# KEY (CORRECT ANSWERS)

| | | | |
|---|---|---|---|
| 1. | B | 6. | D |
| 2. | D | 7. | B |
| 3. | A | 8. | A |
| 4. | C | 9. | A |
| 5. | C | 10. | C |

# TEST 3

DIRECTIONS: Each question or incomplete statement is followed by several suggested answers or completions. Select the one that BEST answers the question or completes the statement. *PRINT THE LETTER OF THE CORRECT ANSWER IN THE SPACE AT THE RIGHT.*

Questions 1-9.

DIRECTIONS: Assume that the Police Department is planning to conduct a statistical study of individuals who have been convicted of crimes during a certain year. For the purpose of this study, identification numbers are being assigned to individuals in the following manner:

The first two digits indicate the age of the individual.
The third digit indicates the sex of the individual:
1. Male
2. Female

The fourth digit indicates the type of crime involved:
1. criminal homicide
2. forcible rape
3. robbery
4. aggravated assault
5. burglary
6. larceny
7. auto theft
8. other

The fifth and sixth digits indicate the month in which the conviction occurred:
01. January
02. February, etc.

Questions 1 through 9 are to be answered SOLELY on the basis of the above information and the following list of individuals and identification numbers.

| | | | |
|---|---|---|---|
| Abbott, Richard | 271304 | Morris, Chris | 212705 |
| Collins, Terry | 352111 | Owens, William | 231412 |
| Elders, Edward | 191207 | Parker, Leonard | 291807 |
| George, Linda | 182809 | Robinson, Charles | 311102 |
| Hill, Leslie | 251702 | Sands, Jean | 202610 |
| Jones, Jackie | 301106 | Smith, Michael | 42108 |
| Lewis, Edith | 402406 | Turner, Donald | 191601 |
| Mack, Helen | 332509 | White, Barbara | 242803 |

1. The number of women on the above list is  1.____
A. 6  B. 7  C. 8  D. 9

2. The two convictions which occurred during February were for the crimes of 2.____
   A. aggravated assault and auto theft
   B. auto theft and criminal homicide
   C. burglary and larceny
   D. forcible rape and robbery

3. The ONLY man convicted of auto theft was 3.____
   A. Richard Abbott B. Leslie Hill
   C. Chris Morris D. Leonard Parker

4. The number of people on the list who were 25 years old or older is 4.____
   A. 6 B. 7 C. 8 D. 9

5. The OLDEST person on the list is 5.____
   A. Terry Collins B. Edith Lewis
   C. Helen Mack D. Michael Smith

6. The two people on the list who are the same age are 6.____
   A. Richard Abbott and Michael Smith
   B. Edward Elders and Donald Turner
   C. Linda George and Helen Mack
   D. Leslie Hill and Charles Robinson

7. A 28-year-old man who was convicted of aggravated assault in October would have identification number 7.____
   A. 281410 B. 281509 C. 282311 D. 282409

8. A 33-year-old woman convicted in April of criminal homicide would have identification number 8.____
   A. 331140 B. 331204 C. 332014 D. 332104

9. The number of people on the above list who were convicted during the first six months of the year is 9.____
   A. 6 B. 7 C. 8 D. 9

Questions 10-19.

DIRECTIONS: The following is a list of patients who were referred by various clinics to the laboratory for tests. After each name is a patient identification number. Questions 10 through 19 are to be answered on the basis of the information contained in this list and the explanation accompanying it.

The first digit refers to the clinic which made the referral:

1. cardiac
2. Renal
3. Pediatrics
4. Ophthalmology
5. Orthopedics
6. Hematology
7. Gynecology
8. Neurology
9. Gastroenterology

The second digit refers to the sex of the patient:
1. male
2. female

The third and fourth digits give the age of the patient
The last two digits give the day of the month the laboratory tests were performed

LABORATORY REFERRALS DURING JANUARY

| | | | |
|---|---|---|---|
| Adams, Jacqueline | 320917 | Miller, Michael | 511806 |
| Black, Leslie | 813406 | Pratt, William | 214411 |
| Cook, Marie | 511616 | Rogers, Ellen | 722428 |
| Fisher, Pat | 914625 | Saunders, Sally | 310229 |
| Jackson, Lee | 923212 | Wilson, Jan | 416715 |
| James, Linda | 624621 | Wyatt, Mark | 321326 |
| Lane, Arthur | 115702 | | |

10. According to the list, the number of women referred to the laboratory during January was 10.____
A. 4 B. 5 C. 6 D. 7

11. The clinic from which the MOST patients were referred was 11.____
A. Cardiac B. Gynecology
C. Ophthalmology D. Pediatrics

12. The YOUNGEST patient referred from any clinic other than Pediatrics was 12.____
A. Leslie Black B. Marie Cook
C. Arthur Lane D. Sally Saunders

13. The number of patients whose laboratory tests were performed on or before January 16 was 13.____
A. 7 B. 8 C. 9 D. 10

14. The number of patients referred for laboratory tests who are under age 45 is 14.____
A. 7 B. 8 C. 9 D. 10

15. The OLDEST patient referred to the clinic during January was 15.____
A. Jacqueline Adams B. Linda James
C. Arthur Lane D. Jan Wilson

16. The ONLY patient treated in the Orthopedics clinic was 16.____
A. Marie Cook B. Pat Fisher
C. Ellen Rogers D. Jan Wilson

17. A woman, age 37 was referred from the Hematology clinic to the laboratory. Her laboratory tests were performed on January 9. Her identification number would be 17.____
A. 610937 B. 623709 C. 613790 D. 623790

18. A man was referred for lab tests from the Orthopedics clinic. He is 30 years old and his tests were performed on January 6. 18.____
His identification number would be
A. 413006 B. 510360 C. 513006 D. 513060

19. A 4-year-old boy was referred from the Pediatrics clinic to have laboratory tests on January 23. 19.____
His identification number was
A. 310422 B. 310423 C. 310433 D. 320403

## KEY (CORRECT ANSWERS)

| | | | |
|---|---|---|---|
| 1. | B | 11. | D |
| 2. | B | 12. | B |
| 3. | B | 13. | A |
| 4. | D | 14. | C |
| 5. | D | 15. | D |
| 6. | B | 16. | A |
| 7. | A | 17. | B |
| 8. | D | 18. | C |
| 9. | C | 19. | B |
| 10. | B | | |

# TEST 4

DIRECTIONS: Each question or incomplete statement is followed by several suggested answers or completions. Select the one that BEST answers the question or completes the statement. *PRINT THE LETTER OF THE CORRECT ANSWER IN THE SPACE AT THE RIGHT.*

Questions 1-10.

DIRECTIONS: Questions 1 through 10 are to be answered on the basis of the information and directions given below.

Assume that you are a Senior Stenographer assigned to the personnel bureau of a city agency. Your supervisor has asked you to classify the employees in your agency into the following five groups:

A. Employees who are college graduates, who are at least 35 years of age but less than 50, and who have been employed by the City for five years or more;
B. Employees who have been employed by the City for less than five years, who are not college graduates, and who earn at least $32,500 a year but less than $34,500;
C. Employees who have been City employees for five years or more, who are at least 21 years of age but less than 35, and who are not college graduates;
D. Employee who earn at least $34,500 a year but less than $36,000 who are college graduates, and who have been employed by the City for less than five years;
E. Employees who are not included in any of the foregoing groups.

NOTE: In classifying these employees you are to compute age and period of service as of January 1, 2003. In all cases, it is to be assumed that each employee has been employed continuously in City service. In each question, consider only the information which will assist you in classifying each employee Any information which is of no assistance in classifying an employee would not be considered.

SAMPLE: Mr. Brown, a 29-year-old veteran, was appointed to his present position of Clerk on June 1, 2000. He has completed two years of college. His present salary is $33,050.

The correct answer to this sample is B, since the employee has been employed by the City for less than five years, is not a college graduate, and earn at least $32,500 a year but less than $34,500.

Questions 1 through 10 contain excerpts from the personnel records of 10 employees in the agency. In the correspondingly numbered space at the right print the capital letter preceding the appropriate group into which you would place each employee.

1. Mr. James has been employed by the City since 1993, when he was graduated from a local college. Now 35 years of age, he earns $36,000 a year. 1.____

2. Mr. Worth began working in City service early in 1999. He was awarded his college degree in 1994, at the age of 21. As a result of a recent promotion, he now earns $34,500 a year. 2.____

3. Miss Thomas has been a City employee since August 1, 1998. Her salary is $34,500 a year. Miss Thomas, who is 25 years old, has had only three years of high school training. 3.____

4. Mr. Williams has had three promotions since entering City service on January 1, 1991. He was graduated from college with honors in 1974, when he was 20 years of age. His present salary is $37,000 a year. 4.____

5. Miss Jones left college after two years of study to take an appointment to a position in the City service paying $33,300 a year. She began work on March 1, 1997 when she was 19 years of age. 5.____

6. Mr. Smith was graduated from an engineering college with honors in January 1998 and became a City employee three months later. His present salary is $35,810. Mr. Smith was born in 1976. 6.____

7. Miss Earnest was born on May 31, 1979. Her education consisted of four years of high school and one year of business school. She was appointed as a typist in a City agency on June 1, 1997. Her annual salary is $33,500. 7.____

8. Mr. Adams, a 24-year-old clerk, began his City service on July 1, 1999, soon after being discharged from the U.S. Army. A college graduate, his present annual salary is $33,200. 8.____

9. Miss Charles attends college in the evenings, hoping to obtain her degree is 2004, when she will be 30 years of age. She has been a City employee since April 1998, and earns $33,350. 9.____

10. Mr. Dolan was just promoted to his present position after six years of City service. He was graduated from high school in 1982, when he was 18 years of age, but did not go on to college. Mr. Dolan's present salary is $33,500. 10.____

## KEY (CORRECT ANSWERS)

| | | | |
|---|---|---|---|
| 1. | A | 6. | D |
| 2. | D | 7. | C |
| 3. | E | 8. | E |
| 4. | A | 9. | B |
| 5. | C | 10. | E |

# TEST 5

DIRECTIONS: Questions 1 through 4 each contain five numbers that should be arranged in numerical order. The number with the lowest numerical value should be first and the number with the highest numerical value should be last. Pick that option which indicates the CORRECT order of the numbers.

Examples: A. 9; 18; 14; 15; 27
B. 9; 14; 15; 18; 27
C. 14; 15; 18; 27; 9
D. 9; 14; 15; 27; 18

The correct answer is B, which contains the proper arrangement of the five numbers.

1. A. 20573; 20753; 20738; 20837; 20098 1.____
B. 20098; 20753; 20573; 20738; 20837
C. 20098; 20573; 20753; 20837; 20738
D. 20098; 20573; 20738; 20753; 20837

2. A. 113492; 113429; 111314; 113114; 131413 2.____
B. 111314; 113114; 113429; 113492; 131413
C. 111314; 113429; 113492; 113114; 131413
D. 111314; 113114; 131413; 113429; 113492

3. A. 1029763; 1030421; 1035681; 1036928; 1067391 3.____
B. 1030421; 1029763; 1035681; 1067391; 1036928
C. 1030421; 1035681; 1036928; 1067391; 1029763
D. 1029763; 1039421; 1035681; 1067391; 1036928

4. A. 1112315; 1112326; 1112337; 1112349; 1112306 4.____
B. 1112306; 1112315; 1112337; 1112326; 1112349
C. 1112306; 1112315; 1112326; 1112337; 1112349
D. 1112306; 1112326; 1112315; 1112337; 1112349

# KEY (CORRECT ANSWERS)

1. D
2. B
3. A
4. C

# TEST 6

DIRECTIONS: The phonetic filing system is a method of filing names in which the alphabet is reduced to key code letters. The six key letters and their equivalents are as follows:

| KEY LETTERS | EQUIVALENTS |
|---|---|
| b | p, f, v |
| c | s, k, g, j, q, x, z |
| d | t |
| l | none |
| m | n |
| r | none |

A key letter represents itself.
Vowels (a, e, i, o, and u) and the letters w, h, and y are omitted.
For example, the name GILMAN would be represented as follows:

G is represented by the key letter C.
I is a vowel and is omitted.
L is a letter and represents itself.
M is a key letter and represents itself.
A is a vowel and is omitted.
N is represented by the key letter M.

Therefore, the phonetic filing code for the name GILMAN is CLMM.

Answer Questions 1 through 10 based on the information below.

1. The phonetic filing code for the name FITZGERALD would be 1.____
   A. BDCCRLD B. BDCRLD C. BDZCRLD D. BTZCRLD

2. The phonetic filing code CLBR may represent any one of the following names EXCEPT 2.____
   A. Calprey B. Flower C. Glover D. Silver

3. The phonetic filing code LDM may represent any one of the following names EXCEPT 3.____
   A. Halden B. Hilton C. Walton D. Wilson

4. The phonetic filing code for the name RODRIGUEZ would be 4.____
   A. RDRC B. RDRCC C. RDRCZ D. RTRCC

5. The phonetic filing code for the name MAXWELL would be 5.____
   A. MCLL B. MCWL C. MCWLL D. MXLL

6. The phonetic filing code for the name ANDERSON would be 6.____
   A. AMDRCM B. ENDRSM C. MDRCM D. NDERCN

7. The phonetic filing code for the name SAVITSKY would be 7.____
   A. CBDCC B. CBDCY C. SBDCC D. SVDCC

8. The phonetic filing code CMC may represent any one of the following names EXCEPT 8.____
   A. James B. Jayes C. Johns D. Jones

9. The ONLY one of the following names that could be represented by the phonetic filing code CDDDM would be 9.____
   A. Catalano B. Chesterton C. Cittadino D. Cuttlerman

10. The ONLY one of the following names that could be represented by the phonetic filing code LLMCM would be 10.____
   A. Ellington B. Hallerman C. Inslerman D. Willingham

## KEY (CORRECT ANSWERS)

| | | | |
|---|---|---|---|
| 1. | A | 6. | C |
| 2. | B | 7. | A |
| 3. | D | 8. | B |
| 4. | B | 9. | C |
| 5. | A | 10. | D |

# PREPARING WRITTEN MATERIAL

# PARAGRAPH REARRANGEMENT COMMENTARY

The sentences that follow are in scrambled order. You are to rearrange them in proper order and indicate the letter choice containing the correct answer at the space at the right.

Each group of sentences in this section is actually a paragraph presented in scrambled order. Each sentence in the group has a place in that paragraph; no sentence is to be left out. You are to read each group of sentences and decide upon the best order in which to put the sentences so as to form a well-organized paragraph.

The questions in this section measure the ability to solve a problem when all the facts relevant to its solution are not given.

More specifically, certain positions of responsibility and authority require the employee to discover connection between events sometimes, apparently, unrelated. In order to do this, the employee will find it necessary to correctly infer that unspecified events have probably occurred or are likely to occur. This ability becomes especially important when action must be taken on incomplete information.

Accordingly, these questions require competitors to choose among several suggested alternatives, each of which presents a different sequential arrangement of the events. Competitors must choose the MOST logical of the suggested sequences.

In order to do so, they may be required to draw on general knowledge to infer missing concepts or events that are essential to sequencing the given events. Competitors should be careful to infer only what is essential to the sequence. The plausibility of the wrong alternatives will always require the inclusion of unlikely events or of additional chains of events which are NOT essential to sequencing the given events.

It's very important to remember that you are looking for the best of the four possible choices, and that the best choice of all may not even be one of the answers you're given to choose from.

There is no one right way to solve these problems. Many people have found it helpful to first write out the order of the sentences, as they would have arranged them, on their scrap paper before looking at the possible answers. If their optimum answer is there, this can save them some time. If it isn't, this method can still give insight into solving the problem. Others find it most helpful to just go through each of the possible choices, contrasting each as they go along. You should use whatever method feels comfortable and works for you.

While most of these types of questions are not that difficult, we've added a higher percentage of the difficult type, just to give you more practice. Usually there are only one or two questions on this section that contain such subtle distinctions that you're unable to answer confidently. And you then may find yourself stuck deciding between two possible choices, neither of which you're sure about.

---

# PREPARING WRITTEN MATERIAL
# PARAGRAPH REARRANGEMENT

## EXAMINATION SECTION

## TEST 1

DIRECTIONS: The sentences that follow are in scrambled order. You are to rearrange them in proper order and indicate the letter choice containing the CORRECT answer. *PRINT THE LETTER OF THE CORRECT ANSWER IN THE SPACE AT THE RIGHT.*

1. Police Officer Jenner responds to the scene of a burglary at 2106 La Vista Boulevard. He is approached by an elderly man named Richard Jenkins, whose account of the incident includes the following five sentences: 1.____
   I. I saw that the lock on my apartment door had been smashed and the door was open.
   II. My apartment was a shambles; my belongings were everywhere and my television set was missing.
   III. As I walked down the hallway toward the bedroom, I heard someone opening a window.
   IV. I left work at 5:30 P.M. and took the bus home.
   V. At that time, I called the police.

   The MOST logical order for the above sentence to appear in the report is
   A. I, V, IV, II, III B. IV, I, II, III, V C. I, V, II, III, IV D. IV, III, II, V, I

2. Police Officer LaJolla is writing an Incident Report in which back-up assistance was required. The report will contain the following five sentences: 2.____
   I. The radio dispatcher asked what my location was and he then dispatched patrol cars for back-up assistance.
   II. At approximately 9:30 P.M., while I was walking my assigned footpost, a gunman fired three shots at me.
   III. I quickly turned around and saw a white male, approximately 5'10", with black hair, wearing blue jeans, a yellow T-shirt, and white sneaker, running across the avenue carrying a handgun.
   IV. When the back-up officers arrived, we searched the area but could not find the suspect.
   V. I advised the radio dispatcher that a gunman had just fired a gun at me, and then I gave the dispatcher a description of the man

   The MOST logical order for the above sentences to appear in the report is:
   A. III, V, II, IV, I B. II, III, V, I, IV C. III, II, IV, I, V D. II, V, I, III, IV

3. Police Officer Durant is completing a report of a robbery and assault. The report will contain the following five sentences: 3.____
   I. I went to Mount Snow Hospital to interview a man who was attacked and robbed of his wallet earlier that night.
   II. An ambulance arrived at 82$^{nd}$ Street and 3$^{rd}$ Avenue and took an intoxicated, wounded man to Mount Snow Hospital
   III. Two youths attacked the man and stole his wallet.

IV. A well-dressed man left Hanratty's Bar very drunk, with his wallet hanging out of his back pocket.
V. A passerby dialed 911 and requested police and ambulance assistance.
The MOST logical order for the above sentences to appear in the report is
A. I, II, IV, III, V  B. IV, III, V, II, I  C. IV, V, II, III, I  D. V, IV, III, II, I

4. Police Officer Boswell is preparing a report of an armed robbery and assault which will contain the following five sentences: 4.____
I. Both men approached the bartender and one of them drew a gun.
II. The bartender immediately went to grab the phone at the bar.
III. One of the men leaped over the counter and smashed a bottle over the bartender's head.
IV. Two men in a blue Buick drove up to the bar and went inside.
V. I found the cash register empty and the bartender unconscious on the floor, with the phone still dangling off the hook.
The MOST logical order for the above sentences to appear in the report is
A. IV, I, II, II, V  B. V, IV, III, I, II  C. IV, III, II, V, I  D. II, I, III, IV, V

5. Police Officer Mitzler is preparing a report of a bank robbery, which will contain the following five sentences: 5.____
I. The teller complied with the instructions on the note, but also hit the silent alarm.
II. The perpetrator then fled south on Broadway.
III. A suspicious male entered the bank at approximately 10:45 A.M.
IV. At this time, an undetermined amount of money has been taken.
V. He approached the teller on the far right side and handed her a note.
The MOST logical order for the above sentences to appear in the report is:
A. III, V, I, II, IV  B. I, III, V, II, IV  C. III, V, IV, I, II  D. III, V, II, IV, I

6. A Police Officer is preparing an Accident Report for an accident which occurred at the intersection of East 119th Street and Lexington Avenue. The report will include the following five sentences: 6.____
I. On September 18, while driving ten children to school, a school bus driver passed out.
II. Upon arriving at the scene, I notified the dispatcher to send an ambulance.
III. I notified the parents of each child once I got to the station house.
IV. He said the school bus, while traveling west on East 119th Street, struck a parked Ford which was on the southwest corner of East 119th Street.
V. A witness by the name of John Ramos came up to me to describe what happened.
The MOST logical order for the above sentences to appear in the Accident Report is:
A. I, II, V, III, IV  B. I, II, V, IV, III  C. II, V, I, III, IV  D. II, V, I, IV, III

7. A Police Officer is preparing a report concerning a dispute. The report will contain the following five sentences: 7.____
I. The passenger got out of the back of the taxi and leaned through the front window to complain to the driver about the fare.

II. The driver of the taxi caught up with the passenger and knocked him to the ground; the passenger then kicked the driver and a scuffle ensued.
III. The taxi drew up in front of the high-rise building and stopped.
IV. The driver got out of the taxi and followed the passenger into the lobby of the apartment building.
V. The doorman tried but was unable to break up the fight, at which point he called the precinct.

The MOST logical order for the above sentences to appear in the report is

A. III, I, IV, II, V  B. III, IV, I, II, V  C. III, IV, II, V, I  D. V, I, III, IV, II

8. Police Officer Morrow is writing an Incident Report. The report will include the following four sentences: 8.____

I. The man reached into his pocket and pulled out a gun.
II. While on foot patrol, I identified a suspect, who was wanted for six robberies in the area, from a wanted picture I was carrying.
III. I drew my weapon and fired six rounds at the suspect, killing him instantly.
IV. I called for back-up assistance and told the man to put his hands up.

The MOST logical order for the above sentences to appear in the report is

A. II, III, IV, I  B. IV, I, III, II  C. IV, I, II, III  D. II, IV, I, III

9. Sergeant Allen responds to a call at 16 Grove Street regarding a missing child. At the scene, the Sergeant is met by Police Officer Samuels, who gives a brief account of the incident consisting of the following five sentences: 9.____

I. I transmitted the description and waited for you to arrive before I began searching the area.
II. Mrs. Banks, the mother, reports that she last saw her daughter Julie about 7:30 A.M. when she took her to school.
III. About 6 P.M., my partner and I arrived at this location to investigate a report of a missing 8-year-old girl.
IV. When Mrs. Banks left her, Julie was wearing a red and white striped T-shirt, blue jeans, and white sneakers.
V. Mrs. Banks dropped her off in front of the playground of P.S. 11.

The MOST logical order for the above sentences to appear in the report is

A. III, V, IV, II, I  B. III, II, V, IV, I  C. III, IV, I, II, V  D. III, II, IV, I, V

10. Police Officer Franco is completing a report of an assault. The report will contain the following five sentences: 10.____

I. In the park I observed an elderly man lying on the ground, bleeding from a back wound.
II. I applied first aid to control the bleeding and radioed for an ambulance to respond.
III. The elderly man stated that he was sitting on the park bench when he was attacked from behind by two males.
IV. I received a report of a man's screams coming from inside the park, and I went to investigate.
V. The old man could not give a description of his attackers.

The MOST logical order for the above sentences to appear in the report is

A. IV, I, II, III, V  B. V, III, I, IV, II  C. IV, III, V, II, I  D. II, I, V, IV, III

11. Police Officer Williams is completing a Crime Report. The report contains the following five sentences: 11.____
I. As Police Officer Hanson and I approached the store, we noticed that the front door was broken.
II. After determining that the burglars had fled, we notified the precinct of the burglary.
III. I walked through the front door as Police Officer Hanson walked around to the back.
IV. At approximately midnight, an alarm was heard at the Apex Jewelry Store.
V. We searched the store and found no one.
The MOST logical order for the above sentences to appear in the report is
A. I, IV, II, III, V B. I, IV, III, V, II C. IV, I, III, II, V D. IV, I, III, V, II

12. Police Officer Clay is giving a report to the news media regarding someone who has jumped from the Empire State Building. His report will include the following five sentences: 12.____
I. I responded to the $86^{th}$ floor, where I found the person at the edge of the roof.
II. A security guard at the building had reported that a man was on the roof at the $86^{th}$ floor.
III. At 5:30 P.M., the person jumped from the building.
IV. I received a call from the radio dispatcher at 4:50 P.M. to respond to the Empire State Building.
V. I tried to talk to the person and convince him not to jump.
The MOST logical order for the above sentences to appear in the report is
A. I, II, IV, III, V B. III, IV, I, II, V C. II, IV, I, III, V D. IV, II, I, V, III

13. The following five sentences are part of a report of a burglary written by Police Officer Reed: 13.____
I. When I arrived at 2400 $1^{st}$ Avenue, I noticed that the door was slightly open.
II. I yelled out, *Police, don't move*!
III. As I entered the apartment, I saw a man with a TV set passing through a window to another man standing on a fire escape.
IV. While on foot patrol, I was informed by the radio dispatcher that a burglary was in progress at 2400 $1^{st}$ Avenue.
V. However, the burglars quickly ran down the fire escape.
The MOST logical order for the above sentences to appear in the report is
A. I, III, IV, V, II B. IV, I, III, V, II C. IV, I, III, II, V D. I, IV, III, II, V

14. Police Officer Jenkins is preparing a report for Lost or Stolen Property. The report will include the following five sentences: 14.____
I. On the stairs, Mr. Harris slipped on a wet leaf and fell on the landing.
II. It wasn't until he got to the token booth that Mr. Harris realized his wallet was no longer in his back pants pocket.
III. A boy wearing a football jersey helped him up and brushed off the back of Mr. Harris' pants.
IV. Mr. Harris states he was walking up the stairs to the elevated subway at Queensborough Plaza.
V. Before Mr. Harris could thank him, the boy was running down the stairs to the street.

The MOST logical order for the above sentences to appear in the report is
A. IV, III, V, I, II B. IV, I, III, V, II C. I, IV, II, III, V D. I, II, IV, III, V

15. Police Officer Hubbard is completing a report of a missing person. The report will contain the following five sentences: 15.____
I. I visited the store at 7:55 P.M. and asked the employees if they had seen a girl fitting the description I had been given.
II. She gave me a description and said she had gone into the local grocery store at about 6:15 P.M.
III. I asked the woman for a description of her daughter.
IV. The distraught woman called the precinct to report that her daughter, aged 12, had not returned from an errand.
V. The storekeeper said a girl matching the description had been in the store earlier, but he could not give an exact time.
The MOST logical order for the above sentences to appear in the report is
A. I, III, II, V, IV B. IV, III, II, I, V C. V, I, II, III, IV D. III, I, II, IV, V

16. A police officer is completing an entry in his Daily Activity Log regarding traffic summonses which he issued. The following five sentences will be included in the entry: 16.____
I. I was on routine patrol parked 16 yards west of 170th Street and Clay Avenue.
II. The summonses were issued for unlicensed operator and disobeying a steady red light.
III. At 8 A.M. hours, I observed an auto traveling westbound on 170th Street not stop for a steady red light at the intersection of Clay Avenue and 170th Street.
IV. I stopped the driver of the auto and determined that he did not have a valid driver's license.
V. After a brief conversation, I informed the motorist that he was receiving two summonses.
The MOST logical order for the above sentences to appear in the report is
A. I, III, IV, V, II B. III, IV, II, V, I C. V, II, I, III, IV D. IV, V, II, I, III

17. The following sentences appeared on an Incident Report: 17.____
I. Three teenagers who had been ejected from the theater were yelling at patrons who were now entering.
II. Police Officer Dixon told the teenagers to leave the area.
III. The teenager said that they were told by the manager to leave the theater because they were talking during the movie.
IV. The theater manager called the precinct at 10:20 P.M. to report a disturbance outside the theater.
V. A patrol car responded to the theater at 10:42 P.M. and two police officers went over to the teenagers.
The MOST logical order for the above sentences to appear in the Incident Report is
A. I, V, IV, III, II B. IV, I, V, III, II C. IV, I, III, V, II D. IV, III, I, V, II

18. Activity Log entries are completed by police officers. Police Officer Samuels has written an entry concerning vandalism and part of it contains the following five sentences: 18.____

I. The man, in his early twenties, ran down the block and around the corner.
II. A man passing the store threw a brick through a window of the store.
III. I arrived on the scene and began to question the witnesses about the incident.
IV. Malcolm Holmes, the owner of the Fast Service Shoe Repair Store, was working in the back of the store at approximately 3 P.M.
V. After the man fled, Mr. Holmes called the police.

The MOST logical order for the above sentences to appear in the Activity Log is

A. IV, II, I, V, III  B. II, IV, I, III, V  C. II, I, IV, III, V  D. IV, II, V, III, I

19. Police Officer Buckley is preparing a report concerning a dispute in a restaurant. The report will contain the following five sentences: 19.____

I. The manager, Charles Chin, and a customer, Edward Green, were standing near the register arguing over the bill.
II. The manager refused to press any charges providing Green pay the check and leave.
III. While on foot patrol, I was informed by a passerby of a disturbance in the Dragon Flame Restaurant.
IV. Green paid the $15.00 check and left the restaurant.
V. According to witnesses, the customer punched the owner in the face when Chin asked him for the amount due.

The MOST logical order for the above sentences to appear in the report is

A. III, I, V, II, IV  B. I, II, III, IV, V  C. V, I, III, II, IV  D. III, V, II, IV, I

20. Police Officer Wilkins is preparing a report for leaving the scene of an accident. The report will include the following five sentences: 20.____

I. The Dodge struck the right rear fender of Mrs. Smith's 2010 Ford and continued on its way.
II. Mrs. Smith stated she was making a left turn from $40^{th}$ Street onto Third Avenue.
III. As the car passed, Mrs. Smith noticed the dangling rear license plate #412AEJ.
IV. Mrs. Smith complained to police of back pains and was removed by ambulance to Bellevue Hospital.
V. An old green Dodge traveling up Third Avenue went through the red light at $40^{th}$ Street and Third Avenue.

The MOST logical order for the above sentences to appear in the report is

A. V, III, I, II, IV  B. I, III, II, V, IV  C. IV, V, I, II, III  D. II, V, I, III, IV

21. Detective Simon is completing a Crime Report. The report contains the following five sentences: 21.____

I. Police Officer Chin, while on foot patrol, heard the yelling and ran in the direction of the man.
II. The man, carrying a large hunting knife, left the High Sierra Sporting Goods Store at approximately 10:30 A.M.

III. When the man heard Police Officer Chin, he stopped, dropped the knife, and began to cry.
IV. As Police Officer Chin approached the man, he drew his gun and yelled, *Police, freeze.*
V. After the man left the store, he began yelling, over and over, *I am going to kill myself!*

The MOST logical order for the above sentences to appear in the report is
A. V, II, I, IV, III B. II, V, I, IV, III C. II, V, IV, I, III D. II, I, V, IV, III

22. Police Officer Miller is preparing a Complaint Report which will include the following five sentences: 22.____
I. From across the lot, he yelled to the boys to get away from his car.
II. When he came out of the store, he noticed two teenage boys trying to break into his car.
III. The boys fled as Mr. Johnson ran to his car.
IV. Mr. Johnson stated that he parked his car in the municipal lot behind Tams Department Store.
V. Mr. Johnson saw that the door lock had been broken, but nothing was missing from inside the auto.

The MOST logical order for the above sentences to appear in the report is
A. IV, I, II, V, III B. II, III, I, V, IV C. IV, II, I, III, V D. I, II, III, V, IV

23. Police Officer O'Hara completes a Universal Summons for a motorist who has just passed a red traffic light. The Universal Summons includes the following five sentences: 23.____
I. As the car passed the light, I followed in the patrol car.
II. After the driver stopped the car, he stated that the light was yellow, not red.
III. A blue Cadillac sedan passed the red light on the corner of 79th Street and 3rd Avenue at 11:25 P.M.
IV. As a result, the driver was informed that he did pass a red light and that his brake lights were not working.
V. The driver in the Cadillac stopped his car as soon as he saw the patrol car, and I noticed that the brake lights were not working.

The MOST logical order for the above sentences to appear in the Universal Summons is
A. I, III, V, II, IV B. III, I, V, II, IV C. III, I, V, IV, II D. I, III, IV, II, V

24. Detective Egan is preparing a follow-up report regarding a homicide on 170th Street and College Avenue. An unknown male was found at the scene. The report will contain the following five sentences: 24.____
I. Police Officer Gregory wrote down the names, addresses, and phone numbers of the witnesses.
II. A 911 operator received a call of a man shot and dispatched Police Officers Worth and Gregory to the scene.
III. They discovered an unidentified male dead on the street.
IV. Police Officer Worth notified the Precinct Detective Unit immediately.
V. At approximately 9:00 A.M., an unidentified male shot another male in the chest during an argument.

The MOST logical order for the above sentences to appear in the report is
A. V, II, III, IV, I  B. II, III, V, IV, I  C. IV, I, V, II, III  D. V, III, II, IV, I

25. Police Officer Tracey is preparing a Robbery Report which will include the following five sentences: 25.____
I. I ran around the corner and observe a man pointing a gun at a taxidriver.
II. I informed the man I was a police officer and that he should not move.
III. I was on the corner of 125th Street and Park Avenue when I heard a scream coming from around the corner.
IV. The man turned around and fired one shot at me.
V. I fired once, shooting him in the arm and causing him to fall to the ground.
The MOST logical order for the above sentences to appear in the report is
A. I, III, IV, II, V  B. IV, V, II, I, III  C. III, I, II, IV, V  D. III, I, V, II, IV

# KEY (CORRECT ANSWERS)

1. B
2. B
3. B
4. A
5. A

6. B
7. A
8. D
9. B
10. A

11. D
12. D
13. C
14. B
15. B

16. A
17. B
18. A
19. A
20. D

21. B
22. C
23. B
24. A
25. C

# TEST 2

DIRECTIONS: The sentences that follow are in scrambled order. You are to rearrange them in proper order and indicate the letter choice containing the CORRECT answer. *PRINT THE LETTER OF THE CORRECT ANSWER IN THE SPACE AT THE RIGHT*

1. Police Officer Weiker is completing a Complaint Report which will contain the following five sentences: 1.____
   I. Mr. Texlor was informed that the owner of the van would receive a parking ticket and that the van would be towed away.
   II. The police tow truck arrived approximately one half hour after Mr. Texlor complained.
   III. While on foot patrol on West End Avenue, I saw the owner of Rand's Restaurant arrive to open his business.
   IV. Mr. Texlor, the owner, called to me and complained that he could not receive deliveries because a van was blocking his driveway.
   V. The van's owner later reported to the precinct that his van had been stolen, and he was then informed that it had been towed.

   The MOST logical order for the above sentences to appear in the report is
   A. III, V, I, II, IV B. III, IV, I, II, V C. IV, III, I, II, V D. IV, III, II, I, V

2. Police Officer Ames is completing an entry in his Activity Log. The entry contains the following five sentences: 2.____
   I. Mr. Sands gave me a complete description of the robber.
   II. Alvin Sands, owner of the Star Delicatessen, called the precinct to report he had just been robbed.
   III. I then notified all police patrol vehicles to look for a white male in his early twenties wearing brown pants and shirt, a black leather jacket, and black and white sneakers.
   IV. I arrived on the scene after being notified by the precinct that a robbery had just occurred at the Star Delicatessen.
   V. Twenty minutes later, a man fitting the description was arrested by a police officer on patrol six blocks from the delicatessen.

   The MOST logical order for the above sentences to appear in the Activity Log is
   A. II, I, IV, III, V B. II IV, III, I, V C. II, IV, I, III, V D. II, IV, I, V, III

3. Police Officer Benson is completing a Complaint Report concerning a stolen taxicab, which will include the following five sentences: 3.____
   I. Police Officer Benson noticed that a cab was parked next to a fire hydrant.
   II. Dawson *borrowed* the cab for transportation purposes since he was in a hurry.
   III. Ed Dawson got into his car and tried to start it, but the battery was dead.
   IV. When he reached his destination, he parked the cab by a fire hydrant and placed the keys under the seat.
   V. He looked around and saw an empty cab with the engine running.

   The MOST logical order for the above sentences to appear in the report is
   A. I, III, II, IV, V B. III, I, II, V, IV C. III, V, II, IV, I D. V, II, IV, III, I

4. Police Officer Hatfield is reviewing his Activity Log entry prior to completing a report. The entry contains the following five sentences: 4.____

I. When I arrived at Zand's Jewelry Store, I noticed that the door was slightly open.
II. I told the burglar I was a police officer and that he should stand still or he would be shot.
III. As I entered the store, I saw a man wearing a ski mask attempting to open the safe in the back of the store.
IV. On December 16, 2020, at 1:38 A.M., I was informed that a burglary was in progress at Zand's Jewelry Store on East 59th Street.
V. The burglar quickly pulled a knife from his pocket when he saw me.

The MOST logical order for the above sentences to appear in the report is

A. IV, I, III, V, II B. I, IV, III, V, II C. IV, III, II, V, I D. I, III, IV, V, II

5. Police Officer Lorenz is completing a report of a murder. The report will contain the following five statements made by a witness: 5.____

I. I was awakened by the sound of a gunshot coming from the apartment next door and I decided to check.
II. I entered the apartment and looked into the kitchen and the bathroom.
III. I found Mr. Hubbard's body slumped in the bathtub.
IV. The door to the apartment was open, but I didn't see anyone.
V. He had been shot in the head.

The MOST logical order for the above sentences to appear in the report is

A. I, III, II, IV, V B. I, IV, II, III, V C. IV, II, I, III, V D. III, I, II, IV, V

6. Police Officer Baldwin is preparing an accident report which will include the following five sentences: 6.____

I. The old man lay on the ground for a few minutes, but was not physically hurt.
II. Charlie Watson, a construction worker, was repairing some brick work at the top of a building at 54th Street and Madison Avenue.
III. Steven Green, his partner, warned him that this could be dangerous, but Watson ignored him.
IV. A few minutes later, one of the bricks thrown by Watson smashed to the ground in front of an old man, who fainted out of fright.
V. Mr. Watson began throwing some of the bricks over the side of the building.

The MOST logical order for the above sentences to appear in the report is

A. II, V, III, IV, I B. I, IV, II, V, III C. III, II, IV, V, I D. II, III, I, IV, V

7. Police Officer Porter is completing an Incident Report concerning her rescue of a woman being held hostage by a former boyfriend. Her report will contain the following five sentences: 7.____

I. I saw a man holding .25 caliber gun to a woman's head, but he did not see me.
II. I then broke a window and gained access to the house.
III. As I approached the house on foot, a gunshot rang out and I heard a woman scream.
IV. A decoy van brought me as close as possible to the house where the woman was being held hostage.

V. I ordered the man to drop his gun, and he released the woman and was taken into custody.

The MOST logical order for the above sentences to appear in the report is

A. I, III, II, IV, V B. IV, III, II, I, V C. III, II, I, IV, V D. V, I, II, III, IV

8. Police Officer Byrnes is preparing a crime report concerning a robbery. The report will consist of the following five sentences: 8.____

I. Mr. White, following the man's instructions, opened the car's hood, at which time the man got out of the auto, drew a revolver, and ordered White to give him all the money in his pockets.
II. Investigation has determined there were no witnesses to this incident.
III. The man asked White to check the oil and fill the tank.
IV. Mr. White, a gas attendant, states that he was working alone at the gas station when a black male pulled up to the gas pump in a white Mercury.
V. White was then bound and gagged by the male and locked in the gas station's rest room.

The MOST logical order for the above sentences to appear in the report is

A. IV, I, III, II, V B. III, I, II, V, IV C. IV, III, I, V, II D. I, III, IV, II, V

9. Police Officer Gale is preparing a report of a crime committed against Mr. Weston. The report will consist of the following five sentences: 9.____

I. The man, who had a gun, told Mr. Weston not to scream for help and ordered him back into the apartment.
II. With Mr. Weston disposed of in this fashion, the man proceeded to ransack the apartment.
III. Opening the door to see who was there, Mr. Weston was confronted by a tall white male wearing a dark blue jacket and white pants.
IV. Mr. Weston was at home alone in his living room when the doorbell rang.
V. Once inside, the man bound and gagged Mr. Weston and locked him in the bathroom.

The MOST logical order for the above sentences to appear in the report is

A. III, V, II, I, IV B. IV, III, I, V, II C. III, V, IV, II, I D. IV, III, V, I, II

10. A police officer is completing a report of a robbery, which will contain the following five sentences: 10.____

I. Two police officers were about to enter the Red Rose Coffee Shop on 47th Street and 8th Avenue.
II. They then noticed a male running up the street carrying a brown paper bag.
III. They heard a woman standing outside the Broadway Boutique yelling that her store had just been robbed by a young man, and she was pointing up the street.
IV. They caught up with him and made an arrest.
V. The police officers pursued the male, who ran past them on 8th Avenue.

The MOST logical order for the above sentences to appear in the report is

A. I, III, II, V, IV B. III, I, II, V, IV C. IV, V, I, II, III D. I, V, IV, III, II

11. Police Officer Capalbo is preparing a report of a bank robbery. The report will contain the following five statements made by a witness: 11.____
    I. Initialing, all I could see were two men, dressed in maintenance uniforms, sitting in the area reserved for bank officers.
    II. I was passing the bank at 8 P.M. and noticed that all the lights were out, except in the rear section.
    III. Then I noticed two other men in the bank, coming from the direction of the vault, carrying a large metal box.
    IV. At this point, I decided to call the police.
    V. I knocked on the window to get the attention of the men in the maintenance uniforms, and they chased the two men carrying the box down a flight of steps.

    The MOST logical order for the above sentences to appear in the report is
    A. IV, I, II, V, III B. I, III, II, V, IV C. II, I, III, V, IV D. II, III, I, V, IV

12. Police Officer Roberts is preparing a crime report concerning an assault and a stolen car. The report will contain the following five sentences: 12.____
    I. Upon leaving the store to return to his car, Winters noticed that a male unknown to him was sitting in his car.
    II. The man then re-entered Winters' car and drove away, fleeing north on 2nd Avenue.
    III. Mr. Winters stated that he parked his car in front of 235 East 25th Street and left the engine running while he went into the butcher shop at that location.
    IV. Mr. Robert Gering, a witness, stated that the male is known in the neighborhood as Bobby Rae and is believed to reside at 323 East 114th Street.
    V. When Winters approached the car and ordered the man to get out, the man got out of the auto and struck Winters with his fists, knocking him to the ground.

    The MOST logical order for the above sentences to appear in the report is
    A. III, II, V, I, IV B. III, I, V, II, IV C. I, IV, V, II, III D. III, II, I, V, IV

13. Police Officer Robinson is preparing a crime report concerning the robbery of Mr. Edwards' store. The report will consist of the following five sentences: 13.____
    I. When the last customer left the store, the two men drew revolvers and ordered Mr. Edwards to give them all the money in the cash register.
    II. The men proceeded to the back of the store as if they were going to do some shopping.
    III. Janet Morley, a neighborhood resident, later reported that she saw the men enter a green Ford station wagon and flee northbound on Albany Avenue.
    IV. Edwards complied after which the gunmen ran from the store.
    V. Mr. Edwards states that he was stocking merchandise behind the store counter when two white males entered the store.

    The MOST logical order for the above sentences to appear in the report is
    A. V, II, III, I, IV B. V, II, I, IV, III C. II, I, V, IV, III D. III, V, II, I, IV

14. Police Officer Wendell is preparing an accident report for a 6-car accident that occurred at the intersection of Bath Avenue and Bay Parkway. The report will consist of the following five sentences: 14.____

I. A 2016 Volkswagen Beetle, traveling east on Bath Avenue, swerved to the left to avoid the Impala, and struck a 2014 Ford station wagon which was traveling west on Bath Avenue.
II. The Seville then mounted the curb on the northeast corner of Bath Avenue and Bay Parkway and struck a light pole.
III. A 2013 Buick Lesabre, traveling northbound on Bay Parkway directly behind the Impala, struck the Impala, pushing it into the intersection of Bath Avenue and Bay Parkway.
IV. A 2015 Chevy Impala, traveling northbound on Bay Parkway, had stopped for a red light at Bath Avenue.
V. A 2017 Toyota, traveling westbound on Bath Avenue, swerved to the right to avoid hitting the Ford station wagon, and struck a 2017 Cadillac Seville double-parked near the corner.

The MOST logical order for the above sentences to appear in the report is

A. IV, III, V, II, I  B. III, IV, V, II, I  C. IV, III, I, V, II  D. III, IV, V, I, II

15. The following five sentences are part of an Activity Log entry Police Officer Rogers made regarding an explosion: 15.____

I. I quickly treated the pedestrian for the injury.
II. The explosion caused a glass window in an office building to shatter.
III. After the pedestrian was treated, a call was placed to the precinct requesting additional police officers to evacuate the area.
IV. After all the glass settled to the ground, I saw a pedestrian who was bleeding from the arm.
V. While on foot patrol near 5th Avenue and 53rd Street, I heard a loud explosion.

The MOST logical order for the above sentences to appear in the report is

A. II, V, IV, I, III  B. V, II, IV, III, I  C. V, II, I, IV, III  D. V, II, IV, I, III

16. Police Officer David is completing a report regarding illegal activity near the entrance to Madison Square Garden during a recent rock concert. The report will obtain the following five sentences: 16.____

I. As I came closer to the man, he placed what appeared to be tickets in his pocket and began to walk away.
II. After the man stopped, I questioned him about *scalping* tickets.
III. While on assignment near the Madison Square Garden entrance, I observed a man apparently selling tickets.
IV. I stopped the man by stating that I was a police officer.
V. The man was then given a summons, and he left the area.

The MOST logical order for the above sentences to appear in the report is

A. I, III, IV, II, V  B. III, I, IV, V, II  C. III, IV, I, II, V  D. III, I, IV, II, V

17. Police Officer Sampson is preparing a report containing a dispute in a bar. The report will contain the following five sentences: 17.____
    I. John Evans, the bartender, ordered the two men out of the bar.
    II. Two men dressed in dungarees entered the C and D Bar at 5:30 P.M.
    III. The two men refused to leave and began to beat up Evans.
    IV. A customer in the bar saw me on patrol and yelled to me to come separate the three men.
    V. The two men became very drunk and loud within a short time.

    The MOST logical order for the above sentences to appear in the report is
    A. II, I, V, III, IV B. II, III, IV, V, I C. III, I, II, V, IV D. II, V, I, III, IV

18. A police officer is completing a report concerning the response to a crime in progress. The report will include the following five sentences: 18.____
    I. The officers saw two armed men run out of the liquor store and into a waiting car.
    II. Police Officers Lunty and Duren received the call and responded to the liquor store.
    III. The robbers gave up without a struggle.
    IV. Lunty and Duren blocked the getaway car with their patrol car.
    V. A call came into the precinct concerning a robbery in progress at Jane's Liquor Store.

    The MOST logical order for the above sentence to appear in the report is
    A. V, II, I, IV, III B. II, V, I, III, IV C. V, I, IV, II, III D. I, V, II, III, IV

19. Police Officers Jenkins is preparing a Crime Report which will consist of the following five sentences: 19.____
    I. After making inquirie in the vicinity, Smith found out that his next door neighbor, Viola Jones, had seen two local teenagers, Michael Heinz and Vincent Gaynor, smash his car's windshields with a crowbar.
    II. Jones told Smith that the teenagers live at 8700 19th Avenue.
    III. Mr. Smith heard a loud crash at approximately 11:00 P.M., looked out of his apartment window, and saw two white males running away from his car.
    IV. Smith then reported the incident to the precinct, and Heinz and Gaynor were arrested at the address given.
    V. Leaving his apartment to investigate further, Smith discovered that his car's front and rear windshields had been smashed.

    The MOST logical order for the above sentences to appear in the report is
    A. III, IV, V, I, II B. III, V, I, II, IV C. III, I, V, II, IV D. V, III, I, II, IV

20. Sergeant Nancy Winston is reviewing a Gun Control Report which will contain the following five sentences: 20.____
    I. The man fell to the floor when hit in the chest with three bullets from 22 caliber gun.
    II. Merriam's 22 caliber gun was seized, and he was given a summons for not having a pistol permit.
    III. Christopher Merriam, the owner of A-Z Grocery, shot a man who attempted to rob him.
    IV. Police Officer Franks responded and asked Merriam for his pistol permit, which he could not produce.

V. Merriam phoned the police to report he had just shot a man who had attempted to rob him.

The MOST logical order for the above sentences to appear in the report is

A. III, I, V, IV, II B. I, III, V, IV, II C. III, I, V, II, IV D. I, III, II, V, IV

21. Detective John Manville is completing a report for his superior regarding the murder of an unknown male who was shot in Central Park. The report will contain the following five sentences: 21.____

I. Police Officers Langston and Cavers responded to the scene.

II. I received the assignment to investigate the murder in Central Park from Detective Sergeant Rogers.

III. Langston notified the Detective Bureau after questioning Jason.

IV. An unknown male, apparently murdered, was discovered in Central Park by Howard Jason, a park employee, who immediately called the police.

V. Langston and Cavers questioned Jason.

The MOST logical order for the above sentences to appear in the report is

A. I, IV, V, III, II B. IV, I, V, II, III C. IV, I, V, III, II D. IV, V, I, III, II

22. A police officer is completing a report concerning the arrest of a juvenile. The report will contain the following five sentences: 22.____

I. Sanders then telephoned Jay's parents from the precinct to inform them of their son's arrest.

II. The store owner resisted, and Jay then shot him and ran from the store.

III. Jay was transported directly to the precinct by Officer Sanders.

IV. James Jay, a juvenile, walked into a candy store and announced a hold-up.

V. Police Officer Sanders, while on patrol, arrested Jay a block from the candy store.

The MOST logical order for the above sentences to appear in the report is

A. IV, V, II, I, III B. IV, II, V, III, I C. II, IV, V, III, I D. V, IV, II, I, III

23. Police Officer Olsen prepared a crime report for a robbery which contained the following five sentences: 23.____

I. Mr. Gordon was approached by this individual who then produced a gun and demanded the money from the cash register.

II. The man then fled from the scene on foot, southbound on 5$^{th}$ Avenue.

III. Mr. Gordon was working at the deli counter when a white male, 5'6", 150-160 lbs., wearing a green jacket and blue pants, entered the store.

IV. Mr. Gordon complied with the man's demands and handed him the daily receipts.

V. Further investigation has determined there are no other witnesses to this robbery.

The MOST logical order for the above sentences to appear in the report is

A. I, III, IV, V, II B. I, IV, II, III, V C. III, IV, I, V, II D. III, I, IV, II, V

24. Police Officer Bryant responded to 285 E. 31st Street to take a crime report of a burglary of Mr. Bond's home. The report will contain a brief description of the incident, consisting of the following five sentences: 24.____

I. When Mr. Bond attempted to stop the burglar by grabbing him, he was pushed to the floor.
II. The burglar had apparently gained access to the home by forcing open the 2nd floor bedroom window facing the fire escape.
III. Mr. Bond sustained a head injury in the scuffle, and the burglar exited the home through the front door.
IV. Finding nothing in the dresser, the burglar proceeded downstairs to the first floor, where he was confronted by Mr. Bond who was reading in the dining room.
V. Once inside, he searched the drawers of the bedroom dresser.

The MOST logical order for the above sentences to appear in the report is

A. V, IV, I, II, III  B. II, V, IV, I, III  C. II, IV, V, III, I  D. III, II, I, V, IV

25. Police Officer Derringer responded to a call of a rape-homicide case in his patrol area and was ordered to prepare an incident report, which will contain the following five sentences: 25.____

I. He pushed Miss Scott to the ground and forcibly raped her.
II. Mary Scott was approached from behind by a white male, 5'7", 150-160 lbs. wearing dark pants and a white jacket.
III. As Robinson approached the male, he ordered him to stop.
IV. Screaming for help, Miss Scott alerted one John Robinson, a local grocer, who chased her assailant as he fled the scene.
V. The male turned and fired two shots at Robinson, who fell to the ground mortally wounded.

The MOST logical order for the above sentences to appear in the report is

A. IV, III, I, II, V  B. II, IV, III, V, I  C. II, IV, I, V, III  D. II, I, IV, III, V

# KEY (CORRECT ANSWERS)

1. B
2. C
3. C
4. A
5. B

6. A
7. B
8. C
9. B
10. A

11. C
12. B
13. B
14. C
15. D

16. D
17. D
18. A
19. B
20. A

21. C
22. B
23. D
24. B
25. D

# PREPARING WRITTEN MATERIAL

# EXAMINATION SECTION

# TEST 1

DIRECTIONS: Each question or incomplete statement is followed by several suggested answers or completions. Select the one that BEST answers the question or completes the statement. *PRINT THE LETTER OF THE CORRECT ANSWER IN THE SPACE AT THE RIGHT.*

1. The one of the following sentences which is LEAST acceptable from the viewpoint of correct usage is: 1.____
   A. The police thought the fugitive to be him.
   B. The criminals set a trap for whoever would fall into it.
   C. It is ten years ago since the fugitive fled from the city.
   D. The lecturer argued that criminals are usually cowards.
   E. The police removed four bucketfuls of earth from the scene of the crime.

2. The one of the following sentences which is LEAST acceptable from the viewpoint of correct usage is: 2.____
   A. The patrolman scrutinized the report with great care.
   B. Approaching the victim of the assault, two bruises were noticed by the patrolman.
   C. As soon as I had broken down the door, I stepped into the room.
   D. I observed the accused loitering near the building, which was closed at the time.
   E. The storekeeper complained that his neighbor was guilty of violating a local ordinance.

3. The one of the following sentences which is LEAST acceptable from the viewpoint of correct usage is: 3.____
   A. I realized immediately that he intended to assault the woman, so I disarmed him.
   B. It was apparent that Mr. Smith's explanation contained many inconsistencies.
   C. Despite the slippery condition of the street, he managed to stop the vehicle before injuring the child.
   D. Not a single one of them wish, despite the damage to property, to make a formal complaint.
   E. The body was found lying on the floor.

4. The one of the following sentences which contains NO error in usage is: 4.____
   A. After the robbers left, the proprietor stood tied in his chair for about two hours before help arrived.
   B. In the cellar I found the watchman's hat and coat.
   C. The persons living in adjacent apartments stated that they had heard no unusual noises.

D. Neither a knife or any firearms were found in the room.
E. Walking down the street, the shouting of the crowd indicated that something was wrong.

5. The one of the following sentences which contains NO error in usage is: 5.____
A. The policeman lay a firm hand on the suspect's shoulder.
B. It is true that neither strength nor agility are the most important requirement for a good patrolman.
C. Good citizens constantly strive to do more than merely comply the restraints imposed by society.
D. No decision was made as to whom the prize should be awarded.
E. Twenty years is considered a severe sentence for a felony.

6. Which of the following sentences is NOT expressed in standard English usage? 5.____
A. The victim reached a pay-phone booth and manages to call police headquarters.
B. By the time the call was received, the assailant had left the scene.
C. The victim has been a respected member of the community for the past eleven years.
D. Although the lighting was bad and the shadows were deep, the storekeeper caught sight of the attacker.
E. Additional street lights have since been installed, and the patrols have been strengthened.

7. Which of the following sentences is NOT expressed in standard English usage? 7.____
A. The judge upheld the attorney's right to question the witness about the missing glove.
B. To be absolutely fair to all parties is the jury's chief responsibility.
C. Having finished the report, a loud noise in the next room startled the sergeant.
D. The witness obviously enjoyed having played a part in the proceedings.
E. The sergeant planned to assign the case to whoever arrived first.

8. In which of the following sentences is a word misused? 8.____
A. As a matter of principle, the captain insisted that the suspect's partner be brought for questioning.
B. The principle suspect had been detained at the station house for most of the day.
C. The principal in the crime had no previous criminal record, but his closest associate had been convicted of felonies on two occasions.
D. The interest payments had been made promptly, but the firm had been drawing upon the principal for these payments.
E. The accused insisted that his high school principal would furnish him a character reference.

9. Which of the following statements is ambiguous? 9.____
   A. Mr. Sullivan explained why Mr. Johnson had been dismissed from his job.
   B. The storekeeper told the patrolman he had made a mistake.
   C. After waiting three hours, the patients in the doctor's office were sent home.
   D. The janitor's duties were to maintain the building in good shape and to answer tenants' complaints.
   E. The speed limit should, in my opinion, be raised to sixty miles an hour on that stretch of road.

10. In which of the following is the punctuation or capitalization faulty? 10.____
   A. The accident occurred at an intersection in the Kew Gardens section of Queens, near the bus stop.
   B. The sedan, not the convertible, was struck in the side.
   C. Before any of the patrolmen had left the police car received an important message from headquarters.
   D. The dog that had been stolen was returned to his master, John Dempsey, who lived in East Village.
   E. The letter had been sent to 12 Hillside Terrace, Rutland, Vermont 05702.

Questions 11-25.

DIRECTIONS: Questions 11 through 25 are to be answered in accordance with correct English usage; that is, standard English rather than nonstandard or substandard. Nonstandard and substandard English includes words or expressions usually classified as slang, dialect, illiterate, etc., which are not generally accepted as correct in current written communication. Standard English also requires clarity, proper punctuation and capitalization and appropriate use of words. Write the letter of the sentence NOT expressed in standard English usage in the space at the right.

11. A. There were three witnesses to the accident. 11.____
   B. At least three witnesses were found to testify for the plaintiff.
   C. Three of the witnesses who took the stand was uncertain about the defendant's competence to drive.
   D. Only three witnesses came forward to testify for the plaintiff.
   E. The three witnesses to the accident were pedestrians.

12. A. The driver had obviously drunk too many martinis before leaving for home. 12.____
   B. The boy who drowned had swum in these same waters many times before.
   C. The petty thief had stolen a bicycle from a private driveway before he was apprehended.
   D. The detectives had brung in the heroin shipment they intercepted.
   E. The passengers had never ridden in a converted bus before.

13. A. Between you and me, the new platoon plan sounds like a good idea. 13.____
B. Money from an aunt's estate was left to his wife and he.
C. He and I were assigned to the same patrol for the first time in two months.
D. Either you or he should check the front door of that store.
E. The captain himself was not sure of the witness's reliability.

14. A. The alarm had scarcely begun to ring when the explosion occurred. 14.____
B. Before the firemen arrived at the scene, the second story had been destroyed.
C. Because of the dense smoke and heat, the firemen could hardly approach the now-blazing structure.
D. According to the patrolman's report, there wasn't nobody in the store when the explosion occurred.
E. The sergeant's suggestion was not at all unsound, but no one agreed with him.

15. A. The driver and the passenger they were both found to be intoxicated. 15.____
B. The driver and the passenger talked slowly and not too clearly.
C. Neither the driver nor his passengers were able to give a coherent account of the accident.
D. In a corner of the room sat the passenger, quietly dozing.
E. the driver finally told a strange and unbelievable story, which the passenger contradicted.

16. A. Under the circumstances I decided not to continue my examination of the premises. 16.____
B. There are many difficulties now not comparable with those existing in 1960.
C. Friends of the accused were heard to announce that the witness had better been away on the day of the trial.
D. The two criminals escaped in the confusion that followed the explosion.
E. The aged man was struck by the considerateness of the patrolman's offer.

17. A. An assemblage of miscellaneous weapons lay on the table. 17.____
B. Ample opportunities were given to the defendant to obtain counsel.
C. The speaker often alluded to his past experience with youthful offenders in the armed forces.
D. The sudden appearance of the truck aroused my suspicions.
E. Her studying had a good affect on her grades in high school.

18. A. He sat down in the theater and began to watch the movie. 18.____
B. The girl had ridden horses since she was four years old.
C. Application was made on behalf of the prosecutor to cite the witness for contempt.
D. The bank robber, with his two accomplices, were caught in the act.
E. His story is simply not credible.

19. A. The angry boy said that he did not like those kind of friends. 19.____
B. The merchant's financial condition was so precarious that he felt he must avail himself of any offer of assistance.
C. He is apt to promise more than he can perform.
D. Looking at the messy kitchen, the housewife felt like crying.
E. A clerk was left in charge of the stolen property.

20. A. His wounds were aggravated by prolonged exposure to sub-freezing temperatures. 20.____
B. The prosecutor remarked that the witness was not averse to changing his story each time he was interviewed.
C. The crime pattern indicated that the burglars were adapt in the handling of explosives.
D. His rigid adherence to a fixed plan brought him into renewed conflict with his subordinates.
E. He had anticipated that the sentence would be delivered by noon.

21. A. The whole arraignment procedure is badly in need of revision. 21.____
B. After his glasses were broken in the fight, he would of gone to the optometrist if he could.
C. Neither Tom nor Jack brought his lunch to work.
D. He stood aside until the quarrel was over.
E. A statement in the psychiatrist's report disclosed that the probationer vowed to have his revenge.

22. A. His fiery and intemperate speech to the striking employees fatally affected any chance of a future reconciliation. 22.____
B. The wording of the statute has been variously construed.
C. The defendant's attorney, speaking in the courtroom, called the official a demagogue who contemepuously disregarded the judge's orders.
D. The baseball game is likely to be the most exciting one this year.
E. The mother divided the cookies among her two children.

23. A. There was only a bed and a dresser in the dingy room. 23.____
B. John was one of the few students that have protested the new rule.
C. It cannot be argued that the child's testimony is negligible; it is, on the contrary, of the greatest importance.
D. The basic criterion for clearance was so general that officials resolved any doubts in favor of dismissal.
E. Having just returned from a long vacation, the officer found the city unbearably hot.

24. A. The librarian ought to give more help to small children. 24.____
B. The small boy was criticized by the teacher because he often wrote careless.
C. It was generally doubted whether the women would permit the use of her apartment for intelligence operations.
D. The probationer acts differently every time the officer visits him.
E. Each of the newly appointed officers has 12 years of service.

25. A. The North is the most industrialized region in the country. 25.____
B. L. Patrick Gray 3d, the bureau's acting director, stated that, while "rehabilitation is fine" for some convicted criminals, "it is a useless gesture for those who resist every such effort."
C. Careless driving, faulty mechanism, narrow or badly kept roads all play their part in causing accidents.
D. The childrens' books were left in the bus.
E. It was a matter of internal security; consequently, he felt no inclination to rescind his previous order.

# KEY (CORRECT ANSWERS)

1. C
2. B
3. D
4. C
5. E

6. A
7. C
8. B
9. B
10. C

11. C
12. D
13. B
14. D
15. A

16. C
17. E
18. D
19. A
20. C

21. B
22. E
23. B
24. B
25. D

# TEST 2

DIRECTIONS: Each question or incomplete statement is followed by several suggested answers or completions. Select the one that BEST answers the question or completes the statement. *PRINT THE LETTER OF THE CORRECT ANSWER IN THE SPACE AT THE RIGHT.*

Questions 1-6.

DIRECTIONS: Each of Questions 1 through 6 consists of a statement which contains a word (one of those underlined) that is either incorrectly used because it is not in keeping with the meaning the quotation is evidently intended to convey, or is misspelled. There is only one INCORRECT word in each quotation. Of the four underlined words, determine if the first one should be replaced by the word lettered A, the second replaced by the word lettered B, the third replaced by the word lettered C, or the fourth replaced by the word lettered D.

1. Whether one depends on fluorescent or artificial light or both, adequate standards should be maintained by means of systematic tests. 1.____
   A. natural B. safeguards C. established D. routine

2. A police officer has to be prepared to assume his knowledge as a social scientist in the community. 2.____
   A. forced B. role C. philosopher D. street

3. It is practically impossible to indicate whether a sentence is too long simply by measuring its length. 3.____
   A. almost B. tell C. very D. guessing

4. Strong leaders are required to organize a community for delinquency prevention and for dissemination of organized crime and drug addiction. 4.____
   A. tactics B. important C. control D. meetings

5. The demonstrators who were taken to the Criminal Courts building in Manhattan (because it was large enough to accommodate them), contended that the arrests were unwarranted. 5.____
   A. demonstraters B. Manhatten
   C. accomodate D. unwarranted

6. They were guaranteed a calm atmosphere, free from harassment, which would be conducive to quiet consideration of the indictments. 6.____
   A. guarenteed B. atmspher
   C. harassment D. inditements

Questions 7-11.

DIRECTIONS: Each of Questions 7 through 11 consists of a statement containing four words in capital letters. One of these words in capital letters is not in keeping with the meaning which the statement is evidently intended to carry. The four words in capital letters in each statement are reprinted after the statement. Print the capital letter preceding the one of the four words which does MOST to spoil the true meaning of the statement in the space at the right.

7. Retirement and pension systems are essential not only to provide employees with with a means of support in the future, but also to prevent longevity and CHARITABLE considerations from UPSETTING the PROMOTIONAL opportunities RETIRED members of the career service. 7.____
   A. charitable B. upsetting C. promotional D. retired

8. Within each major DIVISION in a properly set up public or private organization, provision is made so that each NECESSARY activity is CARED for and lines of authority and responsibility are clear-cut and INFINITE. 8.____
   A. division B. necessary C. cared D. infinite

9. In public service, the scale of salaries paid must be INCIDENTAL to the services rendered, with due CONSIDERATION for the attraction of the desired MANPOWER and for the maintenance of a standard of living COMMENSURATE with the work to be performed. 9.____
   A. incidental B. consideration
   C. manpower D. commensurate

10. An understanding of the AIMS of an organization by the staff will AID greatly in increasing the DEMAND of the correspondence work of the office, and will to a large extent DETERMINE the nature of the correspondence. 10.____
   A. aims B. aid C. demand D. determine

11. BECAUSE the Civil Service Commission strongly feels that the MERIT system is a key factor in the MAINTENANCE of democratic government, it has adopted as one of its major DEFENSES the progressive democratization of its own procedures in dealing with candidates for positions in the public service. 11.____
   A. Because B. merit C. maintenance D. defenses

Questions 12-14.

DIRECTIONS: Questions 12 through 14 consist of one sentence each. Each sentence contains an incorrectly used word. First, decide which is the incorrectly used word. Then, from among the options given, decide which word, when substituted for the incorrectly used word, makes the meaning of the sentence clear.

<u>EXAMPLE</u>:

The U.S. national income exhibits a pattern of long term deflection.
   A. reflection B. subjection C. rejoicing D. growth

The word *deflection* in the sentence does not convey the meaning the sentence evidently intended to convey. The word *growth* (Answer D), when substituted for the word *deflection*, makes the meaning of the sentence clear. Accordingly, the answer to the question is D.

12. The study commissioned by the joint committee fell compassionately short of the mark and would have to be redone. 12.____
    A. successfully B. insignificantly
    C. experimentally D. woefully

13. He will not idly exploit any violation of the provisions of the order. 13.____
    A. tolerate B. refuse C. construe D. guard

14. The defendant refused to be virile and bitterly protested service. 14.____
    A. irked B. feasible C. docile D. credible

Questions 15-25.

DIRECTIONS: Questions 15 through 25 consist of short paragraphs. Each paragraph contains one word which is INCORRECTLY used because it is NOT in keeping with the meaning of the paragraph. Find the word in each paragraph which is INCORRECTLY used and then select as the answer the suggested word which should be substituted for the incorrectly used word.

<u>SAMPLE QUESTION</u>:
In determining who is to do the work in your unit, you will have to decide just who does what from day to day. One of your lowest responsibilities is to assign work so that everybody gets a fair share and that everyone can do his part well.
A. new B. old C. important D. performance

EXPLANATION:
The word which is NOT in keeping with the meaning of the paragraph is *lowest*. This is the INCORRECTLY used word. The suggested word *important* would be in keeping with the meaning of the paragraph and should be substituted for *lowest*. Therefore, the CORRECT answer is choice C.

15. If really good practice in the elimination of preventable injuries is to be achieved and held in any establishment, top management must refuse full and definite responsibility and must apply a good share of its attention to the task. 15.____
    A. accept B. avoidable C. duties D. problem

16. Recording the human face for identification is by no means the only service performed by the camera in the field of investigation. When the trial of any issue takes place, a word picture is sought to be distorted to the court of incidents, occurrences, or events which are in dispute. 16.____
    A. appeals B. description C. portrayed D. deranged

17. In the collection of physical evidence, it cannot be emphasized too strongly that a haphazard systematic search at the scene of the crime is vital. Nothing must be overlooked. Often the only leads in a case will come from the results of this search. 17.____
    A. important B. investigation
    C. proof D. thorough

18. If an investigator has reason to suspect that the witness is mentally stable, or a habitual drunkard, he should leave no stone unturned in his investigation to determine if the witness was under the influence of liquor or drugs, or was mentally unbalanced either at the time of the occurrence to which he testified or at the time of the trial. 18.____
    A. accused B. clue C. deranged D. question

19. The use of records is a valuable step in crime investigation and is the main reason every department should maintain accurate reports. Crimes are not committed through the use of departmental records alone but from the use of all records, of almost every type, wherever they may be found and whenever they give any incidental information regarding the criminal. 19.____
    A. accidental B. necessary C. reported D. solved

20. In the years since passage of the Harrison Narcotic Act of 1914, making the possession of opium amphetamines illegal in most circumstances, drug use has become a subject of considerable scientific interest and investigation. There is at present a voluminous literature on drug use of various kinds. 20.____
    A. ingestion B. derivatives C. addiction D. opiates

21. Of course, the fact that criminal laws are extremely patterned in definition does not mean that the majority of persons who violate them are dealt with as criminals. Quite the contrary, for a great many forbidden acts are voluntarily engaged in within situations of privacy and go unobserved and unreported. 21.____
    A. symbolic B. casual C. scientific D. broad-gauged

22. The most punitive way to study punishment is to focus attention on the pattern of punitive action: to study how a penalty is applied, too study what is done to or taken from an offender. 22.____
    A. characteristic B. degrading C. objective D. distinguished

23. The most common forms of punishment in times past have been death, physical torture, mutilation, branding, public humiliation, fines, forfeits of property, banishment, transportation, and imprisonment. Although this list is by no means differentiated, practically every form of punishment has had several variations and applications. 23.____
    A. specific B. simple C. exhaustive D. characteristic

24. There is another important line of inference between ordinary and professional criminals, and that is the source from which they are recruited. The professional criminal seems to be drawn from legitimate employment and, in many instances, from parallel vocations or pursuits. 24.____
    A. demarcation B. justification C. superiority D. reference

25. He took the position that the success of the program was insidious on getting additional revenue. 25.____
    A. reputed B. contingent C. failure D. indeterminate

## KEY (CORRECT ANSWERS)

| | | | |
|---|---|---|---|
| 1. | A | 11. | D |
| 2. | B | 12. | D |
| 3. | B | 13. | A |
| 4. | C | 14. | C |
| 5. | D | 15. | A |
| 6. | C | 16. | C |
| 7. | D | 17. | D |
| 8. | D | 18. | C |
| 9. | A | 19. | D |
| 10. | C | 20. | B |

| | |
|---|---|
| 21. | D |
| 22. | C |
| 23. | C |
| 24. | A |
| 25. | B |

# TEST 3

DIRECTIONS: Each question or incomplete statement is followed by several suggested answers or completions. Select the one that BEST answers the question or completes the statement. *PRINT THE LETTER OF THE CORRECT ANSWER IN THE SPACE AT THE RIGHT.*

Questions 1-5.

DIRECTIONS: Questions 1 through 5 are to be answered on the basis of the following.

You are a supervising officer in an investigative unit. Earlier in the day, you directed Detectives Tom Dixon and Sal Mayo to investigate a reported assault and robbery in a liquor store within your area of jurisdiction.

Detective Dixon has submitted to you a preliminary investigative report containing the following information:

- At 1630 hours on 2/20, arrived at Joe's Liquor Store at 350 SW Avenue with Detective Mayo to investigate A & R.
- At store interviewed Rob Ladd, store manager, who stated that he and Joe Brown (store owner) had been stuck up about ten minutes prior to our arrival.
- Ladd described the robbers as male whites in their late teens or early twenties. Further stated that one of the robbers displayed what appeared to be an automatic pistol as he entered the store, and said, *Give us the money or we'll kill you.* Ladd stated that Brown then reached under the counter where he kept a loaded .38 caliber pistol. Several shots followed, and Ladd threw himself to the floor.
- The robbers fled, and Ladd didn't know if any money had been taken.
- At this point, Ladd realized that Brown was unconscious on the floor and bleeding from a head wound.
- Ambulance called by Ladd, and Brown was removed by same to General Hospital.
- Personally interviewed John White, 382 Dartmouth Place, who stated he was inside store at the time of occurrence. White states that he hid behind a wine display upon hearing someone say, *Give us the money.* He then heard shots and saw two young men run from the store to a yellow car parked at the curb. White was unable to further describe auto. States the taller of the two men drove the car away while the other sat on passenger side in front.
- Recovered three spent .38 caliber bullets from premises and delivered them to Crime Lab.
- To General Hospital at 1800 hours but unable to interview Brown, who was under sedation and suffering from shock and a laceration of the head.
- Alarm #12487 transmitted for car and occupants.
- Case Active.

Based solely on the contents of the preliminary investigation submitted by Detective Dixon, select one sentence from the following groups of sentences which is MOST accurate and is grammatically correct.

1. A. Both robbers were armed. 1.____
   B. Each of the robbers were described as a male white.
   C. Neither robber was armed.
   D. Mr. Ladd stated that one of the robbers was armed.

2. A. Mr. Brown fired three shots from his revolver. 2.____
   B. Mr. Brown was shot in the head by one of the robbers.
   C. Mr. Brown suffered a gunshot wound of the head during the course of the robbery.
   D. Mr. Brown was taken to General Hospital by ambulance.

3. A. Shots were fired after one of the robbers said, *Give us the money or we'll kill you.* 3.____
   B. After one of the robbers demanded the money from Mr. Brown, he fired a shot.
   C. The preliminary investigation indicated that although Mr. Brown did not have a license for the gun, he was justified in using deadly physical force.
   D. Mr. Brown was interviewed at General Hospital.

4. A. Each of the witnesses were customers in the store at the time of occurrence. 4.____
   B. Neither of the witnesses interviewed was the owner of the liquor store.
   C. Neither of the witnesses interviewed were the owner of the store.
   D. Neither of the witnesses was employed by Mr. Brown.

5. A. Mr. Brown arrived at General Hospital at about 5:00 P.M. 5.____
   B. Neither of the robbers was injured during the robbery.
   C. The robbery occurred at 3:30 P.M. on February 10.
   D. One of the witnesses called the ambulance.

Questions 6-10.

DIRECTIONS: Each of Questions 6 through 10 consists of information given in outline form and four sentences labeled A, B, C, and D. For each question, choose the one sentence which CORRECTLY expresses the information given in outline form and which also displays PROPER English usage.

6. Client's Name: Joanna Jones 6.____
   Number of Children: 3
   Client's Income: None
   Client's Marital Status: Single

   A. Joanna Jones is an unmarried client with three children who have no income.
   B. Joanna Jones, who is single and has no income, a client she has three children.
   C. Joanna Jones, whose three children are clients, is single and has no income.
   D. Joanna Jones, who has three children, is an unmarried client with no income.

7. Client's Name: Bertha Smith 7.____
Number of Children: 2
Client's Rent: $1050 per month
Number of Rooms: 4

A. Bertha Smith, a client, pays $1050 per month for her four rooms with two children.
B. Client Bertha Smith has two children and pays $1050 per month for four rooms.
C. Client Bertha Smith is paying $1050 per month for two children with four rooms.
D. For four rooms and two children client Bertha Smith pays $1050 per month.

8. Name of Employee: Cynthia Dawes 8.____
Number of Cases Assigned: 9
Date Cases were Assigned: 12/16
Number of Assigned Cases Completed: 8

A. On December 16, employee Cynthia Dawes was assigned nine cases; she has completed eight of these cases.
B. Cynthia Dawes, employee on December 16, assigned nine cases, completed eight.
C. Being employed on December 16, Cynthia Dawes completed eight of nine assigned cases.
D. Employee Cynthia Dawes, she was assigned nine cases and completed eight, on December 16.

9. Place of Audit: Broadway Center 9.____
Names of Auditors: Paul Cahn, Raymond Perez
Date of Audit: 11/20
Number of Cases Audited: 41

A. On November 20, at the Broadway Center 41 cases was audited by auditors Paul Cahn and Raymond Perez.
B. Auditors Raymond Perez and Paul Cahn has audited 41 cases at the Broadway Center on November 20.
C. At the Broadway Center, on November 20, auditors Paul Cahn and Raymond Perez audited 41 cases.
D. Auditors Paul Cahn and Raymond Perez at the Broadway Center, on November 20, is auditing 41 cases.

10. Name of Client: Barbra Levine 10.____
Client's Monthly Income: $2100
Client's Monthly Expenses: $4520

A. Barbra Levine is a client, her monthly income is $2100 and her monthly expenses is $4520.
B. Barbra Levine's monthly income is $2100 and she is a client, with whose monthly expenses are $4520.

C. Barbra Levine is a client whose monthly income is $2100 and whose monthly expenses are $4520.
D. Barbra Levine, a client, is with a monthly income which is $2100 and monthly expenses which are $4520.

Questions 11-13.

DIRECTIONS: Questions 11 through 13 involve several statements of fact presented in a very simple way. These statements of fact are followed by 4 choices which attempt to incorporate all of the facts into one logical statement which is properly constructed and grammatically correct.

11. I. Mr. Brown was sweeping the sidewalk in front of his house. 11.____
II. He was sweeping it because it was dirty.
III. He swept the refuse into the street.
IV. Police Officer gave him a ticket.

Which one of the following BEST presents the information given above?
A. Because his sidewalk was dirty, Mr. Brown received a ticket from Officer Green when he swept the refuse into the street.
B. Police Officer Green gave Mr. Brown a ticket because his sidewalk was dirty and he swept the refuse into the street.
C. Police Officer Green gave Mr. Brown a ticket for sweeping refuse into the street because his sidewalk was dirty.
D. Mr. Brown, who was sweeping refuse from his dirty sidewalk into the street, was given a ticket by Police Officer Green.

12. I. Sergeant Smith radioed for help. 12.____
II. The sergeant did so because the crowd was getting larger.
III. It was 10:00 A.M. when he made his call.
IV. Sergeant Smith was not in uniform at the time of occurrence.

Which one of the following BEST presents the information given above?
A. Sergeant Smith, although not on duty at the time, radioed for help at 10 o'clock because the crowd was getting uglier.
B. Although not in uniform, Sergeant Smith called for help at 10:00 A.M. because the crowd was getting uglier.
C. Sergeant Smith radioed for help at 10:00 A.M. because the crowd was getting larger.
D. Although he was not in uniform, Sergeant Smith radioed for help at 10:00 A.M. because the crowd was getting larger.

13. I. The payroll office is open on Fridays. 13.____
II. Paychecks are distributed from 9:00 A.M. to 12 Noon.
III. The office is open on Fridays because that's the only day the payroll staff is available.
IV. It is open for the specified hours in order to permit employees to cash checks at the bank during lunch hour.

The choice below which MOST clearly and accurately presents the above idea is:

A. Because the payroll office is open on Fridays from 9:00 A.M. to 12 Noon, employees can cash their checks when the payroll staff is available.
B. Because the payroll staff is only available on Fridays until noon, employees can cash their checks during their lunch hour.
C. Because the payroll staff is available only on Fridays, the office is open from 9:00 A.M. to 12 Noon to allow employees to cash their checks.
D. Because of payroll staff availability, the payroll office is open on Fridays. It is open from 9:00 A.M. to 12 Noon so that distributed paychecks can be cashed at the bank while employees are on their lunch hour.

Questions 14-16.

DIRECTIONS: In each of Questions 14 through 6, the four sentences are from a paragraph in a report. They are not in the right order. Which of the following arrangements is the BEST one?

14. I. An executive may answer a letter by writing his reply on the face of the letter itself instead of having a return letter typed. 14.____
II. This procedure is efficient because it saves the executive's time, the typist's time, and saves office file space.
III. Copying machines are used in small offices as well as large offices to save time and money in making brief replies to business letters.
IV. A copy is made on a copy machine to go into the company files, while the original is mailed back to the sender.

The CORRECT answer is:
A. I, II, IV, III B. I, IV, II, III C. III, I, IV, II D. III, IV, II, I

15. I. Most organizations favor one of the types but always include the others to a lesser degree. 15.____
II. However, we can detect a definite trend toward greater use of symbolic control.
III. We suggest that our local police agencies are today primarily utilizing material control.
IV. Control can be classified into three types: physical, material, and symbolic.

The CORRECT answer is:
A. IV, II, III, I B. II, I, IV, III C. III, IV, II, I D. IV, I, III, II

16. I. They can and do take advantage of ancient political and geographical boundaries, which often give them sanctuary from effective policy activity. 16.____
II. This country is essentially a country of small police forces, each operating independently within the limits of its jurisdiction.
III. The boundaries that define and limit police operations do not hinder the movement of criminals, of course.
IV. The machinery of law enforcement in America is fragmented, complicated, and frequently overlapping.

The CORRECT answer is:
A. III, I, IV B. II, IV, I, III C. IV, II, III, I D. IV, III, II, I

17. Examine the following sentence, and then choose from below the words which should be inserted in the blank spaces to produce the best sentence. 17.____
The unit has exceeded _____ goals and the employees are satisfied with _____ accomplishments.
A. their, it's B. it's; it's C. its, there D. its, their

18. Examine the following sentence, and then choose from below the words which should be inserted in the blank spaces to produce the best sentence. 18.____
Research indicates that employees who _____ no opportunity for close social relationships often find their work unsatisfying, and this _____ of satisfaction often reflects itself in low production.
A. have; lack B. have; excess C. has; lack D. has; excess

19. Words in a sentence must be arranged properly to make sure that the intended meaning of the sentence is clear. 19.____
The sentence below that does NOT make sense because a clause has been separated from the word on which its meaning depends is:
A. To be a good writer, clarity is necessary.
B. To be a good writer, you must write clearly.
C. You must write clearly to be a good writer.
D. Clarity is necessary to good writing.

Questions 20-21.

DIRECTIONS: Each of Questions 20 and 21 consists of a statement which contains a word (one of those underlined) that is either incorrectly used because it is not in keeping with the meaning the quotation is evidently intended to convey, or is misspelled. There is only one INCORRECT word in each quotation. Of the four underlined words, determine if the first one should be replaced by the word lettered A, the second one replaced by the word lettered B, the third one replaced by the word lettered C, or the fourth one replaced by the word lettered D.

20. The alleged killer was occasionally permitted to excercise in the corridor. 20.____
A. alledged B. ocasionally C. permited D. exercise

21. Defense counsel stated, in affect, that their conduct was permissible under the First Amendment. 21.____
A. council B. effect C. there D. permissable

Question 22.

DIRECTIONS: Question 22 consists of one sentence. This sentence contains an incorrectly used word. First, decide which is the incorrectly used word. Then, from among the options given, decide which word, when substituted for the incorrectly used word, makes the meaning of the sentence clear.

22. As today's violence has no single cause, so its causes have no single scheme. 22.____
    A. deference    B. cure    C. flaw    D. relevance

23. In the sentence, *A man in a light-grey suit waited thirty-five minutes in the ante-room for the all-important document*, the word IMPROPERLY hyphenated is 23.____
    A. light-grey    B. thirty-five
    C. ante-room    D. all-important

24. In the sentence, *The candidate wants to file his application for preference before it is too late*, the word *before* is used as a(n) 24.____
    A. preposition    B. subordinating conjunction
    C. pronoun    D. adverb

25. In the sentence, *The perpetrators ran from the scene*, the word *from* is a 25.____
    A. preposition    B. pronoun    C. verb    D. conjunction

# KEY (CORRECT ANSWERS)

| | | | |
|---|---|---|---|
| 1. | D | 11. | D |
| 2. | D | 12. | D |
| 3. | A | 13. | D |
| 4. | B | 14. | C |
| 5. | D | 15. | D |
| 6. | D | 16. | C |
| 7. | B | 17. | D |
| 8. | A | 18. | A |
| 9. | C | 19. | A |
| 10. | C | 20. | D |

| | |
|---|---|
| 21. | B |
| 22. | B |
| 23. | C |
| 24. | B |
| 25. | A |

# EXAMINATION SECTION

## TEST 1

DIRECTIONS: Each question or incomplete statement is followed by several suggested answers or completions. Select the one that BEST answers the question or completes the statement. *PRINT THE LETTER OF THE CORRECT ANSWER IN THE SPACE AT THE RIGHT.*

1. Following are three statements concerning on-the-job training: 1.____
   I. On-the-job training is rarely used as a method of training employees.
   II. On-the-job training is often carried on with little or no planning.
   III. On-the-job training is often less expensive than other types.
   Which of the following BEST classifies the above statements into those that are correct and those that are not?
   A. I is correct, but II and III are not. B. II is correct but I and III are not.
   C. I and II are correct, but III is not. D. II and III are correct, but I is not.

2. The one of the following which is NOT a valid principle for a supervisor to keep in mind when talking to a subordinate about his performance is: 2.____
   A. People frequently know when they deserve criticism.
   B. Supervisors should be prepared to offer suggestions to subordinates about how to improve their work.
   C. Good points should be discussed before bad points.
   D. Magnifying a subordinate's faults will get him to improve faster.

3. In many organizations information travels quickly through the grapevine. Following are three statements concerning the *grapevine*: 3.____
   I. Information a subordinate does not want to tell her supervisor may reach the supervisor through the *grapevine*.
   II. A supervisor can often do her job better by knowing the information that travels through the *grapevine*.
   III. A supervisor can depend on the *grapevine* as a way to get accurate information from the employees on his staff.
   Which one of the following CORRECTLY classifies the above statements into those which are generally correct and those which are not?
   A. II is correct, but I and III are not. B. III is correct, but I and II are not.
   C. I and II are correct, but III is not. D. I and III are correct, but II is not.

4. Following are three statements concerning supervision: 4.____
   I. A supervisor knows he is doing a good job if his subordinates depend upon him to make every decision.
   II. A supervisor who delegates authority to his subordinates soon finds that his subordinates begin to resent him.
   III. Giving credit for good work is frequently an effective method of getting subordinates to work harder

Which one of the following CORRECTLY classifies the above statements into those that are correct and those that are not?

A. I and II are correct, but III is not.
B. II and III are correct, but I is not.
C. II is correct, but I and III are not.
D. III is correct, but I and II are not.

5. Of the following, the LEAST appropriate action for a supervisor to take in preparing a disciplinary case against a subordinate is to 5.____

A. keep careful records of each incident in which the subordinate has been guilty of misconduct or incompetency, even though immediate disciplinary action may not be necessary
B. discuss with the employee each incident of misconduct as it occurs so the employee knows where he stands
C. accept memoranda from any other employees who may have been witnesses to acts of misconduct
D. keep the subordinate's personnel file confidential so that he is unaware of the evidence being gathered against him

6. Praise by a supervisor can be an important element in motivating subordinates. Following are three statements concerning a supervisor's praise of subordinates: 6.____

I. In order to be effective, praise must be lavish and constantly restated.
II. Praise should be given in a manner which meets the needs of the individual subordinate.
III. The subordinate whose work is praised should believe that the praise is earned.

Which of the following CORRECTLY classifies the above statements into those that are correct and those that are not?

A. I is correct, but II and III are not.
B. II and III are correct, but I is not.
C. III is correct, but I and II are not.
D. I and II are correct, but III is not.

7. A supervisor feels that he is about to lose his temper while reprimanding a subordinate. 7.____
Of the following, the BEST action for the supervisor to take is to

A. postpone the reprimand for a short time until his self-control is assured
B. continue the reprimand because a loss of temper by the supervisor will show the subordinate the seriousness of the error he made
C. continue the reprimand because failure to do so will show that the supervisor does not have complete self-control
D. postpone the reprimand until the subordinate is capable of understanding the reason for the supervisor's loss of temper

8. Following are three statements concerning various ways of giving orders to subordinates: 8.____

I. An implied order or suggestion is usually appropriate for the inexperienced employee.
II. A polite request is less likely to upset a sensitive subordinate than a direct order.
III. A direct order is usually appropriate in an emergency situation.

Which of the following CORRECTLY classifies the above statements into those that are correct and those that are not?

A. I is correct, but II and III are not.
B. II and III are correct, but I is not.
C. III is correct, but I and II are not.
D. I and II are correct, but III is not.

9. The one of the following which is NOT an acceptable reason for taking disciplinary action against a subordinate guilty of serious violations of the rules is that 9._____

A. the supervisor can *let off steam* against subordinates who break rules frequently
B. a subordinate whose work continues to be unsatisfactory may be terminated
C. a subordinate may be encouraged to improve his work
D. an example is set for other employees

10. At the first meeting with your staff after appointment as a supervisor, you find considerable indifference and some hostility among the participants. 10._____
Of the following, the MOST appropriate way to handle this situation is to

A. disregard the attitudes displayed and continue to make your presentation until you have completed it
B. discontinue your presentation but continue the meeting and attempt to find out the reasons for their attitudes
C. warm up your audience with some good-natured statements and anecdotes and then proceed with your presentation
D. discontinue the meeting and set up personal interviews with the staff members to try to find out the reason for their attitude

11. Use a written rather than oral communication to amend any previous written communication. 11._____
Of the following, the BEST justification for this statement is that

A. oral changes will be considered more impersonal and thus less important
B. oral changes will be forgotten or recalled indifferently
C. written communications are clearer and shorter
D. written communications are better able to convey feeling tone

12. Assume that a certain supervisor, when writing important communications to his subordinates, often repeats certain points in different words. 12._____
This technique is GENERALLY

A. *ineffective*; it tends to confuse rather than help
B. *effective*; it tends to improve understanding by the subordinates
C. *ineffective*; it unnecessarily increases the length of the communication and may annoy the subordinates
D. *effective*; repetition is always an advantage in communications

13. In preparing a letter or a report, a supervisor may wish to persuade the reader of the correctness of some idea or course of action. 13._____
The BEST way to accomplish this is for the supervisor to

A. encourage the reader to make a prompt decision
B. express each idea in a separate paragraph

C. present the subject matter of the letter in the first paragraph
D. state the potential benefits for the reader

14. Effective communications, a basic necessity for successful supervision is a two-way street. A good supervisor needs to listen to, as well as disseminate, information and he must be able to encourage his subordinates to communicate with him. 14.____
Which of the following suggestions will contribute LEAST to improving the *listening power* of a supervisor?
A. Don't assume anything; don't anticipate, and don't let a subordinate think you know what he is going to say
B. Don't interrupt; let him have his full say even if it requires a second session that day to get the full story
C. React quickly to his statements so that he knows you are interested, even if you must draw some conclusions prematurely
D. Try to understand the real need for his talking to you even if it is quite different from the subject under discussion

15. Of the following, the MOST useful approach for the supervisor to take toward the informal employee communications network known as the *grapevine* is to 15.____
A. remain isolated from it, but not take any active steps to eliminate it
B. listen to it, but not depend on it for accurate information
C. use it to disseminate confidential information
D. eliminate it as diplomatically as possible

16. If a supervisor is asked to estimate the number of employees that he believes he will need in his unit in the coming fiscal year, the supervisor should FIRST attempt to learn the 16.____
A. nature and size of the workload his unit will have during that time
B. cost of hiring and training new employees
C. average number of employee absences per year
D. number of employees needed to indirectly support or assist his unit

17. An important supervisory responsibility is coordinating the operations of the unit. This may include setting work schedules, controlling work quality, establishing interim due dates, etc. In order to handle this task, it has been divided into the following five stages: 17.____
I. <u>Determine the steps</u> or sequence required for the tasks to be performed.
II. <u>Give the orders</u>, either written or oral, to begin work on the tasks.
III. <u>Check up</u> by following each task to make sure it is proceeding according to plan.
IV. <u>Schedule the jobs</u> by setting a time for each task of operation to begin and end.
V. <u>Control the process</u> by correcting conditions which interfere with the plan.
The MOST logical sequence in which these planning steps should be performed is:
A. I, II, III, IV, V B. II, I, V, III, IV C. I, IV, II, III, V D. IV, I, II, III, V

18. Assume that a supervisor calls a meeting with the staff under his supervision in order to discuss several proposals. After some discussion, he realizes that he strongly disagrees with one proposal that four of the staff have rather firmly favored. 18.____
At this point, he could BEST handle the situation by saying:
   A. *I have the responsibility for this decision, and I must disagree.*
   B. *I am just reminding you that I have had a great deal more experience in these matters.*
   C. *You have presented some good points, but perhaps we could look at it another way.*
   D. *The only way that this proposal can be disposed of is to defer it for further discussion.*

19. As far as the social activities and groups of his subordinates are concerned, a supervisor in a large organization can BEST strengthen his tools of leadership by 19.____
   A. emphasizing the organization as a whole and forbidding the formation of groups
   B. ignoring the groups as much as possible and dealing with each subordinate as an individual
   C. learning about the status structure of employee groups and their values
   D. avoiding any relationship with groups

20. If a subordinate asks you, his superior, for advice in planning his career in the department, you should 20.____
   A. encourage him to feel that he can easily reach the top of his occupational ladder
   B. discourage him from setting his hopes too high
   C. discuss career opportunities realistically with him
   D. explain that you have no control over his opportunities for advancement

21. A supervisor's evaluation of an employee is usually based upon a combination of objective facts and subjective judgments or opinions. 21.____
Which of the following aspects of an employee's work or performance is MOST likely to be subjectively evaluated?
   A. Quantity B. Accuracy C. Attitude D. Attendance

22. Of the following possible characteristics of supervisors, the one MOST likely to lead to failure as a supervisor is 22.____
   A. a tendency to seek several opinions before making decisions in complex matters
   B. lack of a strong desire to advance to a top position in management
   C. little formal training in human relations skills
   D. poor relations with subordinates and other supervisory personnel

23. People who break rules do so for a number of reasons. However, employees will break rules LESS often if 23.____
A. the supervisor uses his own judgment about work methods
B. the supervisor pretends to act strictly, but isn't really serious about it
C. they greatly enjoy their work
D. they have completed many years of service

24. Assume that an employee under your supervision has become resentful and generally non-cooperative after his request for transfer to another office closer to his place of residence was denied. The request was denied primarily because of the importance of his current assignment. The employee has been a valued worker, but you are now worried that his resentful attitude will have a detrimental effect. 24.____
Of the following, the MOST desirable way for you to handle this situation is to
A. arrange for the employee's transfer to the office he originally requested
B. arrange for the employee's transfer to another office, but not the one he originally requested
C. attempt to re-focus the employee's attention on those aspects of his current assignment which will be most rewarding and satisfying to him
D. explain to the employee that, while you are sympathetic to his request, department rules will not allow transfers for reasons of personal convenience

25. Of the following, it would be LEAST advisable for a supervisor to use his administrative authority to affect the behavior and activities of his subordinates when he is trying to 25.____
A. change the way his subordinates perform a particular task
B. establish a minimum level of conformity to established rules
C. bring about change in the attitudes of his subordinates
D. improve the speed with which his subordinates respond to his orders

26. Assume that a supervisor gives his subordinate instructions which are appropriate and clear. The subordinate thereupon refuses to follow these instructions. 26.____
Of the following, it would then be MOST appropriate for the supervisor to
A. attempt to find out what it is that the employee objects to
B. take disciplinary action that same day
C. remind the subordinate about supervisory authority and threaten him with discipline
D. insist that the subordinate carry out the order immediately

27. Of the following, the MOST effective way to identify training needs resulting from gradual changes in procedure is to 27.____
A. monitor on a continuous basis the actual jobs performed and the skills required
B. periodically send out a written questionnaire asking personnel to identify their needs
C. conduct interviews at regular intervals with selected employees
D. consult employees' personnel records

28. Assume that you, as a supervisor, have had a new employee assigned to you. If the duties of his position can be broken into independent parts, which of the following is usually the BEST way to train this new employee? 28.____
Start with
    A. the easiest duties and progressively proceed to the most difficult
    B. something easy; move to something difficult; then back to something easy
    C. something difficult; move to something easy; then to something difficult
    D. the most difficult duties and progressively proceed to the easiest

29. The oldest and most commonly used training technique is on-the-job training. Instruction is given to the worker by his supervisor or by another employee. Such training is essential in most jobs, although it is not always effective when used alone. 29.____
This technique, however, can be effectively used alone if
    A. the skills involved can be learned quickly
    B. a large number of people are to be trained at one time
    C. other forms of training have not been previously used with the people involved
    D. the skills to be taught are mental rather than manual

30. It is generally agreed that the learning process is facilitated in proportion to the amount of feedback that the learner is given about his performance. 30.____
Following are three statements concerning the learning process:
    I. The more specific the learner's knowledge of how he performed, the more rapid his improvement and the higher his level of performance
    II. Giving the learner knowledge of his results does not affect his motivation to learn.
    III. Learners who are not given feedback will set up subjective criteria and evaluate their own performance.
Which of the following choices lists ALL of the above statements that are generally CORRECT?
    A. I and II only    B. I and III only    C. II and III only    D. I, II, and III

# KEY (CORRECT ANSWERS)

| | | | | | |
|---|---|---|---|---|---|
| 1. | D | 11. | B | 21. | C |
| 2. | D | 12. | B | 22. | D |
| 3. | C | 13. | D | 23. | C |
| 4. | D | 14. | C | 24. | C |
| 5. | D | 15. | B | 25. | C |
| 6. | B | 16. | A | 26. | A |
| 7. | A | 17. | C | 27. | A |
| 8. | B | 18. | C | 28. | A |
| 9. | A | 19. | C | 29. | A |
| 10. | D | 20. | C | 30. | B |

# TEST 2

DIRECTIONS: Each question or incomplete statement is followed by several suggested answers or completions. Select the one that BEST answers the question or completes the statement. *PRINT THE LETTER OF THE CORRECT ANSWER IN THE SPACE AT THE RIGHT.*

Questions 1-6.

DIRECTIONS: Questions 1 through 6 are to be answered SOLELY on the basis of the information given in the following paragraph.

The use of role-playing as a training technique was developed during the past decade by social scientists, particularly psychologists, who have been active in training experiments. Originally, this technique was applied by clinical psychologists who discovered that a patient appears to gain understanding of an emotionally disturbing situation when encouraged to act out roles in that situation. As applied in government and business organizations, the purpose of role-playing is to aid employees to understand certain work problems involving interpersonal relations and to enable observers to evaluate various reactions to them. Thus, for example, on the problem of handling grievances, two individuals from the group might be selected to act out extemporaneously the parts of subordinate and supervisor. When this situation is enacted by various pairs among the class and the techniques and results are discussed, the members of the group are presumed to reach conclusions about the most effective means of handling similar situations. Often the use of role reversal, where participants take parts different from their actual work roles, assists individuals to gain more insight into other people's problems and viewpoints. Although role-playing can be a rewarding training device, the trainer must be aware of his responsibilities. If this technique is to be successful, thorough briefing of both actors and observers as to the situation in question, the participants' roles, and what to look for, is essential.

1. The role-playing technique was FIRST used for the purpose of 1.____
   A. measuring the effectiveness of training programs
   B. training supervisors in business organizations
   C. treating emotionally disturbed patients
   D. handling employee grievances

2. When role-playing is used in private business as a training device, the CHIEF aim is to 2.____
   A. develop better relations between supervisor and subordinate in the handling of grievances
   B. come up with a solution to a specific problem that has arisen
   C. determine the training needs of the group
   D. increase employee understanding of the human relation factors in work situations

3. From the above passage, it is MOST reasonable to conclude that when role-playing is used, it is preferable to have the roles acted out by 3.____
   A. only one set of actors
   B. no more than 2 sets of actors
   C. several different sets of actors
   D. the trainer or trainers of the group

4. Based on the above passage, a trainer using the technique of role reversal in a problem of first-line supervision should assign a senior employee to play the part of a(n) 4.____
   A. new employee
   B. senior employee
   C. principal employee
   D. angry citizen

5. It can be inferred from the above passage that a limitation of role-play as a training method is that 5.____
   A. many work situations do not lend themselves to role-play
   B. employees are not experienced enough as actors to play the roles realistically
   C. only trainers who have psychological training can use it successfully
   D. participants who are observing and not acting do not benefit from it

6. To obtain good results from the use of role-playing in training, a trainer should give participants 6.____
   A. a minimum of information about the situation so that they can act spontaneously
   B. scripts which illustrate the best method for handling the situation
   C. a complete explanation of the problem and the roles to be acted out
   D. a summary of work problems which involve interpersonal relations

7. Of the following, the MOST important reason for a supervisor to prepare good written reports is that 7.____
   A. a supervisor is rated on the quality of his reports
   B. decisions are often made on the basis of the reports
   C. such reports take less time for superiors to review
   D. such reports demonstrate efficiency of department operations

8. Of the following, the BEST test of a good report is whether it 8.____
   A. provides the information needed
   B. shows the good sense of the writer
   C. is prepared according to a proper format
   D. is grammatical and neat

9. When a supervisor writes a report, he can BEST show that he has an understanding of the subject of the report by 9.____
   A. including necessary facts and omitting non-essential details
   B. using statistical data
   C. giving his conclusions but not the data on which they are based
   D. using a technical vocabulary

10. Suppose you and another supervisor on the same level are assigned to work together on a report. You disagree strongly with one of the recommendations the other supervisor wants to include in the report but you cannot change his views. 10.____
    Of the following, it would be BEST that
    A. you refuse to accept responsibility for the report
    B. you ask that someone else be assigned to this project to replace you

C. each of you state his own ideas about this recommendation in the report
D you give in to the other supervisor's opinion for the sake of harmony

11. Standardized forms are often provided for submitting reports. 11.____
Of the following, the MOST important advantage of using standardized forms for reports is that
A. they take less time to prepare than individually written reports
B. necessary information is less likely to be omitted
C. the responsibility for preparing these reports can be delegated to subordinates
D. the person making the report can omit information he considers unimportant

12. A report which may BEST be classed as a *periodic* report is one which 12.____
A. requires the same type of information at regular intervals
B. contains detailed information which is to be retained in permanent records
C. is prepared whenever a special situation occurs
D. lists information in graphic form

13. Which one of the following is NOT an important reason for keeping accurate records in an office? 13.____
A. Facts will be on hand when decisions have to be made.
B. The basis for past actions can be determined.
C. Information needed by other bureaus can be furnished.
D. Filing is easier when records are properly made out.

14. Suppose you are preparing to write a report recommending a change in a certain procedure. You learn that another supervisor made a report a few years ago suggesting a change in this same procedure, but that no action was taken. 14.____
Of the following, it would be MOST desirable for you to
A. avoid reading the other supervisor's report so that you will write with a more up-to-date point of view
B. make no recommendation since management seems to be against any change in the procedure
C. read the other report before you write your report to see what bearing it may have on your recommendations
D. avoid including in your report any information that can be obtained by referring to the other report

15. If a report you are preparing to your superior is going to be a very long one, it would be DESIRABLE to include a summary of your basic conclusions 15.____
A. at the end of the report
B. at the beginning of the report
C. in a separate memorandum
D. right after you present the supporting data

16. Suppose that some bureau and department policies must be very frequently applied by your subordinates while others rarely come into use. 16.____
As a supervising employee, a GOOD technique for you to use in fulfilling your responsibility of seeing to it that policies are adhered to is to
   A. ask the director of the bureau to issue to all employees an explanation in writing of all policies
   B. review with your subordinates every week those policies which have daily application
   C. follow up on and explain at regular intervals the application of those policies which are not used very often by your subordinates
   D. recommend to your superiors that policies rarely used be changed or dropped

17. The BASIC purpose behind the principle of delegation of authority is to 17.____
   A. give the supervisor who is delegating a chance to acquire skills in higher level functions
   B. free the supervisor from routine tasks in order that he may do the important parts of his job
   C. prevent supervisors from overstepping the lines of authority which have been established
   D. place the work delegated in the hands of those employees who can perform it best

18. A district commander can BEST assist management in long-range planning by 18.____
   A. reporting to his superiors any changing conditions in the district
   B. maintaining a neat and efficiently run office
   C. scheduling work so that areas with a high rate of non-compliance get more intensive coverage
   D. properly training new personnel assigned to his district

19. Suppose that new quarters have been rented for your district office. 19.____
Of the following, the LEAST important factor to be considered in planning the layout of the office is the
   A. need for screening confidential activities from unauthorized persons
   B. relative importance of the various types of work
   C. areas of noise concentration
   D. convenience with which communication between sections of the office can be achieved

20. Of the following, the MOST basic effect of organizing a department so that lines of authority are clearly defined and duties are specifically assigned is to 20.____
   A. increase the need for close supervision
   B. decreases the initiative of subordinates
   C. lessen the possibility of duplication of work
   D. increase the responsibilities of supervisory personnel

21. An accepted management principle is that decisions should be delegated to the lowest point in the organization at which they can be made effectively. 21.____
The one of the following which is MOST likely to be a result of the application of this principle is that
    A. no factors will be overlooked in making decisions
    B. prompt action will follow the making of decisions
    C. decisions will be made more rapidly
    D. coordination of decisions that are made will be simplified

22. Suppose you are a supervisor and need some guidance from a higher authority. 22.____
In which one of the following situations would it be PERMISSIBLE for you to bypass the regular upward channels of communication in the chain of command?
    A. In an emergency when your superior is not available
    B. When it is not essential to get a quick reply
    C. When you feel your immediate superior is not understanding of the situation
    D. When you want to obtain information that you think your superior does not have

23. Of the following, the CHIEF limitation of the organization chart as it is generally used in business and government is that the chart 23.____
    A. makes lines of responsibility and authority undesirably definite and formal
    B. is often out of date as soon as it is completed
    C. does not show human factors and informal working relationships
    D. is usually too complicated

24. The *span of control* for any supervisor is the 24.____
    A. number of tasks he is expected to perform himself
    B. amount of office space he and his subordinates occupy
    C. amount of work he is responsible for getting out
    D. number of subordinates he can supervise effectively

25. Of the following duties performed by a supervising employee, which would be considered a LINE function rather than a staff function? 25.____
    A. Evaluation of office personnel
    B. Recommendations for disciplinary action
    C. Initiating budget requests for replacement of equipment
    D. Inspections, at irregular times, of conditions and staff in the field

# KEY (CORRECT ANSWERS)

| | | | |
|---|---|---|---|
| 1. | C | 11. | B |
| 2. | D | 12. | A |
| 3. | C | 13. | D |
| 4. | A | 14. | C |
| 5. | A | 15. | B |
| 6. | C | 16. | C |
| 7. | B | 17. | B |
| 8. | A | 18. | A |
| 9. | A | 19. | B |
| 10. | C | 20. | C |

| | |
|---|---|
| 21. | B |
| 22. | A |
| 23. | C |
| 24. | D |
| 25. | D |

# EXAMINATION SECTION

## TEST 1

DIRECTIONS: Each question or incomplete statement is followed by several suggested answers or completions. Select the one that BEST answers the question or completes the statement. *PRINT THE LETTER OF THE CORRECT ANSWER IN THE SPACE AT THE RIGHT.*

1. A supervisor was given a booklet that showed a new work method that could save time. He didn't tell his men because he thought that they would get the booklet anyway. 1.____
For the supervisor to have acted like this is a
   A. *good* idea, because he saves time and both of talking to the men
   B. *bad* idea, because he should make sure his men know about better work methods
   C. *good* idea, because the men would rather read about it themselves
   D *bad* idea, because a supervisor should always show his men every memo he gets from higher authority

2. A supervisor found it necessary to discipline two subordinates. One man had been operating his equipment in a wrong way, while the other man came to work late for three days in a row. The supervisor decided to talk to both men together. 2.____
For the supervisor to deal with the problems in this way is a
   A. *good* idea because each man will learn about the difficulties of the other person and how to solve such difficulties
   B. *bad* idea because the supervisor should wait until he can bring a larger group together and save time in discussing such questions
   C. *good* idea because he will be able to get the men to see that their problems are related
   D. *bad* idea because he should meet with each man separately and give him his full attention

3. A supervisor should try to make his men feel their jobs are important in order to 3.____
   A. get the men to say good things about their supervisor to his own superior
   B. get the men to think in terms of advancing to better jobs
   C. let higher management in the agency know that the supervisor is efficient
   D. help the men to be able to work more efficiently and enthusiastically

4. A supervisor should know approximately how long it takes to do a particular kind of job CHIEFLY because he 4.____
   A. will know how much time to take if he has to do it himself
   B. will be able to tell his men to do it even faster
   C. can judge the performance of the person doing the job
   D. can retrain experienced employees in better work habits

5. Supervisors often get their employees' opinions about better work methods because 5.____
   A. the men will know that they are respected
   B. the men would otherwise lose all their confidence in the supervisor
   C. the supervisor might find in this way a good suggestion he could use
   D. this is the best method for improvement of work methods

6. Right after you have trained your subordinates in doing a new job, you find that they seem to be doing all right, but that it will take them several days to finish. You also have several groups of men working at other locations. 6.____
   The MOST efficient way for you to make sure that the men continue doing the new job properly is to
   A. stay on that job with the men until it is finished just in case trouble develops
   B. visit the men every half hour until the job is done
   C. stay away from their job that day and visit the men the next day to ask them if they had any problems
   D. visit the men a few times each day until they finish the new job

7. Assume that one of your new employees is older than you are. You also think that he may be hard to get along with because he is older than you. 7.____
   The BEST way for you to avoid any problems with the older worker is for you to
   A. lay down the law immediately and tell the man he better not cause you any trouble
   B. treat the man just the way you would any other worker
   C. always ask the older worker for advice in the presence of all the men
   D. ignore the man entirely until he realizes that you are the boss

8. Assume that you have tried a new method suggested by one of your employees and find that it is easier and cheaper than the method you had been using. 8.____
   The PROPER thing for you to do NEXT is to
   A. say nothing to anyone but train your men to use the new method
   B. train your men to use the new method and tell your crew that you got the idea from one of the men
   C. continue using the old method because a supervisor should not use suggestions of his men
   D. have your crew learn the new method and take credit for the idea since you are the boss

9. Suppose you are a supervisor and your superior tells you that the way your men are doing a certain procedure is wrong and that you should re-train our men as soon as possible. 9.____
   When you begin to re-train the men, the FIRST thing you should do is to
   A. tell your men that a wrong procedure had been used and that a new method must be learned as a result
   B. train your employees in the new method with no explanation since you are the boss

C. tell the crew that your superior has just decided that everyone should learn a new method
D. tell the crew that your superior says your method is wrong but that you don't agree with this

10. It is BAD practice to criticize a man in front of the other men because 10.____
A. people will think you are too strict
B. it is annoying to anyone who walks by
C. it is embarrassing to the man concerned
D. it will antagonize the other men

11. A supervisor decides not to put his two best men on a work detail because he knows that they won't like it. 11.____
For the supervisor to make the work assignment this way is a
A. *good* idea because it is only fair to give your best men a break once in a while
B. *bad* idea because you should treat all of your me fairly and not show favoritism
C. *good* idea because you save the strength of these men for another job
D. *bad* idea because more of the men should be exempted from the assignment

12. Suppose you are a supervisor and you find it inconvenient to obey an established procedure set by your agency. You think another procedure would be better. 12.____
The BEST thing to do first about this procedure that you don't like is for you to
A. obey the procedure even if you don't to and suggest your idea to your own supervisor
B. disregard the procedure because a supervisor is supposed to have some privileges
C. follow the procedure some of the time but ignore it when the men are not watching
D. organize a group of other supervisors to get the procedure changed

13. A supervisor estimated that it would take his crew one workday per week to do a certain job each week. However, after a month he noticed that the job averaged two and a half days a week and this delayed other jobs that had to be done. 13.____
The FIRST thing that the supervisor should do in this case is to
A. call him men together and warn them that they will get a poor work evaluation if they do not work harder
B. talk to each man personally, asking him to work harder on the job
C. go back and study the maintenance job by himself to see if more men should be assigned to the job
D. write his boss a report describing in detail how much time it is taking the men to do the job

14. An employee complains to you that some of the work assignments are too difficult to do alone. 14.____
Which of the following is the BEST way for you to handle this complaint?
A. Go with him to see exactly what he does and why he finds it so difficult
B. Politely tell the man that he has to do the job or be brought up on charges
C. Tell the man to send his complaint to the head of your agency
D. Sympathize with the man and give him easier jobs

15. The BEST way for a supervisor to keep control of his work assignments is to 15.____
A. ask the men to report to him immediately when their jobs are finished
B. walk around the buildings once a week and get a first-hand view of what is being done
C. keep his ears open for problems and complaints, but leave the men aloe to do the work
D. write up a work schedule and check it periodically against the actual work done

16. A supervisor made a work schedule for his men. At the bottom of it, he wrote, *No changes or exceptions will be made in this schedule for any reason.* 16.____
For the supervisor to have made this statement is
A. *good*, because the men will respect the supervisor for his attitude
B. *bad*, because there are emergencies and special situations that occur
C. *good*, because each man will know exactly what is expected of him
D. *bad*, because the men should expect that no changes will ever be made in the work schedule without written permission

17. Which one of the following would NOT be a result of a well-planned work schedule? 17.____
The schedule
A. makes efficient use of the time of the staff
B. acts as a checklist for an important job that might be left out
C. will give an idea of the work to a substitute supervisor
D. shows at a glance who the best men are

18. A new piece of equipment you have ordered is delivered. You are familiar with it, but the men under you who will use it do not know the equipment. 18.____
Of the following methods, which is the BEST to take in explaining to them how to operate this equipment?
A. Ask the men to watch other crews using the equipment
B. Show one reliable man how to operate the equipment and ask him to teach the other men
C. Ask the men to read the instructions in the manual for the equipment
D. Call the men together and show them how to operate the equipment

19. One supervisor assigns work to his men by calling his crew together each week and describing what has to be done that week. He then tells them to arrange individual assignments among themselves and to work as a team during the week. 19.____

This method of scheduling work is a
- A. *good* idea because this guarantees that the men will work together
- B. *bad* idea because responsibility for doing the job is poorly fixed
- C. *good* idea because the men will finish the job in less time, working together
- D. *bad* idea because the supervisor should always stay with his men

20. Suppose that an employee came to his supervisor with a problem concerning his assignment. 20.____
For the supervisor to listen to his problem is a
    - A. *good* idea because a supervisor should always take time off to talk when one of his men wants to talk
    - B. *bad* idea because the supervisor should not be bothered during the work day
    - C. *good* idea because it is the job of the supervisor to deal with problems of job assignment
    - D. *bad* idea because the employee could start annoying the supervisor with all sorts of problems

21. Suppose that on the previous afternoon you were looking for an experienced employee in order to give him an emergency job and he was missing from his job location. The next morning, he tells you that he got sick suddenly and had to go home, but could not tell you since you were not around. He has never done this before. 21.____
What should you do?
    - A. Tell the man he is excused and that in such circumstances he did the wisest thing
    - B. Bring the man up on charges because whatever he says he could still have notified you
    - C. Have the man examined by a doctor to see if he really was sick the day before
    - D. Explain to the mean that he should make every effort to tell you or to get a message to you if he must leave

22. An employee had a grievance and went to his supervisor about it. The employee was not satisfied with the way the supervisor tried to help him and told him so. Yet, the supervisor had done everything he could under the circumstances. 22.____
The PROPER action for the supervisor to take at this time is to
    - A. politely tell the employee that there is nothing more for the supervisor to do about the problem
    - B. let the employee know how he can bring his complaint to a higher authority
    - C. tell the employee that he must solve the problem on his own since he did not want to follow the supervisor's advice
    - D. suggest to the employee that he ask for another supervisor for assistance

23. In which of the following situations is it BEST to give your men spoken rather than written orders? 23.____
   A. You want your men to have a record of the instructions.
   B. Spoken instructions are less likely to be forgotten.
   C. An emergency situation has arisen in which there is no time to write up instructions.
   D. There are instructions on time and leave regulations which are complicated.

24. One of your employees tells you that a week ago he had a small accident on the job but he did not bother telling you because he was able to continue working. 24.____
For the employee not to have told his supervisor about the accident was
   A. *good*, because the accident was a small one
   B. *bad*, because all accidents should be reported, no matter how small
   C. *good*, because the supervisor should be bothered only for important matters
   D. *bad*, because having an accident is one way to get excused for the day

25. For a supervisor to deal with each of his subordinate in exactly the same manner is 25.____
   A. *poor*, because each man presents a different problem and there is no one way of handling all problems
   B. *good*, because once a problem is handled with one man, he can handle another man with the same problem
   C. *poor*, because the men will resent it if they are not handled each in a better way than others
   D. *good*, because this assures fair and impartial treatment of each subordinate

---

# KEY (CORRECT ANSWERS)

| | | | |
|---|---|---|---|
| 1. | B | 11. | B |
| 2. | D | 12. | A |
| 3. | D | 13. | C |
| 4. | C | 14. | A |
| 5. | C | 15. | D |
| 6. | D | 16. | B |
| 7. | B | 17. | D |
| 8. | B | 18. | D |
| 9. | A | 19. | B |
| 10. | C | 20. | C |

| | |
|---|---|
| 21. | D |
| 22. | B |
| 23. | C |
| 24. | B |
| 25. | A |

# TEST 2

DIRECTIONS: Each question or incomplete statement is followed by several suggested answers or completions. Select the one that BEST answers the question or completes the statement. *PRINT THE LETTER OF THE CORRECT ANSWER IN THE SPACE AT THE RIGHT.*

1. Jim Johnson has been on your staff for over four years. He has always been a conscientious and productive worker. About a month ago, his wife died; and since that time, his work performance has been very poor. 1.____
As his supervisor, which one of the following is the BEST way for you to deal with this situation?
   A. Allow Jim as much time as he needs to overcome his grief and hope that his work performance improves
   B. Meet with Jim to discuss ways to improve his performance
   C. Tell Jim directly that you are more concerned with his work performance than with his personal problem
   D. Prepare disciplinary action on Jim as soon as possible

2. You are responsible for the overall operation of a storehouse which is divided into two sections. Each section has its own supervisor. You have decided to make several complex changes in the storekeeping procedures which will affect both sections. 2.____
Of the following, the BEST way to make sure that these changes are understood by the two supervisors is for you to
   A. meet with both supervisors to discuss the changes
   B. issue a memorandum to each supervisor explaining the changes
   C. post the changes where the supervisors are sure to see them
   D. instruct one supervisor to explain the changes to the other supervisor

3. You have called a meeting of all your subordinates to tell them what has to be done on a new project in which they will all be involved. Several times during the meeting, you ask if there are any questions about what you have told them. 3.____
Of the following, to ask the subordinates whether there are any questions during the meeting can BEST be described as
   A. *inadvisable*, because it interferes with their learning about the new project
   B. *advisable*, because you will find out what they don't understand and have a chance to clear up any problems they may have
   C. *inadvisable*, because it makes the meeting too long and causes the subordinates to lose interest in the new project
   D. *advisable*, because it gives you a chance to learn which of your subordinates are paying attention to what you say

4. As a supervisor, you are responsible for seeing to it that absenteeism does not become a problem among your subordinates. 4.____
Which one of the following is NOT an acceptable way of controlling the problem of excessive absences?

A. Distribute a written statement to your staff on the policies regarding absenteeism in your organization
B. Arrange for workers who have the fewest absences to talk to those workers who have the most absences
C. Let your subordinates know that a record is being kept of all absences
D. Arrange for counseling of those employees who are frequently absent

5. One of your supervisors has been an excellent worker for the past two years. There are no promotion opportunities for this worker in the foreseeable future. Due to the city's present budget crisis, a salary increase is not possible. 5.____
Under the circumstances, which one of the following actions on your part would be MOST likely to continue to motivate this worker?
A. Tell the worker that times are bad all over and jobs are hard to find
B. Give the worker less work and easier assignments
C. Tell the worker to try to look for a better paying job elsewhere
D. Seek the worker's advice often and show that the suggestions provided are appreciated

6. As a supervisor in a warehouse, it is important that you use your available work force to its fullest potential. 6.____
Which one of the following actions on your part is MOST likely to increase the effectiveness of your work force?
A. Assigning more workers to a job than the number actually needed
B. Eliminating all job training to allow more time for work output
C. Using your best workers on jobs that average workers can do
D. Making sure that all materials and equipment used are maintained in good working order

7. You learn that your storage area will soon be undergoing changes which will affect the work of your subordinates. You decide not to tell your subordinates about what is to happen. 7.____
Of the following, your action can BEST be described as
A. *wise*, because your subordinates will learn of the changes for themselves
B. *unwise*, because your subordinates should be advised about what is to happen
C. *wise*, because it is better for your subordinates to continue working without being disturbed by such news
D. *unwise*, because the work of your subordinates will gradually slow down

8. In making plans for the operation of your unit, you are MOST likely to see these plans carried out successfully if you 8.____
A. allow your staff to participate in developing these plans
B. do not spend any time on the minor details of these plans
C. base these plans on the past experiences of others
D. allow these plans to interact with outside activities in other units

9. As a supervisor in charge of the total operation of a food supply warehouse, you find vandalism to be a potentially serious problem. On occasion, trespassers have gained entrance into the facility by climbing over an unprotected 8-foot fence surrounding the warehouse whose dimensions measure 100 feet by 100 feet. 9.____
Assuming that all of the following would be equally effective ways in preventing these breaches in security in the situation described above, which one would be LEAST costly?
   A. Using two trained guard dogs to roam freely throughout the facility at night
   B. Hiring a security guard to patrol the facility after working hours
   C. Installing tape razor wire on top of the fence surrounding the facility
   D. Installing an electronic burglar alarm system requiring the installation of a new fence

10. The area for which you have program responsibility has undergone recent changes. Your staff is now required to perform many new tasks, and morale is low. 10.____
The LEAST effective way for you to improve long-term staff morale would be to
   A. develop support groups to discuss problems
   B. involve staff in job development
   C. maintain a comfortable social environment within the group
   D. adequately plan and give assignments in a timely manner

11. As a supervisor in a large office, one of your subordinate supervisors stops you in the middle of the office and complains loudly that he is being treated unfairly. The rest of the staff ceases work and listens to the complaint. 11.____
The MOST appropriate action for you to take in this situation is to
   A. ignore this unprofessional behavior and continue on your way
   B. tell the supervisor that his behavior is unprofessional and he should learn how to conduct himself
   C. explain to the supervisor why you believe he is not being treated unfairly
   D. ask the supervisor to come to your office at a specific time to discuss the matter

12. You are told that one of your subordinates is distributing literature which attempts to recruit individuals to join a particular organization. Several workers complain that their rights are being violated. 12.____
Of the following, the BEST action for you to take FIRST is to
   A. ignore the situation because no harm is being done
   B. discuss the matter further with your supervisor
   C. ask the worker to stop distributing the literature
   D. tell the workers that they do not have to read the material

13. You have been assigned to develop a short training course for a recently issued procedure. 13.____
In designing this course, which of the following statements is the LEAST important for you to consider?

A. The learning experience must be interesting and meaningful in terms of the staff member's job.
B. The method of teaching must be strictly followed in order to develop successful learning experiences.
C. The course content should incorporate the rules and regulations of the agency.
D. The procedure should be consistent with the agency's objectives.

14. As a supervisor, there are several newly-promoted employees under your supervision. Each of these employees is subject to a probationary period PRIMARILY to 14.____
A. assess the employee's performance to see if the employee should be retained or removed from the position
B. give the employee the option to return to his former employment if the employee is unhappy in the new position
C. give the employee an opportunity to learn the duties and responsibilities of the position
D. judge the employee's potential for upward mobility in the future

15. An employee under your supervision rushes into your office to tell you he has just received a telephone bomb threat. 15.____
As the administrative supervisor, the FIRST thing you should do is
A. evacuate staff from the floor
B. call the police and building security
C. advise your administrator
D. do a preliminary search

16. After reviewing the Absence Control form for a unit under your supervision, you find that one of your staff members has a fifth undocumented sick leave within a six-month period. 16.____
In this situation, the FIRST action you should take is to
A. discuss the seriousness of the matter with the staff member when he returns to work and fully document the details of the discussion
B. review the case with the location director and warn the staff member that future use of sick leave will be punished
C. submit the proper disciplinary forms to ensure that the staff member is penalized for excessive absences
D. request that the timekeeper put the staff member on doctor's note restriction

17. A subordinate supervisor recently assigned to your office begins his first conference with you by saying that he has learned something that another supervisor is doing that you should know about. 17.____
After hearing this statement, of the following, the BEST approach for you to take is to
A. explain to the supervisor that the conference is to discuss his work and not that of his co-workers
B. tell the supervisor that you do not encourage a spy system among the staff you supervise

C. tell the supervisor that you will listen to his report only if the other supervisor is present
D. allow the supervisor to continue talking until you have enough information to make a decision on how best to respond

18. Assume that you are a supervisor recently assigned to a new unit. You notice that, for the past few days, one of the employees in your unit whose work is about average has been stopping work at about four o'clock and has been spending the rest of the afternoon relaxing at his desk. 18.____
The BEST of the following actions for you to take in this situation is to
A. assign more work to this employee since it is apparent that he does not have enough work to keep him busy
B. observe the employee's conduct more closely for about ten days before taking any more positive action
C. discuss the matter with the employee, pointing out to him how he can use the extra hour daily to raise the level of his job performance
D. question the previous supervisor in charge of the unit in order to determine whether he had sanctioned such conduct when he supervised that unit

19. A new supervisor was assigned to your program four months ago. Although he tries hard, he has been unable to meet certain standards because he still has a lot to learn. As his supervisor, you are required to submit performance evaluations within a few days. 19.____
How would you rate this employee on the tasks where he fails to meet standards because of lack of experience?
A. Satisfactory
B. Conditional
C. Unsatisfactory
D. Unratable

20. You find that there is an important procedural error in a memo which you distributed to your staff several days ago. 20.____
The BEST approach for you to take at this time is to
A. send a corrected memo to the staff, indicating what prior error was made
B. send a corrected memo to the staff without mentioning the prior error
C. tell the staff about the error at the next monthly staff meeting
D. place the corrected memo on the office bulletin board

21. Your superior asks you, a supervisor, about the status of the response to a letter from a public official concerning a client's case. When you ask the subordinate who was assigned to prepare the response to give you the letter, the subordinate denies that it was given to him. You are certain that the subordinate has the letter, but is withholding it because the response has not yet been prepared. 21.____
Of the following, in order to secure the letter from the subordinate, you should FIRST
A. accuse the subordinate of lying and demand that the letter be given to you immediately
B. say that you would consider it a personal favor if the subordinate would find the letter

C. continue to question the subordinate until he admits to having been given the letter
D. offer a face-saving solution, such as asking the subordinate to look again for the letter

22. As a supervisor, you have been assigned to write a few paragraphs to be included in the agency's annual report, describing a public service agency department this year as compared to last year. 22.____
Which of the following elements basic to the agency is LEAST likely to have changed since last year?
A. Mission B. Structure C. Technology D. Personnel

23. As a supervisor, you have been informed that a grievance has been filed against you, accusing you of assigning a subordinate to out-of-title tasks. 23.____
Of the following, the BEST approach for you to take is to
A. waive the grievance so that it will proceed to a Step II hearing
B. immediately change the subordinate's assignment to avoid future problems
C. respond to the grievance, giving appropriate reasons for the assignment
D. review the job description to ensure that the subordinate's tasks are not out-of-title

24. Which of the following is NOT a correct statement about agency group training programs in a public service agency? 24.____
A. Training sessions continue for an indefinite period of time.
B. Group training sessions are planned for designated personnel.
C. Training groups are organized formally through administrative planning.
D. Group training is task-centered and aimed toward accomplishing specific educational goals.

25. As a supervisor, you have submitted a memo to your superior requesting a conference to discuss the performance of a manager under your supervision. The memo states that the manager has a good working relationship with her staff; however, she tends to interpret agency policy too liberally and shows poor administrative skills by missing some deadlines and not keeping proper controls. 25.____
Which of the following steps should NOT be taken in order to prepare for this conference with your superior?
A. Collect and review all your notes regarding the manager's prior performance.
B. Outline your agenda so that you will have sufficient time to discuss the situation.
C. Tell the manager that you will be discussing her performance with your superior.
D. Clearly define objectives which will focus on improving the manager's performance.

# KEY (CORRECT ANSWERS)

| | | | |
|---|---|---|---|
| 1. | B | 11. | D |
| 2. | A | 12. | C |
| 3. | B | 13. | B |
| 4. | B | 14. | A |
| 5. | D | 15. | B |
| 6. | D | 16. | A |
| 7. | B | 17. | D |
| 8. | A | 18. | C |
| 9. | C | 19. | B |
| 10. | C | 20. | A |

| | |
|---|---|
| 21. | D |
| 22. | A |
| 23. | C |
| 24. | A |
| 25. | C |

# SUPERVISION STUDY GUIDE

Social science has developed information about groups and leadership in general and supervisor-employee relationships in particular. Since organizational effectiveness is closely linked to the ability of supervisors to direct the activities of employees, these findings are important to executives everywhere.

IS A SUPERVISOR A LEADER?

First-line supervisors are found in all large business and government organizations. They are the men at the base of an organizational hierarchy. Decisions made by the head of the organization reach them through a network of intermediate positions. They are frequently referred to as part of the management team, but their duties seldom seem to support this description.

A supervisor of clerks, tax collectors, meat inspectors, or securities analysts is not charged with budget preparation. He cannot hire or fire the employees in his own unit on his say-so. He does not administer programs which require great planning, coordinating, or decision making.

Then what is he? He is the man who is directly in charge of a group of employees doing productive work for a business or government agency. If the work requires the use of machines, the men he supervises operate them. If the work requires the writing of reports, the men he supervises write them. He is expected to maintain a productive flow of work without creating problems which higher levels of management must solve. But is he a leader?

To carry out a specific part of an agency's mission, management creates a unit, staffs it with a group of employees and designates a supervisor to take charge of them. Management directs what this unit shall do, from time to time changes directions, and often indicates what the group should not do. Management presumably creates status for the supervisor by giving him more pay, a title, and special privileges.

Management asks a supervisor to get his workers to attain organizational goals, including the desired quantity and quality of production. Supposedly, he has authority to enable him to achieve this objective. Management at least assumes that by establishing the status of the supervisor's position, it has created sufficient authority to enable him to achieve these goals—not his goals, nor necessarily the group's, but management's goals.

In addition, supervision includes writing reports, keeping records of membership in a higher-level administrative group, industrial engineering, safety engineering, editorial duties, housekeeping duties, etc. The supervisor as a member of an organizational network, must be responsible to the changing demands of the management above him. At the same time, he must be responsive to the demands of the work group of which he is a member. He is placed in the difficult position of communicating and implementing new decisions, changed programs and revised production quotas for his work group, although he may have had little part in developing them.

It follows, then, that supervision has a special characteristic: achievement of goals, previously set by management, through the efforts of others. It is in this feature of the supervisor's job that we find the role of a leader in the sense of the following definition: *A leader is that person who <u>most</u> effectively influences group activities toward goal setting and goal achievements.*

This definition is broad. It covers both leaders in groups that come together voluntarily and in those brought together through a work assignment in a factory, store, or government agency. In the natural group, the authority necessary to attain goals is determined by the group membership and is granted by them. In the working group, it is apparent that the establishment of a supervisory position creates a predisposition on the part of employees to accept the authority of the occupant of that position. We cannot, however, assume that mere occupation confers authority sufficient to assure the accomplishment of an organization's goals.

Supervision is different, then, from leadership. The supervisor is expected to fulfill the role of leader but without obtaining a grant of authority from the group he supervises. The supervisor is expected to influence the group in the achieving of goals but is often handicapped by having little influence on the organizational process by which goals are set. The supervisor, because he works in an organizational setting, has the burdens of additional organizational duties and restrictions and requirements arising out of the fact that his position is subordinate to a hierarchy of higher-level supervisors. These differences between leadership and supervision are reflected in our definition: *Supervision is basically a leadership role, in a formal organization, which has as its objective the effective influencing of other employees.*

Even though these differences between supervision and leadership exist, a significant finding of experimenters in this field is that supervisors <u>must</u> be leaders to be successful.

The problem is: How can a supervisor exercise leadership in an organizational setting? We might say that the supervisor is expected to be a natural leader in a situation which does not come about naturally. His situation becomes really difficult in an organization which is more eager to make its supervisors into followers rather than leaders.

LEADERSHIP: NATURAL AND ORGANIZATIONAL

Leadership, in its usual sense of *natural* leadership, and supervision are not the same. In some cases, leadership embraces broader powers and functions than supervision; in other cases, supervision embraces more than leadership. This is true both because of the organization and technical aspects of the supervisor's job and because of the relatively freer setting and inherent authority of the natural leader.

The natural leader usually has much more authority and influence than the supervisor. Group members not only follow his command but prefer it that way. The employee, however, can appeal the supervisor's commands to his union or to the supervisor's superior or to the personnel office. These intercessors represent restrictions on the supervisor's power to lead.

The natural leader can gain greater membership involvement in the group's objectives, and he can change the objectives of the group. The supervisor can attempt to gain employee support only for management's objectives; he cannot set other objectives. In these instances leadership is broader than supervision.

The natural leader must depend upon whatever skills are available when seeking to attain objectives. The supervisor is trained in the administrative skills necessary to achieve management's goals. If he does not possess the requisite skills, however, he can call upon management's technicians.

A natural leader can maintain his leadership, in certain groups, merely by satisfying members' need for group affiliation. The supervisor must maintain his leadership by directing and organizing his group to achieve specific organizational goals set for him and his group by management. He must have a technical competence and a kind of coordinating ability which is not needed by many natural leaders.

A natural leader is responsible only to his group which grants him authority. The supervisor is responsible to management, which employs him, and also to the work group of which he is a member. The supervisor has the exceedingly difficult job of reconciling the demands of two groups frequently in conflict. He is often placed in the untenable position of trying to play two antagonistic roles. In the above instance, supervision is broader than leadership.

ORGANIZATIONAL INFLUENCES ON LEADERSHIP

The supervisor is both a product and a prisoner of the organization wherein we find him. The organization which creates the supervisor's position also obstructs, restricts, and channelizes the exercise of his duties. These influences extend beyond prescribed functional relationships to specific supervisory behavior. For example, even in a face-to-face situation involving one of his subordinates, the supervisor's actions are controlled to a great extent by his organization. His behavior must conform to the organization policy on human relations, rules which dictate personnel procedures, specific prohibitions governing conduct, the attitudes of his own superior, etc. He is not a free agent operating within the limits of his work group. His freedom of action is much more circumscribed than is generally admitted. The organizational influences which limit his leadership actions can be classified as structure, prescriptions, and proscriptions.

The organizational structure places each supervisor's position in context with other designated positions. It determines the relationships between his position and specific positions which impinge on his. The structure of the organization designates a certain position to which he looks for orders and information about his work. It gives a particular status to his position within a pattern of statuses from which he perceives that (1) certain positions are on a par, organizationally, with his, (2) other positions are subordinate, and (3) still others are superior.

The organizational structure determines those positions to which he should look for advice and assistance, and those positions to which he should give advice and assistance.

For instance, the organizational structure has predetermined that the supervisor of a clerical processing unit shall report to a supervisory position in a higher echelon. He shall have certain relationships with the supervisors of the work units which transmit work to and receive work from his unit. He shall discuss changes and clarification of procedures with certain staff units, such as organization and methods, cost accounting, and personnel. He shall consult supervisors of units which provide or receive special work assignments.

The organizational structure, however, establishes patterns other than those of the relationships of positions. These are the patterns of responsibility, authority, and expectations.

The supervisor is responsible for certain activities or results; he is presumably invested with the authority to achieve these. His set of authority and responsibility is interwoven with other sets to the end that all goals and functions of the organization are parceled out in small, manageable lots. This, of course, establishes a series of expectations: a single supervisor can perform his particular set of duties only upon the assumption that preceding or contiguous sets of duties have been, or are being carried out. At the same time, he is aware of the expectations of others that he will fulfill his functional role.

The structure of an organization establishes relationships between specified positions and specific expectations for these positions. The fact that these relationships and expectations are established is one thing; whether or not they are met is another.

## PRESCRIPTIONS AND PROSCRIPTIONS

But let us return to the organizational influences which act to restrict the supervisor's exercise of leadership. These are the prescriptions and proscriptions generally in effect in all organizations, and those peculiar to a single organization. In brief these are the *thou shalt's* and the *thou shalt not's*.

Organizations not only prescribe certain duties for individual supervisory positions, they also prescribe specific methods and means of carrying out these duties and maintaining management-employee relations. These include rules, regulations, policy, and tradition. It does no good for the supervisor to say, *This seems to be the best way to handle such-and-such,* if the organization has established a routine for dealing with problems. For good or bad, there are rules that state that firings shall be executed in such a manner, accompanied by a certain notification; that training shall be conducted, and in this manner. Proscriptions are merely negative prescriptions; you may not discriminate against any employee because of politics or race; you shall not suspend any employee without following certain procedures and obtaining certain approvals.

Most of these prohibitions and rules apply to the area of interpersonal relations, precisely the area which is now arousing most interest on the part of administrators and managers. We have become concerned about the contrast between formally prescribed relationships and interpersonal relationships, and this brings us to the often discussed informal organization.

## FORMAL AND INFORMAL ORGANIZATIONS

As we well know, the functions and activities of any organization are broken down into individual units of work called positions. Administrators must establish a pattern which will link these positions to each other and relate them to a system of authority and responsibility. Man-to-man are spelled out as plainly as possible for all to understand. Managers, then, build an official structure which we call the formal organization.

In these same organizations, employees react individually and in groups to institutionally determined roles. John, a worker, rides in the same carpool as Joe, a foreman. An unplanned communication develops. Harry, a machinist knows more about high-speed machining than his foreman or anyone else in his shop. An unofficial tool boss comes into being. Mary, who fought with Jane, is promoted over her. Jane now gives Mary's directions. A planned relationship fails to develop. The employees have built a structure which we call the informal organization.

> *Formal organization is a system of management-prescribed relations between positions in an organization.*
>
> *Informal organization is a network of unofficial relations between people in an organization.*

These definitions might lead us to the absurd conclusion that positions carry out formal activities and that employe4es spend their time in unofficial activities. We must recognize that organizational activities are in all cases carried out by people. The formal structure provides a needed framework within which interpersonal relations occur. What we call informal organization is the complex of normal, natural relations among employees. These personal relationships may be negative or positive. That is, they may impede or aid the achievement of organizational goals. For example, friendship between two supervisors greatly increases the probability of good cooperation and coordination between their sections. On the other hand, *buck passing* nullifies the formal structure by failure to meet a prescribed and expected responsibility.

It is improbable that an ideal organization exists where all activities are carried out in strict conformity to a formally prescribed pattern of functional roles. Informal organization arises because of the incompleteness and ambiguities in the network of formally prescribed relationships, or in response to the needs or inadequacies of supervisors or managers who hold prescribed functional roles in an organization. Many of these relationships are not prescribed by the organizational pattern; many cannot be prescribed; many should not be prescribed.

Management faces the problem of keeping the informal organization in harmony with the mission of the agency. One way to do this is to make sure that all employees have a clear understanding of and are sympathetic with that mission. The issuance of organizational charts, procedural manuals, and functional descriptions of the work to be done by divisions and sections helps communicate management's plans and goals. Issuances alone, of course, cannot do the whole job. They should be accompanied by oral discussion and explanation. Management must ensure that there is mutual understanding and acceptance of charts and procedures. More important is that management acquaint itself with the attitudes, activities, and peculiar brands of logic which govern the informal organization. Only through this type of knowledge can they and supervisors keep informal goals consistent with the agency mission.

## SUPERVISION STATUS AND FUNCTIONAL ROLE

A well-established supervisor is respected by the employees who work with him. They defer to his wishes. It is clear that a superior-subordinate relationship has been established. That is, status of the supervisor has been established in relation to other employees of the same work group. This same supervisor gains the respect of employees when he behaves in as certain manner. He will be expected, generally, to follow the customs of the group in such matters as dress, recreation, and manner of speaking. The group has a set of expectations as to his behavior. His position is a functional role which carries with it a collection of rights and obligations.

The position of supervisor usually has a status distinct from the individual who occupies it: it is much like a position description which exists whether or not there is an incumbent. The status of a supervisory position is valued higher than that of an employee position both because of the functional role of leadership which is assigned to it and because of the status symbols of titles, rights, and privileges which go with it.

Social ranking, or status, is not simple because it involves both the position and the man. An individual may be ranked higher than others because of his education, social background, perceived leadership ability, or conformity to group customs and ideals. If such a man is ranked higher by the members of a work group than their supervisor, the supervisor's effectiveness may be seriously undermined.

If the organization does not build and reinforce a supervisor's status, his position can be undermined in a different way. This will happen when managers go around rather than through the supervisor or designate him as a straw boss, acting boss, or otherwise not a real boss.

Let us clarify this last point. A role, and corresponding status, establishes a set of expectations. Employees expect their supervisor to do certain things and to act in certain ways. They are prepared to respond to that expected behavior. When the supervisor's behavior does not conform to their expectations, they are surprised, confused, and ill-at-ease. It becomes necessary for them to resolve their confusion, if they can. They might do this by turning to one of their own members for leadership. If the confusion continues, or their attempted solutions are not satisfactory, they will probably become a poorly motivated, non-cohesive group which cannot function very well.

## COMMUNICATION AND THE SUPERVISOR

In a recent survey, railroad workers reported that they rarely look to their supervisor for information about the company. This is startling, at least to us, because we ordinarily think of the supervisor as the link between management and worker. We expect the supervisor to be the prime source of information about the company. Actually, the railroad workers listed the supervisor next to last in the o5rder of their sources of information. Most surprising of all, the supervisors, themselves, stated that rumor and unofficial contacts were their principal sources of information. Here we see one of the reasons why supervisors may not be as effective as management desires.

The supervisor is not only being bypassed by his work group, he is being ignored, and his position weakened, by the very organization which is holding him responsible for the activities of his workers. If he is management's representative to the employee, then management has an obligation to keep him informed of its activities. This is necessary if he is to carry out his functions efficiently and maintain his leadership in the work group. The supervisor is expected to be a source of information; when he is not, his status is not clear, and employees are dissatisfied because he has not lived up to expectations.

By providing information to the supervisor to pass along to employees, we can strengthen his position as leader of the group, and increase satisfaction and cohesion within the group. Because he has more information than the other members, receives information sooner, and passes it along at the proper times, members turn to him as a source and also provide him with information in the hope of receiving some in return. From this, we can see an increase in group cohesiveness because:

- Employees are bound closer to their supervisor because he is *in the know.*
- There is less need to go outside the group for answers
- Employees will more quickly turn to the supervisor for enlightenment

The fact that he has the answers will also enhance the supervisor's standing in the eyes of his men. This increased status will serve to bolster his authority and control of the group and will probably result in improved morale and productivity.

The foregoing, of course, does not mean that all management information should be given out. There are obviously certain policy determinations and discussions which need not or cannot be transmitted to all supervisors. However, the supervisor must be kept as fully informed as possible so that he can answer questions when asked and can allay needless fears and anxieties. Further, the supervisor has the responsibility of encouraging employee questions and submissions of information. He must be able to present information to employees so that it is clearly understood and accepted. His attitude and manner should make it clear that he believes in what he is saying, that the information is necessary or desirable to the group, and that he is prepared to act on the basis of the information.

## SUPERVISION AND JOB PERFORMANCE

The productivity of work groups is a product; employees' efforts are multiplied by the supervision they receive. Many investigators have analyzed this relationship and have discovered elements of supervision which differentiate high and low production groups. These researchers have identified certain types of supervisory practices which they classify as *employee-centered* and other types which they classify as *production centered.*

The difference between these two kinds of supervision lies not in specific practices but in the approach or orientation to supervision. The employee-centered supervisor directs most of his efforts toward increasing employee motivation. He is concerned more with realizing the potential energy of persons than with administrative and technological methods of increasing efficiency and productivity. He is the man who finds ways of causing employees to want to work harder with the same tools. These supervisors emphasize the personal relations between their employees and themselves.

Now, obviously, these pictures are overdrawn. No one supervisor has all the virtues of the ideal type of employee-centered supervisor. And, fortunately, no one supervisor has all the bad traits found in many production-centered supervisors. We should remember that the various practices that researchers have fond which distinguish these two kinds of supervision represent the many practices and methods of supervisors of all gradations between these extremes. We should be careful, too, of the implications of the labels attached to the two types. For instance, being production-centered is not necessarily bad, since the principal responsibility of any supervisor is maintaining the production level that is expected of his work group. Being employee-centered may not necessarily be good, if the only result is a happy, chuckling crew of loafers. To return to the researchers' findings, employee-centered supervisors:

- Recommend promotions, transfers, pay increases
- Inform men about what is happening in the company
- Keep men posted on how well they are doing
- Hear complaints and grievances sympathetically
- Speak up for subordinates

Production-centered supervisors, on the other hand, don't do those things. They check on employees more frequently, give more detailed and frequent instructions, don't give reasons for changes, and are more punitive when mistakes are made. Employee-centered supervisors were reported to contribute to high morale and high production, whereas production-centered supervision was associated with lower morale and less production.

More recent findings, however, show that the relationship between supervision and productivity is not this simple. Investigators now report that high production is more frequently associated with supervisory practices which combine employee-centered behavior with concern for production. (This concern is not the same, however, as anxiety about production, which is the hallmark of our production-centered supervisor.) Let us examine these apparently contradictory findings and the premises from which they are derived.

## SUPERVISION AND MORALE

Why do supervisory activities cause high or low production? As the name implies, the activities of the employee-centered supervisor tend to relate him more closely and satisfactorily to his workers. The production-centered supervisor's practices tend to separate him from his group and to foster antagonism. An analysis of this difference may answer our question.

Earlier, we pointed out that the supervisor is a type of leader and that leadership is intimately related to the group in which it occurs We discover, now, that an employee-centered supervisor's primary activities are concerned with both his leadership and his group membership. Such a supervisor is a member of a group and occupies a leadership role in that group.

These facts are sometimes obscured when we speak of the supervisor as management's representative, or as the organizational link between management and the employee, or as the end of the chain of command. If we really want to understand what it is we expect of the supervisor, we must remember that he is the designated leader of a group of employees to whom he is bound by interaction and interdependence.

Most of his actions are aimed, consciously or unconsciously, at strengthening membership ties in the group. This includes both making members more conscious that he is a member of their group) and causing members to identify themselves more closely with the group. These ends are accomplished by:

- making the group more attractive to the worker: they find satisfaction of their needs for recognition, friendship, enjoyable work, etc.;
- maintaining open communication: employees can express their views and obtain information about the organization
- giving assistance: members can seek advice on personal problems as well as their work; and
- acting as a buffer between the group and management: he speaks up for his men and explains the reasons for management's decisions.

Such actions both strengthen group cohesiveness and solidarity and affirm the supervisor's leadership position in the group.

## DEFINING MORALE

This brings us back to a point mentioned earlier. We had said that employee-centered supervisors contribute to high morale as well as to high production. But how can we explain units which have low morale and high productivity, or vice versa? Usually production and morale are considered separately, partly because they are measured against different criteria and partly because, in some instances, they seem to be independent of each other.

Some of this difficulty may stem from confusion over definitions of morale. Morale has been defined as, or measured by, absences from work, satisfaction with job or company, dissension among members of work groups, productivity, apathy or lack of interest, readiness to help others, and a general aura of happiness as rated by observers. Some of these criteria of morale are not subject to the influence of the supervisor, and some of them are not clearly related to productivity. Definitions like these invite findings of low morale coupled with high production.

Both productivity and morale can be influenced by environmental factors not under the control of group members or supervisors. Such things as plant layout, organizational structure and goals, lighting, ventilation, communications, and management planning may have an adverse or desirable effect.

We might resolve the dilemma by defining morale on the basis of our understanding of the supervisor as leader of a group; morale is the degree of satisfaction of group members with their leadership. In this light, the supervisor's employee-centered activities bear a clear relation to morale. His efforts to increase employee identification with the group and to strengthen his leadership lead to greater satisfaction with that leadership. By increasing group cohesiveness and by demonstrating that his influence and power can aid the group, he is able to enhance his leadership status and afford satisfaction to the group.

SUPERVISION, PRODUCTION, AND MORALE

There are factors within the organization itself which determine whether increased production is possible:

- Are production goals expressed in terms understandable to employees and are they realistic?
- Do supervisors responsible for production respect the agency mission and production goals?
- If employees do not know how to do the job well, does management provide a trainer—often the supervisor—who can teach efficient work methods?

There are other factors within the work group which determine whether increased production will be attained:

- Is leadership present which can bring about the desired level of production?
- Are production goals accepted by employees as reasonable and attainable?
- If group effort is involved, are members able to coordinate their efforts?

Research findings confirm the view that an employee-centered supervisor can achieve higher morale than a production-centered supervisor. Managers may well ask what is the relationship between this and production.

Supervision is production-oriented to the extent that it focuses attention on achieving organizational goals, and plans and devises methods for attaining them; it is employee-centered to the extent that it focuses attention on employee attitudes toward those goals, and plans and works toward maintenance of employee satisfaction.

High productivity and low morale result when a supervisor plans and organizes work efficiently but cannot achieve high membership satisfaction. Low production and high morale result when a supervisor, though keeping members satisfied with his leadership, either has not gained acceptance of organizational goals or does not have the technical competence to achieve them.

The relationship between supervision, morale, and productivity is an interdependent one, with the supervisor playing an integral role due to his ability to influence productivity and morale independently of each other.

A supervisor who can plan his work well has good technical knowledge, and who can install better production methods can raise production without necessarily increasing group satisfaction. On the other hand, a supervisor who can motivate his employees and keep them satisfied with his leadership can gain high production in spite of technical difficulties and environmental obstacles.

## CLIMATE AND SUPERVISION

Climate, the intangible environment of an organization made up of attitudes, beliefs, and traditions, plays a large part in morale, productivity, and supervision. Usually when we speak of climate and its relationship to morale and productivity, we talk about the merits of *democratic* versus *authoritarian* climate. Employees seem to produce more and have higher morale in a democratic climate, whereas in an authoritarian climate, the reverse seems to be true or so the researchers tell us. We would do well to determine what these terms mean to supervision.

Perhaps most of our difficulty in understanding and applying these concepts comes from our emotional reactions to the words themselves. For example, authoritarian climate is usually painted as the very blackest kind of dictatorship. This is not surprising, because we are usually expected to believe that it is invariably bad. Conversely, democratic climate is drawn to make the driven snow look impure by comparison.

Now these descriptions are most probably true when we talk about our political processes, or town meetings, or freedom of speech. However, the same labels have been used by social scientists in other contexts and have also been applied to government and business organizations, without it, it seems, any recognition that the meanings and their social values may have changed somewhat

For example, these labels were used in experiments conducted in an informal classroom setting using 11-year-old boys as subjects. The descriptive labels applied to the climate of the setting as well as the type of leadership practiced. When these labels were transferred to a management setting, it seems that many presumed that they principally meant the king of leadership rather than climate. We can see that there is a great difference between the experimental and management settings and that leadership practices for one might be inappropriate for the other.

It is doubtful that formal work organizations can be anything but authoritarian, in that goals are set by management and a hierarchy exists through which decisions and orders from the top are transmitted downward. Organizations are authoritarian by structure and need; direction and control are placed in the hands of a few in order to gain fast and efficient decision making. Now this does not mean to describe a dictatorship. It is merely the recognition of the fact that direction of organizational affairs comes from above. It should be noted that leadership in some natural groups is, in this sense, authoritarian.

Granting that formal organizations have this kind of authoritarian leadership, can there be a democratic climate? Certainly there can be, but we would want to define and delimit this term. A more realistic meaning of democratic climate in organizations is the use of permissive and participatory methods in management-employee relations. That is, a mutual exchange of information and explanation with the granting of individual freedom within certain restricted and defined limits. However, it is not our purpose to debate the merits of authoritarianism versus democracy. We recognize that within the small work group there is a need for freedom from constraint and an increase in participation in order to achieve organizational goals within the framework of the organizational movement.

Another aspect of climate is best expressed by this familiar, and true, saying: actions speak louder than words. Of particular concern to us is this effect of management climate on the behavior of supervisors, particularly in employee-centered activities.

There have been reports of disappointment with efforts to make supervisors ore employee-centered. Managers state that, since research has shown ways of improving human relations, supervisors should begin to practice these methods. Usually a training course in human relations is established; and supervisors are given this training. Managers then sit back and wait for the expected improvements, only to find that there are none.

If we wish to produce changes in the supervisor's behavior, the climate must be made appropriate and rewarding to the changed behavior. This means that top-level attitudes and behavior cannot deny or contradict the change we are attempting to effect. Basic changes in organizational behavior cannot be made with any permanence, unless we provide an environment that is receptive to the changes and rewards those persons who do change.

IMPROVING SUPERVISION

Anyone who has read this far might expect to find *A Dozen Rules for Dealing With Employees* or *29 Steps to Supervisory Success.* We will not provide such a list.

Simple rules suffer from their simplicity. They ignore the complexities of human behavior. Reliance upon rules may cause supervisors to concentrate on superficial aspects of their relations with employees. It may preclude genuine understanding.

The supervisor who relies on a list of rules tends to think of people in mechanistic terms. In a certain situation, he uses *Rule No. 3.* Employees are not treated as thinking and feeling persons, but rather as figures in a formula: Rule 3 applied to employee X = Production.

Employees usually recognize mechanical manipulation and become dissatisfied and resentful. They lose faith in, and respect for, their supervisor, and this may be reflected in lower morale and productivity.

We do not mean that supervisors must become social science experts if they wish to improve. Reports of current research indicate that there are two major parts of their job which can be strengthened through self-improvement: (1) Work planning, including technical skills, and (2) motivation of employees.

The most effective supervisors combine excellence in the administrative and technical aspects of their work with friendly and considerate personal relations with their employees.

13

CRITICAL PERSONAL RELATIONS

Later in this chapter we shall talk about administrative aspects of supervision, but first let us comment on *friendly and considerate personal relations*. We have discussed this subject throughout the preceding chapters, but we want to review some of the critical supervisory influences on personal relations.

Closeness of Supervision: The closeness of supervision has an important effect on productivity and morale. Mann and Dent found that supervisors of low-producing units supervise very closely, while high-producing supervisors exercise only general supervision. It was found that the low-producing supervisors:

- check on employees more frequently
- give more detailed and frequent instructions
- limit employee's freedom to do job in own way

Workers who felt less closely supervised reported that they were better satisfied with their jobs and the company. We should note that the manner or attitude of the supervisor has an important bearing on whether employees perceive supervision as being close or general.

These findings are another way of saying that supervision does not mean standing over the employee and telling him what to do and when and how to do it. The more effective supervisor tells his employees what is required, giving general instructions.

COMMUNICATION

Supervisors of high-production units consider communication as one of the most important aspects of their job. Effective communication is used by these supervisors to achieve better interpersonal relations and improved employee motivation. Low-production supervisors do not rate communications as highly important.

High-producing supervisors find that an important aid to more effective communication is listening. They are ready to listen to both personal problems or interests and questions about the work. This does not mean that they are *nosey* or meddle in their employees' personal lives, but rather that they show a willingness to listen, and do listen, if their employees wish to discuss problems.

These supervisors inform employees about forthcoming changes in work; they discuss agency policy with employees; and they make sure that each employee knows how well he is doing. What these supervisors do is use two-way communication effectively. Unless the supervisor freely imparts information, he will not receive information in return.

Attitudes and perception are frequently affected by communication or the lack of it. Research surveys reveal that many supervisors are not aware of their employees' attitudes, nor do they know what personal reactions their supervision arouses. Through frank discussion with employees, they have been surprised to discover employee beliefs about which they were ignorant. Discussion sometimes reveals that the supervisor and his employees have totally different impressions about the same event. The supervisor should be constantly on the alert for misconceptions about his words and deeds. He must remember that, although his actions are perfectly clear to himself, they may be, and frequently are, viewed differently by employees.

Failure to communicate information results in misconceptions and false assumptions. What you say and how you say it will strongly affect your employees' attitudes and perceptions. By giving them available information, you can prevent misconceptions; by discussion, you may be able to change attitudes; by questioning, you can discover what the perceptions and assumptions really are. And it need hardly be added that actions should conform very closely to words.

If we were to attempt to reduce the above discussion on communication to rules, we would have a long list which would be based on one cardinal principle: Don't make assumptions!

- Don't assume that your employees know; tell them.
- Don't assume that you know how they feel; find out.
- Don't assume that they understand; clarify.

15

## 20 SUPERVISORY HINTS

1. Avoid inconsistency.
2. Always give employees a chance to explain their action before taking disciplinary action. Don't allow too much time for a "cooling off" period before disciplining an employee.
3. Be specific in your criticisms.
4. Delegate responsibility wisely.
5. Do not argue or lose your temper, and avoid being impatient.
6. Promote mutual respect and be fair, impartial, and open-minded.
7. Keep in mind that asking for employees' advice and input can be helpful in decision making.
8. If you make promises, keep them.
9. Always keep the feelings, abilities, dignity and motives of your staff in mind.
10. Remain loyal to your employees' interests.
11. Never criticize employees in front of others, or treat employees like children.
12. Admit mistakes. Don't place blame on your employees, or make excuses.
13. Be reasonable in your expectations, give complete instructions, and establish well-planned goals.
14. Be knowledgeable about office details and procedures, but avoid becoming bogged down in details.
15. Avoid supervising too closely or too loosely. Employees should also view you as an approachable supervisor.
16. Remember that employees' personal problems may affect job performance, but become involved only when appropriate.
17. Work to develop workers, and to instill a feeling of cooperation while working toward mutual goals.
18. Do not overpraise or underpraise, be properly appreciative.
19. Never ask an employee to discipline someone for you.
20. A complaint, even if unjustified, should be taken seriously.

# NOTES

# POLICE COMMUNICATIONS & TELETYPE OPERATIONS

## TABLE OF CONTENTS

# POLICE COMMUNICATIONS & TELETYPE OPERATIONS

## I. COMMUNICATIONS

### A. RADIOS IN AUTOMOBILES

It is an Unclassified misdemeanor for any person who is not a peace officer to either equip an automobile with or knowingly use an automobile equipped with a radio receiving set capable of receiving signals on the frequencies allocated to police use. Excepted are holders of Federal amateur radio operator's licenses operating a receiver in connection with a mobile transmitter (V&T Sec. 397).

### B. POLICE RADIO MESSAGES

It is a like misdemeanor to in any way knowingly interfere with the transmission of radio messages by police without first having secured a permit to do so from the person authorized to issue such a permit by the local municipal governing body or board. Offenses are punishable by fine not over $1,000, imprisonment not more than 6 months, or both (V&T Sec. 397).

The law excepts persons who hold a valid amateur radio operator's license issued by the Federal Communications Commission and who operate a duly licensed portable transmitter-receiver on frequencies allocated by the Federal Communications Commission to licensed radio amateurs (V&T Sec. 397).

### C. TAMPERING WITH PRIVATE COMMUNICATIONS

A person is guilty of Tampering with Private Communications when, knowing that he does not have the consent of the sender or receiver, he obtains or attempts to obtain from an employee, officer or representative, of a telephone or telegraph corporation, by connivance, deception, intimidation or in any other manner, information with respect to the contents or nature thereof of a telephonic or telegraphic communication (P.L. Sec. 250.25, subd. 3).

A person is also guilty of Tampering with Private Communications when, knowing that he does not have the consent of the sender or receiver, and being an employee, officer or representative of a telephone or telegraph corporation, he knowingly divulges to another person the contents or nature thereof of a telephonic or telegraphic communication. The provisions of this subdivision do not apply to such person when he acts to report a criminal communication under the requirements of Penal Law Section 250.35 (see next paragraph) (P.L. Sec. 250.25, subd. 4). Tampering with Private Communications is a Class B misdemeanor.

### D. FAILING TO REPORT CRIMINAL TELEPHONE OR TELEGRAPH COMMUNICATIONS

It is the duty of a telephone or telegraph corporation and of any employee, officer or representative thereof having knowledge that the facilities of such corporation are being used to conduct any criminal business, traffic or transaction, to furnish or attempt to furnish to an appropriate law enforcement officer or agency, all pertinent information within his possessionrelating to such matter, and to cooperate fully with any law enforcement officer or agency investigating such matter. A person is guilty of Failing to Report Criminal Communications when he knowingly violates any duty prescribed in this section (P.L. Sec. 250.35).

Failing to Report Criminal Communications is a Class B misdemeanor.

The prohibitions in Section 250.25, Penal Law do not apply to a law enforcement officer who obtains information from a telephone or telegraph corporation pursuant to Section 250.35 of the Penal Law (P.L. Sec. 250.25, subd.3).

E. UNLAWFULLY OBTAINING COMMUNICATIONS INFORMATION

A person is guilty of Unlawfully Obtaining Communications Information when, knowing that he does not have the authorization of a telephone or telegraph corporation, he obtains or attempts to obtain, by deception, stealth or in any other manner, from such corporation or from any employee, officer or representative thereof:

1. Information concerning identification or location of any wires, cables, lines, terminals or other apparatus used in furnishing telephone or telegraph service; or
2. Information concerning a record of any communication passing over telephone or telegraph lines of any such corporation (P.L. Sec. 250.30).

Unlawfully Obtaining Communications Information is a Class B misdemeanor.

F. TAMPERING WITH LETTERS, MAIL, ETC.

A person is guilty of Tampering with Private Communications when:

1. Knowing that he does not have the consent of the sender or receiver, he opens or reads a sealed letter or other sealed private communication (P.L. Sec. 250.25, subd. 1); or
2. Knowing that a sealed letter or other sealed private communication has been opened or read in violation of subdivision one of this section, he divulges, without the consent of the sender or receiver, the contents of such letter or communication, in whole or in part, or a resume of any portion of the contents thereof (P.L. Sec. 250.25, subd. 2).

Tampering with Private Communications is a Class B misdemeanor.

It is a Federal crime, punishable by $2,000 fine or 5 years imprisonment or both, to take a letter, postcard or package out of any post office or authorized depository or from a mail carrier or to take such thing which has been in the mails before it is delivered to a person to whom directed, with intent to obstruct the correspondence or to pry into the business or secrets of another. This violation includes taking mail left by the carrier, including from private mail boxes where deposited by the carrier.

It is also a Federal violation to steal or obtain mail by fraud from the post office or any postal facility.

These Federal violations are investigated by U.S. Postal Inspectors, who should be promptly notified of offenses (Title 18 U.S. Code, Secs. 1703, 1708).

## II. OFFENSES IN USE OF COMMUNICATION MEDIA

A. PARTY LINES

A person commits the crime of Unlawfully Refusing to Yield a Party Line when being informed that a party line is needed for an emergency call, he refuses to immediately relinquish the line (P.L. Sec 270.15, subd. 2).

Unlawfully Refusing to Yield a Party Line is a Class B misdemeanor. A "party line" is a subscriber's line telephone circuit, consisting of two or more main telephone stations connected therewith, each station with a distinctive ring or telephone number (P.L. Sec. 270.15, subd. 1-a). An "emergency call" is a telephone call to a police or fire department, or for medical aid or ambulance service, necessitated by a situation in which human life or property is in jeopardy and prompt summoning of aid is essential (P.L. Sec. 270.15, subd. 1-b).

B. ANNOYING OR ALARMING COMMUNICATIONS

It is the crime of Aggravated Harassment to communicate with a person anonymously or otherwise, by telephone, telegraph, mail or any other form of communication, in a manner likely to cause annoyance or alarm, with intent to harass, annoy or alarm another (P.L. Sec. 240.30, subd.1). Aggravated Harassment is a Class A misdemeanor.

C. JAMMING, OTHER NON-LEGITIMATE PHONE CALLS

It is also Aggravated Harassment for any person to make a telephone call, whether or not a conversation ensues, with no purpose of legitimate communication and with intent to harass, annoy or alarm another (P.L. Sec. 240.30, subd. 2).

D. THEFT OF SERVICES (TELEPHONE, TELEGRAPH)

A person is guilty of Theft of Services when, with intent to avoid payment by himself or another person of the lawful charge for any telecommunications service, he obtains or attempts to avoid payment therefor by himself or another person by means of:

1. Tampering or making connection with the equipment of the supplier, whether by mechanical, electrical, acoustical, or other means, or
2. Any misrepresentation of fact which he knows to be false, or
3. Any other artifice, trick,deception, code or device (P.L. Sec. 165.15, subd. 4).

Theft of Services is a Class A misdemeanor. It includes use of illicit credit cards

## III. INVESTIGATIONS

In any case involving police-frequency radio in automobiles, care must be taken to ensure that an actual test of the illicit receiver is made, to establish receipt of police frequencies. In addition, an expert in radio matters should make an examination of the radio, for expert testimony that the radio could receive police frequencies.

In taking complaints dealing with Tampering with Private Communications, the officer must be certain to pin down specific facts and details of the matter divulged, with exact times, dates and facts as to identification of violators.

In cases involving *"jamming"* telephones, it is proper to take detailed written statements from complaints, setting down the time and date of the calls and specific words said. Any factual information the victim may have to identify the offender should be obtained in detail. Where positive proof of identity is lacking, obtain permission to monitor the victim's telephone and consider obtaining an order to monitor the telephone of any suspect. Telephone companies may be able to offer valuable technical assistance in respect to crimes of this kind and the possibilities should be explored with ranking telephone company officals in proper cases.

In party line telephone cases, the officer must establish that the offender was in fact informed that the line was needed for an emergency call and that the emergency met the terms of the statute. A factor of identification of the offender is always present and if the complainant is not familiar with the offender, arrangements may be made for telephone and personal confrontation of the complainant and each potential user of the party line who could be the offender, for identification purposes. Officers should not overlook the value of proper interrogation of suspects in this kind of case.

In cases involving Theft of Services, officers should always work closely with telephone company sections assigned responsibility for attempting to determine to whom calls should properly be billed, since these persons are frequently able to make associations of persons and numbers which cannot be done by anyone not constantly working with such things.

# IV. POLICE RADIO COMMUNICATIONS

Police radio transmitters must be licensed by the Federal Communications Commission (FCC). Each Base Station transmitter must be licensed. All mobile stations are included under the main license. The FCC will assign appropriate frequencies and call letters. Police radio falls in the category of "Public Safety Radio Services" in FCC terminology and is covered by FCC Rules and Regulations, Part 89.

All adjustments and tests which may affect the proper operation of police radios must be made only by holders of first or second class commercial radio operator's licenses. Such license holders may be either a department member or an outsider, such as a radio shop owner or employee.

Police officers and dispatchers broadcasting over police voice radios are not required to have individual licenses.

FCC Rules and Regulations, Sec. 89.151, require that all police transmissions, regardless of their nature, shall be restricted to the minimum practical transmission time.

In all police agencies with radio broadcasting systems, clear general instructions should be in effect to ensure that the headquarters transmitter is in charge of the air and may order other units silenced for priority messages, regardless of the rank of persons using mobile equipment, including radio cars, in the field.

In an emergency, the headquarters transmitter can temporarily transfer command of the air to a ranking officer in the field. This should be a rare occasion and should be done on a formal basis. There should be no informal monopolizing of the air by mobile units in the field.

A list of emergency telephone numbers should be maintained at the dispatcher's desk. The list should be regularly checked and kept current and complete. It should include hospitals, ambulance service, doctors available for emergencies, fire departments, coroner and medical examiners, garages, etc.

## A. GENERAL REQUIREMENTS FOR PROPER TRANSMISSIONS

All transmission must be clearly enunicated. The microphone should be held exactly in front of the speaker's lips and about two inches away. The voice should always be free of emotion or stress. The speaker must be certain that a very brief pause is made after pressing the transmitter button and before speaking and that another very brief pause is made before releasing the button after speaking, to avoid chopping off parts of the transmission.

Inexperienced officers commonly fail to clearly enunciate and often chop off parts of their transmissions by pressing or releasing the transmitter button too late or too soon. All officers using any transmitter should receive substantial training to ensure that they use it properly. (A microphone-amplifier-loudspeaker or a tape recorder set-up should be used in training and not any actual radio transmissions.)

Training should include practice in the use of established radio procedure of the department and in brief, clear wording of transmissions, whether information messages, requests for information or instructions.

Headquarters radio transmitters are distinguishable by sound from the mobile transmitters. It is thus not necessary for headquarters to always identify itself. FCC rules require only that the main station shall identify itself with its assigned call letters at least once each thirty minutes during each period of operation. Mobile transmitters (radio cars, walkie-talkies, etc.) must identify themselves with the geographic name of the governmental subdivision under whose name the main station is licensed (e.g., car two of the Southton, N.Y., Police Department would call itself "Southton two").

A usual, clear and brief routine would thus be: "Car two" (from headquarters); "Southton two" (from the mobile unit), "Compliant, Mrs. John Doe, one Main Street, family disturbance" (from Headquarters); "Southton two okay" (from the mobile unit). With these brief messages, headquarters has located car two "in service," issued instructions to investigate a family disturbance based on a complaint, given the identity of the complainant and the location of the disturbance and has been informed by car two that the message was understood and that the instructions would be complied with.

Established procedures should also include routing for mobile units to inform headquarters when they go into service at the beginning of a tour of duty and when they go out of service from time to time during the tour. The initial call at the beginning of the tour will automatically give a check of the operating condition of the mobile units' radio equipment. The officer or officers using the equipment during the tour should be identified in this initial call.

A usual routing would be: "Southton two" (from the mobile unit); "Car two" (from headquarters); "In service, occupant 113" (from the mobile unit); "'Okay two" (acknowledgment from headquarters, specifying which car is being acknowledged).

"Occupant 113" identifies the officers in Southton Car two in the preceding example. It is best to use numbers, usually badge or shield numbers, to identify officers on the air. It is more secure against unauthorized listeners and is more accurate and brief than using names. The headquarters radioman should of course have a complete list of officers' names and numbers, arranged in numerical sequence and also in name order. He should record the mobile units in use and the officers using them, as they call in.

In larger departments, where air-time is limited, due to the large number of mobile units requiring air-time, it is desirable to use a code to save time on the air. The *"ten-signal"* code is widely used. It provides codes for a major part of the information constituting police radio traffic, thus cutting down words and saving substantial amounts of air-time. Some departments may add security to their use of radio by assigning numbers "post numbers") to key locations in their territory and then describing locations by giving distance and direction from a post number. The following are frequently used *"ten-signals"* of the system recommended by the Associated Public Safety Communications Officers, Inc. (APCO);

TEN-SIGNAL CODE

10-1 Unable to copy, change your location
10-2 Signals good
10-3 Stop transmitting
10-4 Acknowledgment
10-5 Relay
10-6 Busy, stand by unless urgent
10-7 Out of service atreport (give location or telephone number)
10-16 Domestic trouble at
10-17 Meet complainant at
10-18 Complete assignment quickly
10-19 Return to
10-20 My location is (or what is your location)

10- 8 In Service
10- 9 Repeat, please
10-10 Fight in progress at
10-11 Dog case (describe - e.g., *"fight," "biting," "rabid")*
10-12 Stand by (or "stop")
10-13 Weather and road
10-14 Report of prowler at
10-15 Civil disturbance at
10-48 Traffic standard needs repairs at
10-49 Traffic light out at
10-50 Accident (Kind, location)
10-51 Wrecker needed at

10-21 Call by telephone
10-22 Disregard
10-23 Arrived at scene
10-24 Assignment completed
10-25 Report in person to (meet)
10-26 Holding subject - expedite reply
10-27 Diver's license information
10-29 Check records for wanted
10-30 Illegal use of radio
10-31 Crime in progress at
10-32 Man with gun at
10-33 Emergency
10-36 Correct time is
10-37 Investigate suspicious vehicle (describe)
10-38 Stopping suspicious vehicle (Give description and location before stopping)
10-41 Beginning tour of duty
10-42 Ending tour of duty
10-43 Inform me about
10-44 Request permission to leave patrol for
10-45 Animal carcass in lane at
10-46 Assist motorist at
10-47 Emergency road repairs needed at or stolen
10-52 Ambulance needed at
10-53 Road blocked at
10-54 Livestock on highway
10-55 Intoxicated driver
10-56 Intoxicated pedestrian
10-57 Hit-and-run (fatal personal injury, property damage)
10-58 Direct traffic at
10-59 Convoy or escort (specify)
10-62 Reply to message
10-63 Prepare to make written copy
10-64 Message for local delivery
10-65 Net message assignment
10-66 Message cancellation
10-67 Clear to read net message
10-68 Dispatch information
10-69 Message received
10-70 Fire alarm at
10-74 Negative
10-75 In contact with
10-76 En Route
10-77 Estimated time of arrival
10-78 Need assistance at
10-90 Bank alarm at
10-94 Drag racing at
10-96 Mental subject
10-99 Records indicate wanted

Accuracy is of prime importance in radio work. Names should be spelled out in any instance where a file check is required or it is otherwise important that the correct spelling be known. Names should be spelled with a word-code by the officer transmitting. The following word code is good:

WORD CODE

| | | | | | |
|---|---|---|---|---|---|
| A | Adam | I | Ida | R | Robert |
| B | Boy | J | John | S | Sam |
| C | Charles | K | King | T | Tom |
| D | David | L | Lincoln | U | Union |
| E | Edward | M | Mary | V | Victor |
| F | Frank | N | Nora | W | William |
| G | George | O | Ocean | X | X-ray |
| H | Henry | P | Paul | Y | Young |
| | | Q | Queen | Z | Zebra |

In using the word-code for spelling, transmit as follows:

"... JONES, J-JOHN, O-OCEAN, N-NORA, E-EDWARD, S-SAM." Do not say: "J AS IN JOHN" or "J LIKE IN JOHN" or similar wordy recitals.

In cases where numbers must be transmitted, such as license and serial numbers, the receiving officer should repeat each completed number on the air so that the sending officer can verify that it was correctly heard and understood.

B. HEADQUARTERS TRANSMISSIONS

A ranking officer should always be in command of headquarters radio. A dispatcher trained in radio procedures may be permitted to send out routine complaints or other items as received, but all important messages, including instructions to make arrests, alarms of major crimes and similar things should be screened by the ranking officer to insure that proper instructions are issued, that important instructions are not overlooked and that problems of identification, force to be used, road blocks and similar matters requiring police skill and experience are correctly handled. It should be the ranking officer's duty to also coordinate closely the work of the radio dispatcher and any complaint desk or officer, if complaint duties are not handled by the radio dispatcher.

C. FIELD TRANSMISSIONS

In order to keep transmission brief, officers should eliminate the use of unnecessary expressions or formal courtesies, such as "Roger," "Wilco," "Over and out," "Do you want to," "Will you please," "Yes, sir," "Thank you," and so on. Transmissions must be brief, businesslike and impersonal.

D. LISTENERS

It must always be remembered that police frequencies may be overheard by anyone on a large number of radio receivers purchasable almost anywhere. Consequently, matters of a confidential nature should not be put over the air except in extreme emergencies.

E. AUTHORITY

Standing instructions should exist in all departments having radio as to the authority of the headquarters dispatcher to make assignments of mobile units and officers and procedures for instances where mobile units have current assignments when they are called by the dispatcher to take a new assignment, or to take some police action of higher priority.

Generally speaking, the dispatcher should have final and complete authority as to assignments and all should understand that he is working closely with and expressing the instructions of the ranking officer in charge of communications.

The dispatcher should log all assignments as made and the exact time, for immediate reference and for a permanent record.

F. RADIO LOGS

Federal Communications Commission rules require that a radio log be maintained at each base (fixed) station from which transmissions are made (Federal Communications Commission Rules and Regulations, Section 89.175). Maintaining a log is also in accordance with proper police practice and procedure. Logs maintained by police agencies should include all transmissions and messages received and the exact time of each. Abbreviations may be used to reduce the work involved. These logs should also contain notations of exact time station identifying call letters were broadcast, and the full signature of the operator, showing time at beginning and end of his period of responsibility or tour of duty.

Mobile unit operators should not be required to keep radio logs. It is dangerous, since they will often be driving while receiving or transmitting.

# V. POLICE TELETYPE NETWORKS

Chapter 533, Laws of 1931, established a basic system of coordinated teletypewriter communications, "for the purpose of prompt collection and distribution of information throughout the State of New York as the police problems of the state may require" (Exec. L. Sec. 217).

The Superintendent of State Police is responsible for the system's installation, operation and maintenance. The system is available for use by any department or division of the government of New York State, or by any municipal, county, town, village, railroad or other special police department lawfully maintained by any New York corporation (Exec. L. Sec. 219).

The original "basic system" has been expanded over the years since it was established. The current system is operated in conjunction with computers which do both data recording and message routing. Its modern and current name is "Computer Oriented Police information System," and it is commonly referred to by police officers as "COPS."

The COPS teletype network connects with and is part of the Nationwide Law Enforcement Teletype System (known to police as "LETS" or "N-LETS"). LETS covers the 48 continental states (not Alaska or Hawaii).

COPS is also directly connected to the National Crime Information Center ("NCIC") operated by the FBI in Washington, DC, and the NCIC computers. These computers store crime data from throughout the United States.

## A. DESCRIPTION OF "COPS"

The Computer Oriented Police-information System of New York is a teletype network divided into districts, under the control of New York State Police Headquarters. Each district is generally co-extensive with the territory assigned to the various State Police stations. State and Troop Headquarters are "control points."

"Control points" control the teletypewriter circuits in the geographical area assigned them. The individual circuits have varying numbers of teletype machines and stations. All circuits terminate in the computer located at State Police Headquarters in Albany. The teletypewriter stations are located in municipal police departments, sheriff's offices, and other law enforcement agencies, including, of course, New York State Police installations.

All teletypewriter machines on the COPS system are equipped with "selective coding equipment" which permits each teletype machine to receive only those messages addressed to it.

Messages to police departments and other law enforcement agencies not on the COPS network are sent to the station nearest or most accessible to the department to which directed, to be forwarded by telephone or personal delivery. No special instructions in messages are required to secure this service. However, it will only be done in case of messages sent direct to or for the attention of a particular department. An "All Points Bulletin" ("APB") will be sent only to stations on the COPS network. If it is desired that one or more police agencies not on COPS receive an alarm, an individual direction to such agency(ies) is necessary.

## B. COMPUTER CONTROL

The entire COPS network is under the control of its computer in Albany. All messages are transmitted by the computer exactly as received from the sending machines. It is thus essential that every person preparing teletype messages for sending via a COPS teletypewriter shall make certain that only correct messages are delivered to communications personnel for sending.

1. Through selective coding and automatic switching by the computer, the various teletype machines receive only messages addressed to them, except that "control points" receive also all messages on the "circuits" which they control.

2. The computer is designed to hold up and store teletype traffic for any station when the station is out of service due to routine maintenance, mechanical or electronic trouble, change of paper, etc. It will then send the traffic when the station returns to service.

C. OPERATING RULES AND PROCEDURES

Operating rules and detailed procedures for sending messages on the basic system are set out in the COPS Operating Manual. Copies may be obtained from the New York State Police. Operating rules and procedures must be strictly adhered to. Unless there is exact adherence to proper message construction and-to proper codes, the computer will not accept or will misdirect messages.

1. Officers must be familiar with and comply with the following basic Regulations:
   a. Message traffic shall be brief and in the form prescribed.
   b. No message may be sent without proper authorization.
   c. All message traffic must be official business.
   d. Only the messages of duly authorized member agencies shall be transmitted.
   e. Member stations shall transmit official messages without charge for State Police personnel and for members of police departments without teletypewriter service.
   f. Requests of military authorities for use of system to report the arrest of deserters or other military personnel shall be honored.
   g. All messages are confidential and shall not be divulged to unauthorized persons.
   h. The official time of the system is Eastern Standard except that Daylight Saving Time shall be used whenever it is officially in effect.

D. TELETYPE MESSAGES REQUIRED BY LAW

When any peace officer or police agency in New York receives a complaint that a felony has been committed and if the perpetrator thereof has not been apprehended within five hours after such complaint was received, such police agency must cause information of such felony to be dispatched over the police communications system. Police agencies not connected with basic system must transmit such information to the nearest or most convenient teletypewriter station, from where it will be immediately dispatched in conformity with the regulations governing the system (Exec. L. Sec. 221).

1. The paramount consideration in respect to the messages sent in compliance with this law is that they shall accurately inform all police agencies that criminals are abroad and could be in any one of their jurisdictions.

2. Any classification of teletype which conforms to COPS regulations will comply with this law.

E. PERSONS WANTED

Section 173 of the Criminal Procedure Law provides that when a warrant has been issued in New York for the arrest of a person for a crime or offense, any officer having received a communication in the official course of business of the existence of such warrant may arrest such person, although the officer does not have the warrant in his possession at the time of arrest, if the arrest would otherwise have been proper if the officer had the warrant in his possession. The officer must advise the person arrested of the crime or offense charged and of the fact that a warrant has been issued.

Any officer originating any communication in the official course of business involving the commission of a misdemeanor or lesser offense must include therein the fact that a warrant of arrest has or has not been issued and further indicate, when appropriate, that the warrant has been endorsed for "nighttime" and Sunday execution."

Messages on persons wanted from police agencies in states other than New York are covered by Section 843 of the Criminal Procedure Law, which permits arrest without a warrant upon reasonable information that the defendant stands charged in the courts of another state with a crime punishable by death or imprisonment for a term exceeding one year. The official teletype message will constitute "reasonable information."

1. Messages on persons wanted from Canada or any foreign country must be handled in accordance with Federal law. Defendants can only be extradited by Canada or other foreign countries through the government of the United States, in accordance with Federal statute, treaties and conventions. Section 3184 of Title 18, United States Code, provides that any justice or judge of the United States, any United States Commissioners authorized by a US District Court or any New York judge of a court of record of general jurisdiction may, on complaint made under oath, issue a warrant of arrest for a person charged with a crime in the jurisdiction of any foreign government, if the crime is one provided for by treaty or convention between the United States and that foreign government. The teletype message may be used as the basis for complaint by New York officers in such cases.

F. WARRANT AND EXTRADITION

All messages on persons wanted (whether File 5, or other classifications) must state whether a warrant has been issued or facts justifying arrest without a warrant. If no warrant has been issued and one is required, the message must state "CHECKING ON WARRANT."

1. If a message is directed outside New York State, it must also state whether the requesting authority will extradite (e.g., "WARRANT ISSUED, WILL EXTRADITE," or "WAREX") and, if this fact has not been determined, must state "CHECKING ON EXTRADITION."
2. No message concerning a person wanted will be relayed outside New York State unless it has a statement as to warrant and extradition.
3. An "ADDED INFORMATION" message should be directed to the same points as the original message as soon as the facts have been ascertained as to warrant and extradition if the original message stated "CHECKING ON WARRANT" or "CHECKING ON WARRANT AND EXTRADITION" or "WARRANT ISSUED, CHECKING ON EXTRADITION."
4. Wording such as "HOLD FOR INVESTIGATION," "DETAIN FOR THIS DEPARTMENT," etc., cannot be used in any messages on persons wanted, and messages containing such phrases will not be forwarded.

Messages on persons wanted should include all available information required to accurately identify the persons to be taken into custody, including the exact time of the crime or incident, when known, in order to protect arresting officers.

1. When the fingerprint classification (abbreviated "FPC") of a wanted person is known, it must be included in the person wanted message.
2. Such messages shall also include any information known that wanted persons are armed with a dangerous weapon or are otherwise dangerous or have suicidal tendencies.

G. RETENTION OF TELETYPE MESSAGE COPIES

The printed message or "printout" which teletype machines produce (both inquiries of and answers from the computer or other agencies) is a necessary link in establishing "probable cause" warranting the arrest of an individual and should be preserved with the case file. It is not critical whether the document preserved is the original or the copy, but the original is best. The printout should go directly into the file of the agency taking arrest action, to be preserved for any necessary future use.

If a police agency having no teletypewriter terminal of its own has an officer who stops a suspicious car and the officer communicates with a police agency which has a terminal, and is told moments later that he has a "hit," the terminal employee who answers the officer's inquiry should note in writing on the printout sheet how, when and to whom he furnished the information. He should initial his notation, and then forward the printout to the inquiring officer's agency for retention in that agency's case file. This establishes a chain of evidence for the official police communication.

There is no set time as to how long a message printout should be retained. It should be retained as long as there is any chance the defendant will raise a question on the probable cause for his arrest. Some persons arrested and prosecuted in state courts, after arrest on a printout, may receive long sentences and be confined in a penitentiary for several years. Subsequently they may decide to raise the question of arrest in Federal Court on an appeal of some kind. Permanent retention of the printout would seem to be the most desirable rule in any case where an actual arrest is made based on the message.

H. CASES INVOLVING PROPERTY

In any case involving property in which the complainant's only or primary interest is recovery of the property, a message must not be sent unless a warrant has been issued. This rule is for the protection of arresting officers.

I. STOLEN CARS

Whenever a stolen car is reported by a message on the basic system, and is recovered, it should not be released to any person unless and until a full cancellation of the message reporting it stolen has been sent by the department which originated the stolen message and has been received by the department which recovered the car.

J. EMERGENCY MESSAGES

Emergency messages may include only matters requiring immediate transmission and attention, such as hit-and-run, armed robbery, temporary whereabouts of wanted persons, or other urgent matters.

K. CRIMINAL RECORD REQUESTS

*New York State Identification and Intelligence System* (NYSIIS). - Requests directed to NYSIIS for record information will be sent to and handled by NYSHS, day or night, seven days a week.

1. NYSIIS does its utmost to handle teletypewriter messages requesting information on an immediate basis. It is an imposition to request and in most cases, an impossibility for them to check and reply to a long list of names on a teletype request. Except in a rare case of extreme emergency, lengthy lists of names to be checked should be sent by mail or otherwise and not over the "COPS" system.

L. FIREARMS RECORDS

New York State Police Headquarters (Pistol Permit Section) maintains records of all pistol licenses issued in New York. It also keeps a lost or stolen weapons file, licensed pistol registration file and records of weapons purchased and sold by gun dealers (except gun dealers' records on purchases and sales in New York City). These files will be searched on request. Messages should be directed to "SP ALBANY, ATTN: PISTOL PERMIT SECTION." Requests to check New York City files on gun dealers' purchases and sales should be directed to the New York City Police Department.

M. DEFINITIONS

A full list of definitions applicable to all phases of operation of the basic system is published in the COPS Manual; however, the following teletype terms should be understood by all officers:

ACKNOWLEDGMENT - act by which an operator or machine signifies that a message has been received.

ADDED INFORMATION - message sent to supplement an original message and referred thereto.

APB (ALL POINTS BULLETIN) - a general alarm, to all terminals.

AUTHORITY - person responsible for the origination of a message.

BROADCAST - the transmission of a message on all circuits.

CANCELLATION - a message sent to cancel an original alarm.

CDC (CALL DIRECTING CODE) - directs message to its proper destination.

CORRECTION - a message sent to amend a previous message.

DIRECT MESSAGE - a message addressed to a specific agency or receiver.

EMERGENCY CANCELLATION - a message sent to cancel, without delay, previous message.

FINGERPRINT CLASSIFICATION - a listing of the kinds of fingerprint patterns, ridge counts and tracings and missing fingers in a subject's fingerprints, using a code notation for each of the ten fingers.

JUNK - any message or part thereof which is unintelligible by reason of mechanical or electrical difficulties.

MESSAGE NUMBER - numerals in the upper left-hand corner of a teletypewriter communication to distinguish it from other communications having the same point of origin.

MESSAGE TIME - the figures placed on a message after the sender's name, to indicate the time the typing was completed. Time based on the conventional time designator of ante meridian (AM) and post meridian (PM) (noon and midnight designated as 12-00 N and 12-00 MID, respectively). Eastern Standard Time used except when Daylight Saving Time is in effect.

PART CANCELLATION - a message sent by the originating station to cancel some portion of an original and/or previous message, using a new message number and the same file classification as the original.

REFERENCE - data by which an original message is identified, i.e., the message and file numbers, place and date of origin, message direction and subject.

REPLY - a message that answers a previous teletype message; must refer to the original and be designated by the word "REPLY."

SENDER - surname of operator who originally transmits a message.

N. AUTHORIZED ABBREVIATIONS

The following abbreviations may be used in teletype messages:

| | |
|---|---|
| AA | Control Point, Troop "A," Batavia |
| ADDED INFO | Added information |
| AKA | Also known as |
| AM | Ante Meridian - (Between Midnight and Noon) |
| APB | All Points Bulletin |
| ASSIGN | Assignment |
| ASST | Assistant |
| ATL | Attempt to locate |
| ATTN | Attention |
| AUTH | Message sent on authority of |
| BB | Control Point, Troop "B," Malone |
| BCI | Bureau of Criminal Investigation |
| BLD | Build |
| BLK | Black |
| BRN | Brown |
| CC | Control Point, Troop "C," Sidney |
| C (in description) | Chinese |
| CANCEL | Cancellation |
| CAPT | Captain |
| CCT | Circuit |
| CHIEF INSPR | Chief Inspector |
| CODE SIG | Code Signal |
| COL | Colonel |
| COMP | Complexion |
| CORRECT | Correction |
| CP | Chief of Police |
| CPL | Corporal |
| CT/SGT | Chief Technical Sergeant |
| DD | Control Point, Troop "D," Oneida |
| DATA | We request owner's name, address, make of car, motor number, etc., on the following registration |
| DCT | Direct |
| DEP | Deputy |
| DK | Dark |
| DMV | Department of Motor Vehicles, Albany, NY |
| DOA | Dead on arrival |
| DOB | Date of birth |
| EE | Control Point, Troop "E," Canandaigua |

| | |
|---|---|
| ETA | Estimated time of arrival |
| F | Female |
| FF | Control Point, Troop "F." Middletown |
| FILE | File classification number |
| F/SGT | First Sergeant |
| FOA | For other authorities |
| FPC | Fingerprint classification |
| GG | Control Point, Troop "G," Loudonville |
| HQ | Division Headquarters, Albany |
| I | Indian |
| INV | Investigator |
| INSPR | Inspector |
| J | Japanese |
| KK | Control Point, Troop "K," Hawthorne |
| LETS | Nationwide Law Enforcement Teletype System |
| LIC | License number |
| LIEUT | Lieutenant |
| M | Male |
| MAJ | Major |
| MED | Medium |
| MESA | Referring to your message |
| MEX | Mexican |
| MID | Midnight |
| MOT | Motor |
| NCIC | National Crime Information Center |
| NFC | Negative file check |
| NYSIIS | New York State Identification and Intelligence System |
| NMN | No middle name |
| NYS | New York State |
| O (in description) | Other (meaning any other racial abbreviation not listed herein) |
| OFF | Officer |
| OPR | Operator |
| PART CANCEL | Partial cancellation |
| PD | Municipal Police Department |
| PD NYC | Police Department, City of New York |
| PM | Post Meridian (Between Noon and Midnight) |
| PTL | Patrolman |
| QQ | Control Point, Division Headquarters, Albany |
| REF | Please refer to our message |
| REG | Registration number |
| ROIR | Reply only if record |
| RP | Message repeated by |
| SER | Serial |
| SGT | Sergeant |
| SO | Sheriff |
| SP | State Police |
| SR INV | Senior Investigator |
| S/SGT | Staff Sergeant |
| SUPT | Superintendent |
| TT | Control Point, Troop "T," Elsmere |
| TOT | Turned over to |
| TPR | Trooper |
| T/SGT | Technical Sergeant |
| TWX | Teletypewriter Exchange System |

| | |
|---|---|
| UNK | Unknown |
| VIN | Vehicle Identification Number |
| VOID | Cancel our message |
| W | White |
| WAREX | Warrant issued will extradite |
| Z/SGT | Zone Sergeant |

The permissible abbreviations for states of the United States, and for foreign countries, Canadian Provinces and Mexican states are set out In the COPS manual, phone book and postal directory.

## VI. PREPARING TELETYPE MESSAGES

All messages for transmission over the basic system must be in the prescribed form and as brief as possible without losing clarity. Conformance with instructions for message construction set out in the COPS Manual is not only essential for use on the basic system of New York State but also permits the message to be correctly carried to other states in the continental United States over the Nationwide Law Enforcement Teletype System (LETS) and to the National Crime Information Center (NCIC) computers at the FBI in Washington, DC.

COPS Manuals may be found at all stations on the basic system, including local police stations as well as State Police stations and may be procured from the New York State Police at Albany.

### A. MESSAGE FORM

Messages which do not conform (in construction or content) to the requirements set out in the COPS Manual will not be sent but will be returned to the point of origin for correction. Conformity is necessary so that every department in the state may operate with a minimum of delay and to give maximum protection to the individual officer who acts on the basis of information received in a teletype message over the basic system.

### B. MESSAGE EXAMPLE

All messages on the basic system must have a heading, a body, an authority and a sender, in the form indicated by the following example:

EXAMPLE:
Line 1 ... NYAZ
Line 2 ... 6214 FILE 12 PD NYC APR 4-10 REPLY
Line 3 ... TO PD JAMESTOWN NY CODE 77
Line 4 ...
Line 5 ... MESA 381 FILE APR 3-10 APB UNK W M
Line 6 ... SUSPECT HARRY ROE WAS AT QUEENS COUNTY ADDRESS FROM 8-30 AM TO 12-00 MID APR 2-10 ACCORDING TO RELIABLE WITNESSESNO FURTHER INVESTIGATION BEING CONDUCTED. WRITTEN REPORT FOLLOWS.
2nd line below
body ..... AUTH LT MURPHY BROWN 6-17 PM
3rd line below
body ..... NY03030

1. File 1 Messages (Stolen Motor Vehicles, Trailers or Motorcycles) and File 16 Messages (Lost and Stolen License Plates) are the only exceptions to the preceding rule as to form of teletype messages. They must be prepared in a special format, as shown later in this ongoing section.

2. All departments have been assigned NCIC code numbers, whether or not they have teletype facilities on the basic system are assigned two-letter call directing codes ("CDC's"). Both NCIC codes and CDC's are listed in the COPS Manual.
3. The individual lines of the sample message were prepared in accordance with the following rules:
   a. Line 1 contains a message's "call directing codes" (or "CDC's"). These are the means by which the computer determines the destination of the message. The police officer preparing the message must decide on its destination and use. It is the responsibility of the teletype operator to translate these into the proper CDC's (and "Function Codes," if any -the Function Codes give instructions as to computer activity in respect to the message). CDC's and Function Codes are all set out in the COPS Manual.
      (1) The first two letters in the example, on Line 1, are the CDC for the agency originating the message (i.e,. NY for New York City Police Department). The next two letters are the CDC for the department to which the message is destined (i.e. AZ for Jamestown Police Department). The correct CDC must always be ascertained from the COPS Manual
      (2) The CDC "SP" will send the message to all New York State Police teletype stations. The CDC "PD" will send it to all police agencies and sheriff's offices in New York. If a message is to go out of New York to an out-of-state law enforcement agency, the CDC for out-of-state is "IS" and must be followed by the CDC for the out-of-state destination.
      (3) If a message has an inquiry of or information for the New York State Identification and Intelligence System (NYSIIS), the proper CDC for NYSIIS is "QC."
   b. Lines 2 and 3 constitute the "heading" of the message. They show the identity of the message and its origin and destinations, spelled out in words and abbreviations. In the example, the message is the 6,214th message sent by the Police Department, New York City. It is a "File 12" (message concerning homicide). Line 3 (the second line of the heading) shows the message's destination and the code signal for special handling desired ("Code 77").
      (1) Every message must be designated by a number (in the example, "6214"). For every teletype station on the basic system, message numbering always begins with "1" for the first message sent after midnight of December 31 annually and messages are thereafter numbered consecutively throughout the year, straight through the last message sent on the following December 31st.
   c. Line 4 is always left blank
   d. Line 5 is always the reference line, if a reference is required and shows to what prior message, if any, the message relates.
   e. Line 6 and following are the body of the message. The body always begins on line 6 unless there is no reference, when it begins on line 5.
   f. The authority, sender and time sent are the next to last line of every message (in the example, this line is marked "2nd line below body" to show its placement when teletyped). The "authority" is the identity and rank of the officer who authorized the message, "Lt. Murphy" in the

example. "Brown" in the example is the teletype operator who sent the message.

g. The last line of the message is the "NCIC Code" of the sending agency. Frequently a sending agency is not one with a station on the basic system and thus has no CDC. The NCIC code will be its identifier. In the example this is "NY 03030," marked "3rd. line below body" to show its placement when typed on the teletype machine.

C. FILE 1 AND FILE 16 MESSAGES

File 1 (Stolen Motor Vehicles, Trailers, and Motorcycles) and File 16 (Lost or Stolen License Plates) messages have a special format of their own. All the data on the stolen or lost item which the message sets out are automatically entered in the memory banks of the computer the instant the teletype message is received by it when the proper function code is included with the call directing codes (CDC's). Examples of a proper File 1 and a proper File 16 original message are as follows:

EXAMPLE, File 1:
Line 1 ... KORESPPDQLQJNX
Line 2 ... 235 FILE 1 SP CLAVERACK NY MAY 1-10
Line 3 ... TO APB
Line 4 ...
Line 5 ... 4A7528.NY.10..
Line 6 ... 09ME44217CO.
Line 7 ... 09.MERC.COU.2T. GRN/LGR
Line 8 ... 050170
Line 9 ... NY11001
Line 10 .. K0235.
Line 11 .. STOLEN GHENT NY 9 TO 11 PM-OWNER CHARLES A. DOE-
1 MAIN-CLAVERACK NY 2nd line below
body ..... AUTH SGT ROE GREEN 11-50 PM
3rd line below body ..... NY 11001

EXPLANATION

1. The above message concerns a 2009 Mercury Cougar, color top green over light green body, hardtop, two-door, 2010 New York license plates 4A7528, owned by Charles A. Doe, 1 Main Street, Claverack, NY, and stolen at Ghent, NY, sometime between 9:00 and 11:00 PM on May 1, 2010. The individual lines of the example were prepared under the following rules:
   a. Line 1 contains the "CDC's" and "KO" is the CDC for the State Police at Claverack. In addition, this line has the function code "RE," a direction to the computer to include the data in the message in the computer memory bank. Function code "RE" is the same for all File 1 messages. "SP" is the CDC for all State Police installations with teletype. "PD" is the CDC for all police and sheriffs' offices with teletype installations. "QL" is the CDC for the New York State Motor Vehicle Department at Albany; "QJ" is the CDC for New York State Police Communications Headquarters, Albany, and "NX" is the CDC for the National Auto Theft Bureau (NATB) in New York City.
   b. Line 2 is the same as any other message and carries the message number, the "file, originating agency and date sent."

c. Line 3 is the same as any other message, showing the distribution desired - in the example, APB (the abbreviation for "all points bulletin" to all teletype installations on the basic system).
d. Line 4 is left blank as in other messages.
e. Line 5 gives the license plate data. These are always set out in this order: plate number, issuing state and year, followed by two periods for a private plate or an appropriate abbreviation from the COPS Manual for any other kind of plate (e.g., "DL" for dealers' plates, "OB" for passenger bus plates, "TK" for truck plates, etc.). Only private passenger automobile plates are represented solely by two periods, as in the example.
f. Line 6 gives the stolen vehicle's identification number its "VIN."
g. Line 7 sets out the description of the vehicle, using the codes set out in the COPS Manual for motor vehicles, always in the following order: year, make, model, style, color. In the example, these are: "09," "Merc" for Mercury, "COU" for Cougar model, "2T" for two-door hardtop style, and GRN/LGR for green top, light green body. Periods must be used in line 7 just as shown in the example (see paragraph on "Punctuation" later in this section).
h. Line 8 is the date of occurrence of the incident . The date must be set out with numerals for month, day and year. If the month or day is a single numeral it is preceded by 0. February third would thus be entered 0203, followed by the year or "020304" for February 3, 2004. October 20, 2004, would be "102004."
i. Line 9 carries the NCIC code of the originating police agency (SP Claverack is "NY 11001").
j. Line 10 is always the CDC of the originating agency and the message number (KO is the CDC for SP Claverack and the message number is 235).
k. Line 11 carries any pertinent information desired as to the theft, such as owner, time of theft, place of theft. Such data are restricted to a total of 42 characters and nothing past the 42 characters will be entered into the computer, although anything past 42 characters will be transmitted to all receiving an actual copy of the message. This is similar to the "body" of other teletype messages. Any readily recognizable abbreviations pertinent and suitable may be used in the 42 characters, contrary to the general rules that only authorized abbreviations may be used in other messages.
   (1) To include material information in 42 characters requires some thought and economy of phrasing but is not difficult. For example, the characters "ARMED V M" indicate an armed white male, the characters "STOLEN 32 CAL COLT REV GLV COMPT" indicate a .32 caliber Colt revolver which was in the glove compartment was stolen.
l. Second line below the body is the same as other messages, showing the authority for the message and the sender.
m. Third line below the body is also the same as in other messages, carrying the NCIC Code for the originating agency (same as Line 9 of File 1's).

EXAMPLE, File 16:

Line 1 ... KORGQLQJ
Line 2 ... 236 FILE 16 SP CLAVERACK NY MAY 1-10
Line 3 ... TO APB
Line 4 ...
Line 5 ... .2A2314.NY.10..1.
Line 6 ... 050110
Line 7 ... NY11001.
Line 8 ... K0236
Line 9 ... STOLEN GHENT
2nd line below
body ..... AUTH SGT ROE GREEN 11-52 PM
3rd line below body ..... NY11001

EXPLANATION

1. The above message concerns the loss of a single license plate at 7:00 p.m. in Ghent, NY. The license plate is numbered "2A2314" and is a 2010 New York Plate, The individual lines of the message conform to rules as follows:
   a. Line 1 contains the CDC of the originating agency ("KO" for SP, Claverack) and the function code for the computer of "RG" which directs the computer to store the data in its memory bank and is the same for all File 16's. "QL" and "QJ" are the CDC's for the New York State Department of Motor Vehicles and the Communications Headquarters of the State Police, both at Albany.
   b. Line 2 is the same as both prior message examples.
   c. Line 3 is the same as both prior message examples, i.e. shows the destination of the message.
   d. Line 4 is blank, same as prior message example.
   e. Line 5 is same as in a File 1 message, showing the license plate in order of plate number, state of issue and year of issue. The periods indicated in the example must be used in all messages. The example shows one lost or stolen plate. If both plates had been lost or stolen, Line 5 would be: "2A2314.NY.10..2.".
   f. Line 6 shows date lost or stolen, same as Line 8 of a File 1 message.
   g. Line 7 shows the NCIC Code of the originating agency, same as Line 9 of a File 1 message.
   h. Line 8 shows the CDC of the originating agency and its message number, same as Line 10 of a File 1 message.
   i. Line 9 carries any pertinent information desired on the lost or stolen plates, usually in briefest form, as not over 11 characters will be included in the computer memory bank.
   j. Second line below body is authority and sender, same as any other message.
   k. Third line below body is NCIC Code for originating agency, same as any other message, and is same as in Line 7 of the example.

D. PUNCTUATION

In sending messages, the usual punctuation marks cannot be used. Instead of commas, colons, semi-colons and periods, a dash must be used, except in File 1 message lines 5, 6, 7, 8, 9 and 10 and File 16 message lines 5, 6, 7 and 8. The reason for use of periods in File 1 and File 16 messages is that the data they contain on the indicated lines must be fed into the computer in specific segments and the segments must be separated and indicated by periods. If a necessary character is missing from any one of the segments, a period must be put in its place in the message.

NUMBERS IN MESSAGES

All numbers used in teletype messages must be in numerals (e.g., 1, 2, 10, etc.) and not spelled out (e.g. "one," "two," "ten," etc.) except that decimals and fractions must be spelled out in words (e.g. "one-half," "ten and sixteen hundredths," etc., instead of "1/2," "10 16/100," etc.

F. ADDED INFORMATION, CORRECTION, REPLY, CANCELLATION

Every message except an original message must show in Line 2, as in the first message example herein, whether it is an "Added Information," "Correction," "Reply" or a "Cancellation." The proper designation, of course, is determined by the purpose or nature of the message.

G. CODE SIGNALS

A Code Signal is a number which, when included on Line 3 of a message ("CODE 77" in the first example prior), directs certain specific handling of the message by addressees. More than one code signal may be used in a message. Approved code signals and their meanings may be found in the COPS Manual.

H. FIFTH LINE, OTHER THAN ORIGINAL MESSAGES

The fifth line of all messages other than original messages is the reference line. The reference line shall show: (1) whether the message relates to a prior message from the sending station ("REF," or "VOID" on cancellations), or from another station ("MESA"); (2) the message number of the original message; (3) the date of the original message; (4) whether the original message was sent direct ("DCT") or to all points ("APB"); and (5) the subject of the original message, including the name of persons first listed on the fifth line of the original message (if any such listing in the original).

1. The license plate number of any stolen motor vehicle, motorcycle, trailer or lost or stolen plate must be on line five of any message relating to stolen vehicles or lost or stolen plates ("File 1" or "File 16" messages).

I. BODY OF MESSAGE

The body of every message should be as brief as possible. All messages are required to be clear and accurate. Telegraph style must be used in messages, leaving out all connecting words and other words not essential to clarity.

CONTENT

1. The first word in the body of every original message should where possible, indicate the purpose of the message, e.g., "STOLEN," "WANTED," "BURGLARY," "RECOVERED," etc. This rule does not apply to File 1 or File 16 messages.
2. The crime involved must be specified by name in all original messages relating to crimes. The pertinent section of the Penal Law, Criminal Procedure Law, etc., may be added for clarity where deemed necessary.
3. Where the bare name of the crime is not sufficiently descriptive, a brief notation of what the crime involved may be added, e.g., "CRIMINALLY NEGLIGENT HOMICIDE-HUNTING."
4. Messages concerning persons wanted or missing should list the persons' full names or brief descriptions, if names are unknown (e.g., "unknown white male," "unknown colored female"), and the license plate number of any vehicle in their possession, on the fifth line of the message.
5. Stolen motor vehicle, trailer or motorcycle ("File 1") messages must carry the license plate number as the first item on line five in all such messages.

6. The license number shall be shown on the fifth line of all messages dealing with vehicles used in or connected with a crime.
7. The plate number of lost or stolen license plates must be shown as the first item on the fifth line of all messages dealing with such plates ("File 16" messages).

The time and place of the crime must always be set out in an original message. They should be set out in the first part of the message.

Information in the body of a message shall be set out in the following sequence, when applicable:

SEQUENCE

1. Name of subject (unless listed above the body of the message on the fifth line of an original message or in the reference line of any other message).
2. Name and brief facts of crime.
3. Time and place of crime.
4. Warrant data, whether will extradite.
5. Description of persons, with items of description set out in the following order:
   Racial description (White, Colored, American
   Indian, Chinese, etc.);
   Sex, age, height, weight, color hair and eyes;
   Complexion, build;
   Clothing, marks and scars, peculiarities;
   Addresses, occupation, relatives.
   EXAMPLE:
   "W-F-28-5-5-120 LIGHT BRN HAIR-BRN EYES-FAIR
   COMP-MED BLD-BLUE PLAID KERCHIEF ON HEAD-BLK
   TOPCOAT-DK GREEN DRESS-BLK LOW HEEL SHOES-BLK
   BAG OVER SHOULDER-NO MARKS OR SCARS-UNDER
   MENTAL STRAIN-RESIDES 1 MAIN STREET-COHOES
   NY-UNEMPLOYED-MOTHER MRS JOHN R. DOE-SAME
   ADDRESS"
6. Description of Motor Vehicles, with items of description set out in the following order: License plate number, motor number and/or vehicle serial or identification number, year, make, model, color, distinguishing marks.
7. Description of Property, with items of description set out in the following order: Name, make, model, serial number, color, material, size, peculiarities and markings.
   EXAMPLES:
   TYPEWRITER-ROYAL PORTABLE-SER 1J4813996-GREEN PLASTIC
   FRAME-CHEMICAL SYMBOLS ON KEYBOARD-NO CASE
   WRISTWATCH-WALTHAM-SPRITE-SER UNK-WHITE GOLD-SMALL
   BAGUETTE DIAMONDS EACH SIDE-BRAIDED NARROW YELLOW GOLD
   WRIST BAND-ENGRAVED ON BACK CASE-TO JANE WITH LOVE

J. AUTHORITY FOR MESSAGES

Every message must show the rank and surname of the police member authorizing and responsible for the message (and his department if different from the department sending the message). "Authority" is shown by typing at left margin, on the second line below the body of the message, the abbreviation "AUTH" followed by the rank and name of authorizing officer.

K. FILE CLASSIFICATION CHART

The following File Classification Chart is required to be posted at every teletypewriter location associated with the basic system. This chart must be rigidly adhered to and the proper File Classification Number placed on every message. The File Classification Number assigned an original message must be used on all subsequent messages pertaining to and sent in connection with the same case. The File Classification number is used for message filing.

FILE CLASSIFICATION CHART

| FILE | CLASSIFICATION |
|---|---|
| 1 | STOLEN MOTOR VEHICLES AND MOTORCYCLES |
| 2 | MOTOR VEHICLES - INFORMATION REQUESTS |
| 3 | EMERGENCY REPORTS TO DIVISION HEADQUARTERS |
| 4 | HIT AND RUN DRIVER |
| 5 | PERSONS - WANTED OR ESCAPED |
| 6 | PERSONS - MISSING |
| 7 | BURGLARY |
| 8 | ROBBERY AND HOLD UP |
| 9 | PROPERTY - LOST OR MISSING |
| 10 | PROPERTY - STOLEN (LARCENY) |
| 11 | ASSAULT |
| 12 | HOMICIDE |
| 13 | GENERAL POLICE INFORMATION |
| 14 | ORDERS AND ADMINISTRATIVE MESSAGES |
| 15 | REQUESTS FOR INFORMATION (MISC.) |
| 16 | LOST OR STOLEN LICENSE PLATES |
| 20 | CRIMINAL INVESTIGATIONS (BCI ONLY) |
| 24 | LEGAL BULLETINS AND OPINIONS |
| 25 | MISCELLANEOUS MESSAGES |
| 26 | TROUBLE REPORTS |
| 27 | WEATHER BUREAU FALLOUT DATA |
| 28 | ROAD CONDITIONS AND WEATHER REPORTS |
| 44 | TEST MESSAGES |

DESCRIPTION

FILE 1: Use for all messages reporting stolen motor vehicles, trailers or motorcycles. In some agencies associated with the basic system, outside New York, stolen car messages are filed by license number and in others by motor, serial or identification number. It is thus necessary that all cancellations of File 1 messages list not only the license number but also the motor, serial or identification number, exactly as set out in the original message. The license plate number of the stolen vehicle must always be the first item on line five of any File 1 message except cancellations.

FILE 2: Use only for messages involving requests for motor vehicle, trailer, motorcycle or drivers' license information either from outside New York or from the New York State Department of Motor Vehicles. Whenever possible, File 2 messages must include the subject's full name, including middle name or initial and his address and date of birth.

1. Where a message is sent to the New York State Department of Motor Vehicles concerning only a check of a name, the message should be directed to one of

three sections of that Department, depending on the first letter of the subject's last name, as follows:
"TO DMV SEC 1" (for A through G)
"TO DMV SEC 2" (for H through O)
"TO DMV SEC 3" (for P through Z)

2. Whenever a license plate number check is desired, the direction should be merely "TO DMV."
3. Department of Motor Vehicles conviction records are maintained on electronic data processing equipment and it takes several days to furnish complete information, as the data tapes are not updated every day, but at stated intervals. Accurate and prompt service can only be provided if the Department is given accurate and complete information. The subject's name, date of birth, sex and license identification number must be furnished exactly as they appear on the person's operator's or chauffeur's license.
4. The following information should be considered as a guide to requesting information from the New York State Department of Motor Vehicles files to avoid unnecessary work and delayed communications:
    a. Where only the previous record for Driving While Intoxicated or while Ability is Impaired is required, do not request complete record of all convictions.
    b. Where only data on previous suspension or revocation of license are wanted, do not request complete record of all convictions.
    c. Where only convictions in past 18 months are wanted, so specify.
    d. In requesting check on nonresidents, specify that the subject is a nonresident, and pinpointing information desired. DMV maintains a file specifically showing speeding convictions and all vehicle and traffic misdemeanors involving nonresidents arrested in New York.
5. The electronic data processing includes only moving violations, vehicle and traffic misdemeanors and suspension and revocation data. Equipment violations, overload violations and non-moving violations (other than misdemeanors) are not included.
6. Where a complete accident and conviction record (known as a "safety record") is desired on a driver, the message should be sent promptly after the driver's arrest since the limitations of the electronic data processing will delay the reply. The request should specify "COMPUTER ABSTRACT REQUIRED."

Photostats from Department of Motor Vehicles: When photostats of drivers' licenses or any records are desired from the Department of Motor Vehicles, they should be requested directly of the Department by mail and no teletype message should be sent requesting photostats.

FILE 3: This classification is only used by the Few York State Police.

FILE 4: This classification is solely for hit-and-run (leaving the scene of accident) motor vehicle or motorcycle violations. Original messages must always include as much information as possible pertinent to the wanted motor vehicle and driver. File 4 classification applies whether the hit-and-run involves property damage, personal injury or both.

FILE 5: Use for messages concerning crimes other than assaults, burglaries, homicides and robberies (which are File 11, File 7, File 12 and File 8 respectively). File 5 should also be used for messages requesting arrest or announcing that persons are wanted and subject to arrest, including escapees from prisons, jails and mental institutions. File 5 sconcerning escapees from mental institutions should be restricted to New York only, unless the authorities of the institution specifically desire dissemination outside New York. All File 5 original messages on persons wanted must begin the body of the message with "WANTED," followed by the name of the crime or other item justifying the arrest.

FILE 6: Do not use for persons wanted for a crime. Use only in cases of persons missing over 24 hours, except no waiting period is required in case of young children, females 18 years of age and under, mentally incompetent persons or persons known to have been operating a motor vehicle. All File 6 messages must include the time or approximate time the subject left home and must indicate that either the sending authorities or the family or parents will promptly assume the duty of returning children, youths and mentally incompetent persons when located. If the missing person was known to be using a motor vehicle, the license plate number should be included in the message.

FILE 7: Use specifically for burglary. Do not include any larceny without burglary. File 7 original messages must state the type of building burglarized, methods of entry, and complete description of property taken and persons wanted.

FILE 8: Use for all robbery. Messages must adequately describe property taken and persons wanted.

FILE 9: Use for all messages relating to property which has been lost or is missing, except motor vehicle license plates (which are classified in File 16). Stolen property cannot be the subject of a File 9 message, nor any property which has been the subject of a crime. Original messages must adequately describe the property involved.
FILE 10: Use for all messages dealing with stolen property or property which has been the subject of any larceny. This includes aircraft and boats (but not motor vehicles, trailers, motorcycles or vehicle license plates, as these are File 1 and File 16, respectively). Property involved must be adequately described. Long lists of unidentifiable property have little value and should not be sent.

FILE 11: Use only for assault cases. (Motor vehicle hit-and-run cases are not included in File 11 but are classified in File 4).

FILE 12: All messages concerning homicides must be classified in File 12, including all criminal negligence homicides, whether vehicle or other.

FILE 13: Messages are to be classified in File 13 when they do not relate to a specific crime or arrest request in other file classifications and are of interest to police generally or in a special area. They may be sent direct to one or more stations or as all points bulletin as the facts indicate. File 13 messages would include reports of confidence games, notice that specific persons have been apprehended who may be wanted by other departments and their modus operandi (specifying distinctive or unusual features thereof). File 13's would also include notice that specific property has been recovered (including adequate description) and general police warnings. In all instances where a person is arrested for a serious crime, his name, aliases, description and fingerprint analysis or classification should be sent as an all points bulletin under File 13 for the information of all departments on the basic system.

FILE 14: This classification is only used by the New York State Police.

FILE 15: Use on messages requesting information from special files, arrest or criminal records, firearms records, dog licenses, ear tags, birth, marriage and death records, aircraft license data, lost, missing or overdue aircraft and other types of information.

FILE 16: Use only for messages dealing with motor vehicle or motorcycle license plates, whether lost or stolen. List plate numbers at beginning of 5th message line. The plate number must always be the first item on the fifth line of any File 16 message.

FILE 20: This classification is only used by the New York State Police.

FILE 24: Use on all messages concerning notice of new laws, legal opinions, legal bulletins and inquiries concerning laws or legal opinions. It is largely used by the New York State Police but may be used by any agency.

FILE 25: Use for all messages not dealing with crime and which do not fall within any file classification previously set out. It would include messages concerning notification of relatives of persons who have been killed. No messages may be sent under a File 25 classification in criminal cases.

FILE 26: Any report of trouble on the basic system or with a teletypewriter installation should be File Classification 26.

FILE 27: This classification is used solely for official fallout data.

FILE 28: This is used for road condition and weather reports.

FILE 44: Used for test messages.

L. DATA AVAILABLE ON PERSONS OR PROPERTY

The COPS computer is located at Communications Headquarters, New York State Police, Albany. On receipt of properly coded messages, it stores in its memory banks for later search all File 1 and File 16 message data on stolen motor vehicles, trailers, motorcycles and lost or stolen license plates. It also stores data as to vehicles used in commission of a crime and as to lost or stolen vehicle parts (by identification or serial number). Data on vehicles are stored by both license plate number and vehicle identification number ("VIN").

In addition, Communications Headquarters, State Police, Albany, maintains manual record files on stolen property and guns and on lost property. These will be automatically checked on receipt of messages concerning recovered property or guns.

The National Crime Information Center (NCIC) at Washington, DC, stores in its computers information on stolen vehicles and license plates, stolen or missing property and guns and on persons wanted for felonies or missing. Data on property is stored in the NCIC computers for individual items valued at $500 or more, or on loot from a single "job" worth $2,000.00 or more.

The New York State Identification and Intelligence System (NYSIIS) maintains files on persons wanted or missing covering New York. NYSIIS may be checked directly for wanted or missing persons data, by teletype message, or otherwise, such as direct telephone inquiry.

M. COMPARISON OF NCIC, NYSIIS, COPS DATA

The NCIC computer in Washington, DC, stores data received from the continental United States, including, of course, data from New York. Its "wanted" data cover the whole country. The same is true of its stolen car, stolen property or other banks of data. NYSIIS files cover only "wanted" or "missing" from New York state.

The COPS computer at Communications Headquarters, State Police, Albany, also stores only New York data. This includes New York vehicles or plates stolen anywhere and any vehicles or plates stolen in New York.

N. ENTERING DATA AND MAKING INQUIRIES

The COPS computer file on lost or stolen license plates and vehicle identification numbers and license plates is made up of data from File 1 and File 16 messages which automatically go into the computer when the proper function code is stated in Line 1 of the message. If the message's data meet the criteria required for entry into the NCIC computer in Washington, DC, the message is also automatically switched to the NCIC computer by the COPS computer.

Wanted data on persons should be forwarded to NYSIIS in accordance with the instructions pertaining thereto, as well as by appropriately coded message to NCIC, Washington, DC.

In checking on whether a "want" is outstanding for an individual, an inquiry should be sent to the NCIC Computer in Washington, DC. If a negative reply is received, inquiry will then be made automatically, by the State Police, by *"hot line"* telephone to NYSIIS at Albany, and the inquiring agency will be automatically informed of the result of the NYSIIS inquiry.

The COPS computer and the basic system are directly connected with the NCIC computers in Washington, DC. This *"interface"* makes all the information stored in the NCIC computers automatically available to those making inquiries on the basic system. Inquiries to NCIC and COPS can be made from any teletype machine on the basic system. If a *"no record"* reply is received by an inquirer, from the COPS computer in Albany, on a license plate or "*VIN*" inquiry, the inquiry is automatically routed to the NCIC computers in Washington. A reply will be sent from NCIC within approximately two minutes.

O. MESSAGE RECORD SHEET

Each teletypewriter control point must list and periodically check status of all teletype messages originating in its area which are subject to cancellation. A form similar to the one shown should be used by other stations. Messages should not be entered on the form until they are ready for filing on the fourth day after their receipt.

1. Each teletype installation is expected to use the form to list in numerical order all messages originating at the installation. Messages which are subject to future cancellation should be checked at least once each month, to keep all files clear of inactive messages.
2. In Column 2, *"origin,"* designate for each message the agency originating the message.
3. Sample form:

HASKINS POLICE DEPARTMENT
TELETYPE MESSAGE NUMBER AND
CANCELLATION RECORD

| MSG. # | *ORIGIN* | *FILE* | *DATE* | *SUMMARY* | *CANCEL MSG. #* |
|---|---|---|---|---|---|
| 1 | Haskins | 4 | 4-15-08 | Hit-Run A/A | |
| 2 | " | 5 | 4-15-08 | John Jones,Petit Larc.36 | |
| 3 | " | 11 | 4-16-08 | Assault Case | |
| 4 | Lake Como | 6 | 4-16-08 | Leo Moran, Missing | |

P. CANCELLATIONS AND CORRECTIONS

A cancellation is advice that a prior message is no longer valid and that no further action is to be taken in respect to the prior message. A correction amends a previous message. Stations are responsible for promptly sending all necessary full or part cancellations and all corrections. Failure to cancel or correct a message or part of a message may result in serious harm when police action is taken on the basis of a message which should have previously been cancelled or corrected and was not. The responsibility for any such occurrence will be placed squarely on the offending department and its responsible personnel.

[illegible]